Toltec
Dreaming

Toltec Dreaming

Don Juan's Teachings on the Energy Body

Ken Eagle Feather

Bear & Company
Rochester, Vermont

Bear & Company
One Park Street
Rochester, Vermont 05767
www.BearandCompanyBooks.com

Bear & Company is a division of Inner Traditions International

Portions of this text are excerpted from the following previously published works by the author: *Tracking Freedom, Traveling with Power,* and *The Dream of Vixen Tor.*

Text illustrations of the energy body are by David Brown, and Biocognitive Technology kindly grants permission to reproduce them.

Poems are by Harriet Coleman, and Biocognitive Technology kindly grants permission to reproduce them.

Edgar Cayce Readings © 1971, 1993–2006 by the Edgar Cayce Foundation. Used by permission.

Library of Congress Cataloging-in-Publication Data
Eagle Feather, Ken.
  Toltec dreaming : Don Juan's teachings on the energy body / Ken Eagle Feather.
    p. cm.
  Summary: "A metaphysical instruction manual on the role of dreaming in the Toltec tradition"—Provided by publisher.
  Includes bibliographical references and index.
  ISBN-13: 978-1-59143-072-8
  ISBN-10: 1-59143-072-0
  1. Dreams. 2. Toltecs—Miscellanea. 3. Juan, Don, 1891– I. Title.

BF1078.E23 2007
299.7—dc22
                                         2007007956

Printed and bound in the United States by Lake Book Manufacturing

10 9 8 7 6 5 4 3 2 1

Text design and layout by Jon Desautels
This book was typeset in Sabon, with Oxford used as a display typeface

To send correspondence to the author of this book, mail a first-class letter to the author c/o Inner Traditions • Bear & Company, One Park Street, Rochester, VT 05767, and we will forward the communication.

Dedicated to the spirit of
Albion and Merlin's Enclosure,
without which there could be no tomorrow.

Contents

Note to Readers

Quotations from Carlos Castaneda's works are cited in the text using the following abbreviations:

ABBREVIATED TITLE	FULL BOOK TITLE
Teachings	The Teachings of Don Juan
Separate	A Separate Reality
Journey	Journey to Ixtlan
Tales	Tales of Power
Gift	The Eagle's Gift
Second Ring	The Second Ring of Power
Fire	The Fire from Within
Silence	The Power of Silence
Dreaming	The Art of Dreaming

Acknowledgments

A hearty thanks to those who contributed in many ways: Arana, now residing in who knows what world; Laeticia, a lovely dream within a dream; the most impeccable Simon Buxton, founder of the Sacred Trust and beekeeper extraordinaire; Caroline and Harriet Coleman, poets in a world in need of such; Alex Hrynash, a Toltec scientist; Peri Champine, Jon Graham, and Anne Dillon of Inner Traditions for their thoughtful contributions; and, of course, all of my petty tyrants for jobs well done.

Introduction

The navy shore patrolman carried me through the door of our government housing apartment. Shocked, my mother who was standing near the kitchen, was fixed in place like a mannequin in a store window. She watched the patrolman place me carefully on the living room sofa. *My father stood next to my mother, his arm around her shoulders. He smiled at me as he hugged her.*

The patrolman told my mother that he and his partner had been on their way home after work when they saw me being pulled from Lake Michigan. They stopped to help out. By then the man who sold bait at the fishing pier had already pulled me from the water. I accepted a blanket from one of the people who had been watching me drown; the patrolman and his partner volunteered to drive me home.

After explaining all of this to my mother, they said goodbye to her and left. My father was nowhere to be seen.

While fishing, I had lost my balance and had fallen into the water. On the second or third time up for air, gasping and clawing at the water, I saw horrified people thoroughly engaged as they lined up along a cement embankment for a better view of a drowning kid. Even though I felt distressed about my chances for rescue, I remember I also felt aloof about the whole matter. Part of me simply viewed the scene with detached interest, as though I were one of the onlookers.

When I went under water again, I saw a shadow off in the distance.

Up for air and back down, the shadow remained. *Strange*, I remember thinking, *that all my thrashing doesn't scare that fish away*. Up for air and back down. This time I knew I would stay under. The shadow drew closer. Now I saw that it was not a fish but a cloaked figure. The cowl of the cloak covered a faceless shadow. It glided closer with timeless, graceful motion. The shadow began to cover me and I slipped into quiet and total peace.

I felt a jolt and instinctively hugged the flesh that pulled me back into the sunlight. I was eight years old and still alive. A couple of hours after I was taken home, my father came through the door. After dropping me off at the pier earlier that day, he had gone to see his friends. Only now had he returned home.

Not until some thirty years and many experiences later did some of the pieces become clear. Even though I had a memory of my father returning and asking what had happened, I still had the earlier memory of him with his arm around my mother. Years later, my mother assured me that my father was not at home when I was carried through the door. I then realized that the memory had been of a vision, a dream, a nonordinary perception. By this time, I had learned that under the veil of nonordinary perception, rigid rules and interpretations of reality fall away, delivering one to a world filled with mystery and intrigue.

Interpretations of reality originate from the prevailing models of what people hold to be true. People have experiences, then make sense of them by making them fit with their agreements. These agreements form the glue that holds all the elements of a model of reality together. The model then becomes reality itself, rather than a tool to approach and use reality. "Feeling" is the glue that binds all the aspects of a reality into a stable cohesion where you may then be part of that consensus. The net effect is that we typically confine ourselves to a very limited dream, indeed.

This finding of fact, this discovery of what is true, is governed by considerations of what we *think* is true. Interpretations stem from what is being lived; they are the subjective experience of physical events. If enough people agree on how those subjective experiences should be interpreted, then we have what is known as objectivity. There is great power in this, as objectivity enables us to build the elements of our world, constructing such things as buildings, roads, and airplanes. At the same time, objectivity diminishes our thirst for what lies ahead as we cut ourselves off from the value of forging our way into uncharted territories; in other words, we cut ourselves off from the value of dreaming. By gluing ourselves to the thoughts that allow us to build our world, we inadvertently work at disallowing the magic of our dreams, avenues that enable us to build new constructions wherever and however they occur.

The findings of Copernicus, followed by the evidence of Galileo, turned the world on its ear. The voyages of Columbus and other explorers did the same. So why should we not expect our perception of the world to keep turning into a greater version of what came before?

At the time of my childhood accident in the water, I had no vocabulary or perspective with which to make sense of the nonordinary experiences surrounding it. Looking back, however, I see that day as a turning point. Before, I led an ordinary life, with ordinary aspirations. Afterward, everything felt lackluster. I had no sense of meaning or true connection with the world. So I lost myself in comic books that dealt with psychic and other kinds of strange phenomena. But from a distant perspective that I was not yet aware of, I was already traveling a route that would transport me into a totally nonordinary way of perceiving the world and my life.

One stop along the way occurred when I was a high school freshman. My family then lived in Virginia Beach, Virginia, home of the Edgar Cayce Foundation and its sister organization, the Association for Research and Enlightenment (A.R.E.). Edgar Cayce was born in 1877 and died in 1945, leaving over 14,000 documented psychic readings. He read the Holy Bible once for every year of his life and this may account for the fact that his readings contain a strong Christian flavor.

While he initially gave readings on health-related matters, his work eventually branched out and covered a variety of topics, including spiritual development, astrology, and even business. The Cayce Foundation maintains archives for the readings and for Edgar Cayce memorabilia, and runs one of the largest metaphysical libraries in the country. It was in this library that I researched a high school geography term paper on the lost continent of Atlantis. I don't remember ever discussing Atlantis with family or friends. It just seemed like something I ought to study. When the paper received an "A" (which kept me from failing the course) I received a befuddled smile from the teacher; a very memorable dream.

Another stop along the way was experiencing war. I joined the U.S. Navy at the age of seventeen and a few years later I served in Vietnam. After a mortar attack during the first night, something within me deeply shifted. In retrospect, this process took root while undergoing a weapons training course courtesy of the U.S. Marine Corps. I remember pumping .50 caliber bullets into the earth and vaguely wondering about the effects of my actions. I was simultaneously captivated by the awesome power of this weapon and repelled by the utter destruction it wrought.

As I had been raised in a military environment, my priorities had been country, family, and God. But now that I was living the bottom-line effects of that lifestyle, I found these views coming up short on my personal reality meter. As a result, I felt even further separated from life. After another mortar attack, I began noticing unusual energy that looked like heat waves rising from hot pavement. This energy permeated everything. And while I still had no insight on such matters, I dimly recognized a strange force affecting my life.

During the next few months, I unexpectedly received several sets of orders, which took me from a Marine Corps base in Danang to a naval installation near Saigon. I then went upriver from Saigon to a remote, river-patrol boat outpost. After being in Saigon for a few weeks, I was then transferred to a small, riverboat support detachment in the Mekong Delta. I had wanted to travel throughout Vietnam in order to experience different facets of it, something few people had the opportunity to do. I got my wish by having a nightmare.

All the while, I felt an unidentified power guiding my travels. When I felt like I wanted to leave Danang, a set of orders to Saigon appeared. When I grew tired of Saigon, another set of orders came through. Each time, I traveled to a place I wanted to experience. Again, only through looking back did I recognize I was beginning to become aware of "power," a guiding force of creation according to the Toltec worldview. I did not intentionally ask to be transferred place to place. I simply had wanted to go; the results came of their own.

During this time, I also came face-to-face with other forms of power. As I regularly called in air strikes, I commanded the initial, utterly fierce actions of helicopter gunships, Black Ponies (small, fixed-wing aircraft), and even Phantom jets. The results were invariably the same: the bad guys were destroyed or at least halted. While this was often accompanied by an adrenaline-induced euphoria, calling in medical evacuations proved hauntingly soulful. Perhaps the mix of the two eventually brought me to the awareness that humans just didn't have it right with the world at all. We live in blind madness; demonstrating a consistent lack of regard for children, families, villages, and Earth. Indeed, even though Earth has no ideology or skin color, the very source of our physical sustenance is viewed as an expendable resource. Worse yet, it doesn't even register that bombing the hell out of something directly affects the Earth as well as affecting people. So why should we automatically assume civilization has achieved anything notable? Surely there are better options, better dreams.

Some years ago, a new picture of the world was given to us through the teachings of modern Toltecs. According to the works of Carlos Castaneda (perhaps the Copernicus of our time), a principal feature of these Toltec teachings is that perception occurs through the interaction and regulation of internal and external energy fields. How you manage your internal energy determines what you connect with and, therefore, what you perceive.

As you may know, the central figure in the best-selling books of Carlos Castaneda is don Juan Matus.[1] Pointing the way into a magical and mystical avenue of human experience, the association between Carlos Castaneda and don Juan has fired the imaginations of people the world over.

Don Juan came into public view in the late 1960s as a result of Castaneda's first book, *The Teachings of Don Juan*. While this book offers some of don Juan's philosophy regarding the nature of human existence, it primarily portrays Castaneda's experiences while under the influence of psychotropic, or mind-altering, drugs. Castaneda was a graduate anthropology student at U.C.L.A. at the time and wanted to research psychotropic substances used by American Indians. This interest led him to don Juan, who grew into the role of teacher extraordinaire.

Castaneda's second book, *A Separate Reality*, also concerned the use of drugs that provide unusual and dramatic perceptions. However, in the introduction to his third book, *Journey to Ixtlan*, Castaneda tells us that the drugs were administered only because he was too slow to catch on to don Juan's teachings that used meditative and other exercises to enhance perception. And so in this third book, Castaneda returns to day one, giving the lessons don Juan provided *without* the use of drugs. Since then, in several other books, Castaneda has elaborated on don Juan's instruction, and on the effect those teachings have had on his life.

Much of don Juan's instruction stemmed from an ancient lineage, or system, for the development of consciousness; a system developed by the Toltecs. According to don Juan, during ancient times Toltecs were men and women highly skilled in controlling perception (*Fire*, 15–24). This skill set, aligned with an overarching, guiding philosophy, is known as the Toltec Way. It combines techniques and exercises with perspectives and theory, to take awareness beyond ordinary perception. In the process, the practitioner learns how to achieve balance in everyday life, how to generate personal and professional interests that last a lifetime, how to access different modes of perception, and most important, how to leave theory and technique behind en route toward an even greater freedom. Don Juan's overriding concern was to enable his apprentices to transcend dogma in order to live full, complete lives. The process is not unlike the discipline of a mathematician, automobile mechanic, or priest, who undergoes a set regimen of training and ends up with a standardized set of skills and vocabulary.

The Toltec Way goes back thousands of years. In fact, don Juan maintains that the Toltecs actually ruled central Mexico some three thousand to seven thousand years ago. He goes on to portray the evolution of their practice, from being comprised of bizarre, power-based rituals where greed and dominance prevailed, to a practice characterized by the pursuit of freedom. During this time, Toltecs gave form to their nonordinary perceptions, which had been gained from quite remarkable travels in consciousness. As a result, a philosophy embracing both physical and nonphysical levels of reality was established. Views and techniques were engendered to develop an awareness of relationships between these levels. Don Juan refers to this period as the "old cycle" (*Dreaming*, 59).

This was the heyday of magical potions, talismans, witchcraft, and sorcery, when humans turned against other humans for the sake of enhancing their own power. Indeed, an identifying feature of this cycle is the misuse of knowledge. This contrived relation to the world turned against those who misused power, by reducing their awareness of a reality beyond themselves and their physical world, causing the system to fall into disarray.

The mid-1700s marked the end of this cycle and the beginning of the "new cycle." The hallmark of this new cycle was the introduction of ethics. Practices were streamlined and aberrations reduced. The participants overhauled the system in order to regain the sense of evolving beyond the physical world. In doing so, many of the dark side practices were thrown out. The idea that the system should be used for the development of awareness rejuvenated the participants and realigned their behavior. They became singularly interested in freedom beyond perceptual conventions, beyond the confines of reason as it governs socially formed reality (*Fire*, 15–24; *Dreaming*, 98–99).

Castaneda's involvement provides an interesting twist to the Toltec tradition in that, by presenting the most salient or critical components of the system in his books, he built a bridge that took the system into yet another cycle. The oral tradition gave way to a codified, standard reference. Although much of what Castaneda experienced with don Juan was lost due to this process of setting down, in writing, some of the components of the system and not others, this reduction served to enable even more streamlining, which actually complements the new cycle's goal of refining the system. While Castaneda does present some old-cycle practices (such as the use of mirrors to pull entities out of other dimensions to this dimension), I found his work geared toward presenting perspectives and exercises specifically for the enhancement of perception (*Fire*, 87–112). In written form, the teachings have gained uniformity and in this, I think that Castaneda also acts as a bridge that leads from considerations of old and new cycles, to a new order consisting of the first, second, third, and fourth cycles. The first cycle is the initial awareness that something exists beyond ordinary, earth-bound consciousness; the second is synonymous with the old cycle; the third is synonymous with the new cycle; and the fourth is what will transpire in coming years.

Serving as a bridge, Castaneda found himself between cycles, a role that partially separated him from his own kind, both in the anthropological and Toltec communities. In turn, his work is a significant anthropological accomplishment, making him one of the prominent figures in the Toltec tradition. Indeed, it was by using his books as textbooks that I and others have gained access to that world.

All of my experiences, awakenings, and realizations, particularly those that came to me when I was in Vietnam, led me to Carlos Castaneda and his work. And although much of what he said in his books jived with what I had been experiencing, his work ultimately raised more questions than they could answer. Such was their profound effect on me that, three years after returning from Vietnam, I found myself on another journey. I pulled myself together and made a very conscious decision to move to Tucson, Arizona. I would either find a shaman who would help me to figure out Castaneda's riddles once and for all, or die trying. I didn't have a clue that I would actually meet the man himself.

I first passed don Juan Matus on a main drag in Tucson, Arizona while hurriedly walking to a class I was attending at the local university. I first talked with him in the parking lot of a small market on the outskirts of Tucson. I first *saw* him when we were both in a rather nondescript section of the city. And the last time I was physically with him was near the same market where I had first engaged him face-to-face.

These encounters illustrate a blueprint—an omen, if you will—of our association. On our initial encounter, in the hubbub of the city, I simply noted his presence and passed on—I was too caught up in my own life to pay any attention to this man who appeared to be just another stranger, even though I had moved to Tucson with the intent of meeting a Toltec seer on a par with don Juan.

A few days after passing don Juan in the street, a meeting occurred between us on the outskirts of city life (which was very appropriate in that Toltec knowledge currently exists on the outskirts of contemporary civilization!). Years later, I would *see* don Juan as a pure energy body, in exquisite balance with the world, in a setting that de-emphasized the material world. By the end of our association, he and I had come full circle to wrap things up just where we had begun.

My encounters with don Juan turned my world upside down until I eventually could tell what was right side up. Prior to our meeting, my busy and frenetic life had lost all meaning. Languishing in doubt, I didn't know where I was or where I should go. This emotional malaise was only one of my problems, my health was another. Due to internal bleeding, on more than one occasion I vomited blood and had to be hospitalized. In short, I was leading a wretched existence and was on a fast track to the grave. Life as I knew it was no longer sustainable. Practicing the exercises in Castaneda's books brought the only healing I could find, giving me some slight respite from the surgeons who wanted to remove parts of my guts. Indeed, over the years, don Juan's Toltec world has given me physical, emotional, mental, and spiritual renewal. His teachings literally saved my life as they opened an avenue into a new relationship with the world.

My apprenticeship with don Juan was similar to, yet different from, the experience that Castaneda had. While I have had many experiences that parallel his, my character and temperament are different from Castaneda's. This resulted in different methods of instruction by don Juan. For instance, Castaneda was with don Juan for extended periods; I was only with don Juan for short visits. Don Juan fully explained his teachings to Castaneda, whereas he required that *I* obtain additional instruction from other sources in order to understand his teachings. Much of this extracurricular training occurred after I left Arizona and had returned to the East Coast, where don Juan's instructions came to me in visions and dreams. These conveyed a general sense of guidance and a sense that my life was being shaped by a force that I was not consciously in control of.

Don Juan indicated that I should write two books about Castaneda's books, to shed light on them. Accomplishing this naturally required that I earnestly learn what was in them. Completing this task took eighteen years to the month. For sixteen of those years, I worked on the task without ever missing a day. The first of my books, *Traveling with Power*, provided an account of how I met don Juan, as well as basic procedures for entering the Toltec world. My second book, *A Toltec Path*, provided what I consider to be the overall structure of don Juan's teachings. For good measure, I then wrote *Tracking Freedom* to consolidate and synthesize Toltec teachings with other systems of learning. In addition, during a workshop I was giving in England, I had a remarkable dreaming-while-awake experience, which I translated into another book, *The Dream of Vixen Tor*.[2]

As time would have it, *A Toltec Path* was subsequently published as a Tenth Anniversary Edition and retitled *On the Toltec Path*, which is a very tracking-oriented perspective of the Toltec world. This book, as you might easily imagine, pertains more to the dreaming side. It consists of parts taken from *Traveling with Power*, *Tracking Freedom*, and *The Dream of Vixen Tor* as well as offering new material and a theme for a specific purpose. Following the course of my publishing career, my first set of books were placed out-of-print with one publisher and now, signing on with another publisher, I have two books dealing with the principal division of tracking and dreaming. That events have tuned out as they have causes me to once again evaluate the effects and meaning of a learning task given to me some thirty years ago.

You, too, will be evaluating all of this along with me, so why don't we start right now?

1

A Toltec Dream

Whispers of Reality

There're different worlds out there.
I try to stretch out but can't reach them.
People are calling from another time,
but I cannot hear them.
I can smell a memory of an old place,
the taste of bitter herbs cleanses my body.
I see things in the corner of my eye,
but when I look, there's nothing there.
My senses bring whispers of reality.

The books of Carlos Castaneda contain a sophisticated worldview to focus energy, as well as disciplines and techniques to harness energy. The metaphysical philosophy known as the Toltec Way deals with the nature of reality, including how reality is perceived, formulated, and experienced. Furthermore, it is not only a system of thought; it is a philosophy of action, of behavior.

A good metaphysical philosophy always has two elements. First, it has within it the seeds of its own destruction, or its own transcendence, whichever way you care to look at it. Consistent with don Juan's teaching, a system is a tool to enhance personal development. It's not something to be blindly followed. This is partly why he shuns being anyone's master, and pokes fun at those who consider themselves official sorcerers in residence (*Dreaming*, 2). It is also why he accents developing raw potential over living by the dictums of a philosophy. His overriding goal is to become a person of knowledge, a person of freedom, not a Toltec with the stripes, medals, and terminology to prove it.

Second, a viable system is non-exclusive. That is, if you're a practicing Toltec, Hindu, Christian, or whatever, and someone from another faith or discipline offers a tool that works well for you, you don't arbitrarily ignore it because it's not *your* philosophy.

When developing Toltec abilities—such as dreaming, feeling, and *seeing*—it's best to lay a precise and lasting foundation. This enables you to aim for the highest good and stay on the truest path. Although you may have already built a foundation, taking extra time to get a feel for different approaches to the development of perception grants additional freedom and a stronger, more resilient foundation. You then achieve more control of your life because the wider scope of your involvements permits greater integrity. Building a foundation also helps ensure that your priorities are in order and keeps you from straying into dreams where you don't want to travel. In short, a good foundation provides an orientation that allows the development of perception to remain a source of joy and positive expectation.

To build such a foundation, one of the first things don Juan did early in my apprenticeship was to start feeding me a new description of the world. Since he did not speak fluent English, I read and reread Castaneda's books for the basic theoretical structure and practices. Through brief conversations and nonverbal communication, don Juan also directed me to read a wide selection of books, ranging from the lesser known occult traditions, to academic texts on religion and psychology, to the holy books of the world's principal religions.

Exercising awareness-expanding techniques from various traditions also paid off as the subsequent experiences resulting from actively engaging various philosophical worldviews enabled me to dream deeper within myself. In addition, I gained more clarity regarding Toltec techniques, as I had something with which to compare them. Moreover, by requiring me to acquaint myself with other means of orientation, don Juan prevented me from losing myself in the Toltec Way; rather, he sought that I should balance, not lock in to, Toltec views. I could then arrive at a place in between worldviews.

During these early explorations, I discovered that many age-old methods of developing awareness share common components. In general, these systems recognize a primary, or source, reality from which physical and nonphysical worlds emanate. Ordinary and nonordinary worlds both form secondary realities, backdrops against an often invisible, transcendent, and infinite reality. As such, they are mere reflections of primary reality. These disciplines also consider that at least a part of us is similar to—perhaps identical with—primary reality. From this perspective, we always remain connected with the source of creation rather than feeling estranged from our world. As a result, systems that point the way to primary reality enable a journey to emotional, mental, and spiritual health.

These methods also establish doctrines that describe what it is like to perceive primary reality, and they provide techniques that enable participation with that awareness. These are the classic traditions, as they intend freedom instead of a dream of living solely by doctrine. These are the systems that teach how to leave the system, and not to consider the system as exclusive knowledge; they teach us how to *be*.

While these systems appeared to pave the way for the traveler to reach a similar destination, the paths themselves had different colors, flavors, textures. One is not necessarily better than another, save for the effect it has on the practitioner. Different temperaments require different approaches.

Christian traditions, for example, practice meditation, contemplation, and prayer—often to the light of Christ. Meditation involves less mental articulation than contemplation. It develops complete, inner stillness and is often more rigorous to perform. Contemplation gently, intimately, and deliberately mulls over features of the idea or object placed under subtle consideration. It often seems gentler than meditation but can also deliver intense and insightful awareness. Prayer artfully establishes deeper and deeper levels of communication. It carries enormous power, especially when the communication is between God, Christ, or another divine figure—and oneself.

Symbols of Christian mysticism include the crucifix, stained glass, and the pilgrimage. The crucifix represents the magnificent power behind the passion and resurrection of Jesus. To me, more than any other religious symbol, the crucifix reminds me of a relentless adherence to the will of God. Stained glass provides a soothing way to express meanings, historical figures, or events behind particular denominations within the overall Christian heritage.

The pilgrimage involves a long journey, often by foot, to a place of religious prominence. The traveler often seeks healing, wishes to receive a communication, or simply pays special reverence. The paths that Christians travel have a rich heritage of religious personages, and offer a view where Jesus, the Christ, is the central figure who acts as an intermediary to the highest divine order—God. Pilgrimages are also part of the landscape of other traditions such as Islam.

A Zen Buddhist, looking at another path, seeks Mu, or a loss of self to what *Is*, to a clear and basic perception of whatever is at hand. In a way, the Zen practitioner steps over intermediary religious figures in order to cultivate a direct communion between inner and outer awareness. Supports to accomplish this are a blank white wall and a vase.

The wall is an excellent tool to assist in opening or expanding focus. By unfocusing the eyes and allowing awareness to flow out in all directions, it is a simple matter to allow perception to unfold. The trick, however, is to not hold on to whatever perceptions surface. The practice involves a continual letting go. In turn, the vase is a valuable hinge used to hone and purposefully direct perception. Rather than widening concentration, focusing solely on the vase exercises single-mindedness.

Both the expansive- and single-focus approaches aim for achieving awareness beyond the individual self and arriving at an awareness of the whole. This enables the meditator to step out of preconceived patterns and arrive at a point where neither duality (where self and other are separate) nor unity (where self and other are one) exist, yet the meditator is able to retain the awareness that duality and unity do exist. Whether or not they exist in the eyes of the perceiver becomes a matter of where attention is focused. From this point, reality becomes whatever is experienced from moment to moment.

Although Zen also has a rich history of people influencing its development, since this way does not focus on religious figures, people often regard it as dry and sterile. I have found just the opposite to be true. I see it as very personal in that the connectedness engendered by a loss of superficial identity enables an exquisite feeling that transcends identity. In this loss of self, one gains everything. The key is not to cling to any sense of connection, in order to allow oneself to experience more and more of everything.

Rather than seeking Christ or Mu, traditional American Indian practices seek partnership with the Great Spirit. This does not mean that Christ or Mu must be left behind. It is possible to abide by Indian traditions and practice Christianity or Zen Buddhism, just as it is possible to be Christian and practice Zen. Commonly recognized symbols to assist the Indian journey include power objects, the medicine wheel, and the vision quest.

Each of these orientations aspires to generate awareness beyond the individual. Each describes and provides ways to build a secondary reality and then step away from it to touch primary reality. And each has its own way of going about the task. This inherent strength of individual character provides strong support to explore consciousness. Each speaks to or resonates with innate tendencies of the individual, offering the traveler a different experience, and different shades of meaning along similar paths. But regardless of the differences of method, the processes influencing perceptual development remain constant. So whether your goal is learning a specific discipline, developing dreaming-body states, or whether you're heading elsewhere, having knowledge and understanding of relationships among the influences of perception is the foundation that will help ensure that you meet your goals.

A powerful transformation occurs as you develop a worldview that helps connects you with primary reality. At the same time, while the inherent character of a discipline can help open perception, it can also trap perception. As you expand your worldview, for instance, you might tend to regard the expanded version of reality as *the* truth. Whereas you once regarded ordinary reality as truth, you now have learned the folly of your ways and now know your new reality is the real truth. If this happens, all you have done is to duplicate the error of perceiving any given reality (ordinary, nonordinary, or otherwise) as truth, as the end result, rather than as organized impressions and interpretations of perception. You are now having the dream of being a dogmatic fundamentalist. And often it's not fun.

The cumulative effect of organizing perception is the construction of a reality, and the process of isolating its individual features is called *selective cueing*. Selective cueing pertains to placing specific emphasis or de-emphasis on perceptions. For example, from childhood to adolescence to adulthood we are constantly told what to perceive. Our parents say, "This a chair. It has legs, a seat, and a back." We are also told what functions the chair performs. This gradually hones our perception along a certain path. Eventually each piece of the description falls into place and—almost as though it were magic at some point—we suddenly recognize the concept "chair."

Parents, peers, teachers, and associates all provide information that channels perception along specific avenues. The benefit is taking seemingly isolated pieces of information, and organizing and applying them to create something meaningful. In the same way we create a "chair," we create entire realities.

The cost of this natural activity is the amount of energy directed to specific features you are asked (and sometimes demanded) to accept, thereby excluding other perceptions. In the same manner of cueing what to look for, you are also taught what to avoid looking for. For instance, if a child reports seeing an apparition glide through the room, the child is often told it is simply their imagination. As a result, you may repress part of your awareness because you want to work for something meaningful.

Typically, much of our meaning comes from the social groups to which we belong. So we gradually wean away certain perceptions in the pursuit of harmonizing ourselves with the group. In striving to belong to the group, we achieve mastery of the group's version of reality. This is a momentous accomplishment. The process, though, often reduces an infinite, primary reality to a finite, secondary reality.

Building a reality is ongoing. Interest in doll houses turns to interest in cars, and interest in cars changes from a borrowed set of keys for a Saturday night date, to monthly payments to ensure you get to work on time. Perceptions, meanings, and values change as your world changes. Your world changes as your values change.

Piece by piece, through adding and subtracting, elements of your worldview fall into place or are removed. Your reality then determines what you think about; what you think about determines how you feel; how you feel determines what you think about and your behavior; how you behave determines what you think about. Thought, feeling, and behavior all work hand in hand, give and take.

Don Juan recognized the limitations of worldviews; he used them to provide points of comparison and reference. To get to a point where you can experience the world without the ballast of a worldview is a piece of work, to say the least. When you stabilize a new cohesion, a new stage, you'll feel natural in that energy. But remember that all secondary realities feel like home; feel natural . . . until they exhaust you from complacency. Building an energy field relating to primary reality reflects a magnificent, awe-inspiring dream. It is a stage beyond stages. Don't settle for less.

THE EVOLUTION OF THE TOLTEC WAY

The Toltec Way has spawned many lineages, many variations of the essential dream. Don Juan says he is part of a specific line dating back to 1723. This is when his Toltec ancestor Sebastian reclaimed many lost Toltec practices (*Fire*, 233). This is also the beginning of the new cycle. With Sebastian's discoveries, Toltecs had even more experience with which to compare and contrast. As a result, they were able to foster an understanding of personal evolution. Although the old cycle was locked up in a prison of its own doings, it also served as a bridge. Without the efforts, explorations, and examinations of its practitioners, we would not have such a rich philosophy today. While the old cycle lost itself in sorcery, it led to the new cycle's interest in freedom.

Modern Toltecs examine the world from the premise that it is made up of energy. This includes studying the dynamics of emanations, different dimensions of reality, other forms of organic and inorganic life, and the human energy body; the procedures to do this separate one metaphysical path from another. Toltecs, for instance, use death as an advisor, work to remain inaccessible, divvy up energies between tracking and dreaming, and use a theoretical structure of three energy fields. Zen Buddhists, on the other hand, often strive to stay away from the use of "power-based" abilities such as psychic development and various types of dreaming. They do, however, accentuate basic exercises for non-attachment, inaccessibility, and minimizing self-reflection. An overview of these exercises will be presented in later chapters.

A remarkable example of Toltec studies, Castaneda's books provide a common reference to modern Toltec teachings. As more people follow a Toltec path, various sects will most likely sprout. Just as Buddhism and Christianity have sects, there will be groups of like-minded people who get to a certain stage and put their own spin on the Toltec system. They will define particular options and will want to follow those options. For example, one group might *see* chakras as part of the human energy band, while another group *sees* it differently. One group might be more traditional, and another group more avant garde.

As these tributaries form from the greater river, there will be costs and benefits. One cost is that the Toltec system may become bureaucratic, organized, and strictly consensual. Remember, this is what don Juan warned us of when he advised against becoming "official sorcerers in residence." To become part of a status quo automatically removes awareness from the flow of evolution as perception becomes locked in a secondary reality. This will happen because this is what humans do, or at least it's what they have done time and time again. People want to know, and ordinary knowing is based on having a fixed foundation of knowledge. To think that there really is no fixed knowledge is not rational. And by all means, we must be rational . . . even if it means harming, in thought or flesh, our neighbors. That's right, the ones who don't agree with our reasonableness.

Then, too, some people may not feel compelled to journey completely to freedom. Some might find value in just developing their path with heart. So compared with those aiming for third-field freedom, this group might seem tame. But if the overall path helps someone, then that's great. It's like the pioneers who picked up stakes with the intention of traveling to California, only to settle down in Kansas. These people also possessed courage, and, hey, I hear Kansas is where the Wizard of Oz lives!

One benefit of managing a variety of views is that people learn that their views are just that—views. So if folks don't start thinking theirs is *the* right view, then perhaps we'll all realize that different groups are all expressions of Spirit. All denominations should recognize the value of other paths, and partake in that value, while steadfastly awakening their own nature. Remember, when a person lashes out against others, it's projection in motion. And haven't we figured out that the world holds infinite potential and holds possibilities beyond projection?

There will be Toltecs who will bring forward yet another new cycle. This will be done not by their intent, but by Spirit working through them. By ruthless adherence to discipline and strategy, they will allow the force of Spirit to call forth another dawn, a new and masterful expression of the Toltec Way.

2

A Dream
of Completeness

The Journey

Half of me swims under the sea,
and half walks as a spiritual woman.
My golden hair flows from side to side;
my fins glide through the marine-salty water.
One step is a memory,
and the other step is a new journey.
When I go, I hear a hummingbird
reminding me of a dream:
My friends were fish;
my world was blue.
Now I'm astonished,
I can remember all these moments.

Awakening the energy body is the primary goal within the modern Toltec path. This energetic configuration accounts for everything said, heard, imagined, and done. As such, it offers a radical reaccounting of what it means to be human. Not accounting for it and its influence automatically deprives us of our completeness. Walking down the street without awareness of your energy body is akin to not being aware of your legs.

Humans, like no other creature on Earth, adds don Juan, take notice of what is inside their energy bodies (*Fire*, 83). This is an important point as it addresses the key to awakening the energy body: the handling of what Castaneda calls *self-importance* (*Journey*, 37–45). Self-importance, or what I prefer to call *self-reflection*, consists of the stream of thoughts and feelings we have *about* the world. It is by definition self-limiting, as our thoughts and feelings cannot possible capture the entire universe in order to portray an entire view of the world. There is also an emotional aspect: self-reflection. Feeling too good for something, or not good enough, maps the end of a spectrum relating to emotional reflections. The common denominator of mental and emotional reflection is the snare they create to hold perception back. It is a self-serving loop created by having the world mirror our thoughts and feelings rather than ascertaining what the world actually *is*.

In other words, we have a highly refined sense of self. However, we usually get lost in ourselves and forget about the rest of the world as we spend most of our energy reflecting to ourselves about our world. Lost within a mirror-bubble of our own making, we prattle on and on without ever going anywhere. We build a complex inventory without really challenging the content, value, or effects of it. The idea is that we isolate and build upon specific elements of our reality. These items are the inventory. But they are only reference points within the infinity of awareness.

Boyfriends and girlfriends, patriotism, the pursuit of material wealth, the world as physical objects, reincarnation or not . . . all of these are pieces of an inventory and so allow us to entertain and use the world. They also hold the power to hem us in, to restrain the recognition that other inventories, other cohesions, other worlds, exist. An inventory gives us things to look for, and if something is not in our inventory, we may not even recognize it when we do perceive it. Inventories are the stuff of dreams, large and small. It is the shared, vivid dreams that are eventually brought into the daily world to become a socially agreed upon *reality*. Pieces of an inventory are established and are bound together through the selective cueing process that we have discussed earlier—the deliberate calling to our attention features of the world. Repetitive selective cueing is how inventories are built and maintained, then somehow become reality.

Toltecs add considerably to their inventory by including a description of and uses for the energy body—such as dreaming. This automatically sets up the condition that awareness can move beyond the ordinary human region. The idea that this is even possible allows the possibility of opening up to a nonordinary inventory. The modern Toltec is also interested in stepping away from all inventories and into a relationship with the world of pure *being*, the quintessential human dream of completeness. Dreaming is a way to accelerate this process by awakening the entire energy body; a fully awake energy body produces *being*.

A WORLD OF ENERGY

The human energy body rests in a sea of energy emanating from a source. Toltecs often refer to this source as the *Eagle*, yet doing so is a contrivance, simply a way to recognize a higher power (*Fire*, 51). Perhaps source may also be considered to be a theological God, which I personally have no problem with, as a Toltec rendering doesn't necessarily counter-argue the existence of God. It's simply a matter of one's inventory.

The emanations of energy from source are consistent and stable. That is, they exist as objective portions of the universe, just as inventories of the physical universe (such as the Earth, the solar system, various galaxies, etc.) exist (*Dreaming*, 6). And just as there are energetic attributes of the physical universe—electromagnetic bandwidth spectrums, radios, and cell phones, for example—emanations of energy from source comprise different bandwidths (although they are perhaps not yet mapped). In these terms, the energy body belongs to a specific band of energy; naturally enough, the human emanation of the Eagle. Within this band are a number of narrower bands, just as an AM or FM radio band has numerous stations. The process of dreaming is actually the process of observing, hooking on to, and traveling along these emanations.

From ancient times, such observation has typically been undertaken by mystics and prophets and done via innate capacities of perception such as *seeing*, a faculty of perception where one directly perceives energy. Through *seeing* it is plainly evident that there is a nonphysical energy that surrounds and permeates the physical body. When first *seeing* the energy body, people often observe a haze, a very soft rain of light, or a band of white energy around a person's physical body. Continued practice yields the perception of an oblong ball of light. Within this ball are ropes of light that resemble a bundle of fiber optics. Don Juan says that the ancient Toltecs discovered that this glowing energy associated with the energy body is responsible for awareness (*Dreaming*, 8). Just as the physical body has various systems (respiratory, circulatory, skeletal, etc.) the energy body has distinct features and systems. Here are a few components of this specific inventory of the energy body:

The first energy field. For most people the right side of the energy body is only a narrow slice of the entire body and so this ordinary awareness is relegated to what is known by social agreement or standards of "accepted" knowledge. By adopting a nonordinary reality, Toltecs deliberately expand their known world and, therefore, their right side becomes larger than normal, indicating increased awareness.

The second energy field. The larger area of the energy body contains the unknown. It also holds the energy of dreaming. Dreaming as dealt with this book is the process of engaging this energy field. In so doing, the unknown becomes realized as part of the known world as measured by an increased first field. Another way of saying this is that as you develop awareness through dreaming, the first and second fields merge. This produces yet another dynamic, one associated with the state of *being*; this will be covered in greater detail later in the book.

The third energy field. This energy is all that is outside the energy body. In other words, it is the domain of all emanations, those of humanness and those not. Awakening the entire energy body not only provides *being* but also sets the stage to catapult awareness beyond all human confines into the complete unknowable, a procedure Toltecs refer to as "burning with the Fire from Within" (*Silence*, 228).

The first, second, and third energy fields permeate all creation. This Toltec trinity of known, unknown, and unknowable may also be thought of as order, entirely new levels of order, and the driving force or spirit of the whole operation. Using terms such as the first, second, and third energy fields provides a vehicle with which to refocus ourselves. This selective cueing calls our attention to them. Searching for recognition, our perception then tracks the concept, looking to match it with experience. However, we often interpret the vehicle as the reality. We turn a definition into reality itself. Doing so, we again remove ourselves from primary reality—all that is without interpretation—and captivate ourselves with our shenanigans of creating a way to make sense of our experiences.

A secondary reality—ordinary or nonordinary—results as we interpret and give form to our experiences. In itself, this is not good or bad. It's what we humans do. In terms of exploring and developing perception, the problems begin when we give so much form to our experiences that we shut down the flow of formless, pure energy, the energy of God, Spirit, primary reality, whatever you want to call it, resulting in a stagnation of awareness. And then we think and act like we *really* know what's going on. But as we cultivate a sense of the third attention, a realization that something is always just out of reach, we begin to spread ourselves across all levels of attention. We unfold into new worlds and perceive new and more flexible relations among the contents of a secondary reality. As we do this, we incorporate primary reality into our secondary reality. This is the essential maneuver of dreaming while awake and of *being*.

According to the Toltec Way, additional components of this inventory include the following.

Regions

Don Juan says that the energy body is a bundle of several regions. Some regions hold awareness of organic life, some inorganic life, and some no life; they are solely organizations of energy. Only one of these regions is what we associate with human activity (*Fire*, 161–65).

Uniformity

This pertains to the overall shape of the energy body. Don Juan maintains that this shape changes over time (*Dreaming*, 5). Over the course of millennia, it has gone from being football-shaped to egg-shaped, perhaps on its way to becoming a perfect sphere. Hence, uniformity directly relates to evolution. It may well be that this shape has changed over time as a result of the energy bodies of many people becoming more awake and thereby creating pressure from within that has changed uniformity across the species. It could also be an external force causing the shift as well. The bottom line is that perception changes as uniformity changes.

Cohesion

The pattern of energy inside the energy body is *cohesion*. Uniformity plays a determining role in what types of patterns may form as the nature of the container effects that which is within it. While Toltecs think the Eagle bestows awareness through its emanations, exactly *what* is perceived by the individual occurs through cohesion. It is an energetic signature, a pattern of energy that perceives similar patterns. So what you experience throughout the day reflects your cohesion (*Fire*, 163; *Dreaming*, 40).

Your cohesion also changes throughout the day. You might get angry, tired, pumped up, or glued to a television. Plus, different cultures have slightly different cohesions. However, these variations are all very minor changes. They might even be thought of as fluctuations within one cohesion, and this one cohesion is known as *reality*. So within a cohesion there are many options.

While several regions exist within the energy body, cohesion typically brings our attention to only one, the ordinary human region. But change your cohesion and you change your perception. Change it enough and you enter new worlds. When don Juan says he turns into a crow, for instance, he attributes this to reconfiguring his energy. And the capacity for this marvel, he insists, rests within the personal energy body (*Dreaming*, 217). How's that for an option? On a more ordinary scale, cohesion determines all of the options within your inventory and an inventory holds cohesion in place. They contain that much power.

Clarity of perception is governed by how well cohesion has been formed. This makes perfect sense. The more proficient with you become with something—anything—the more skill you have and the clearer you are about it. And dreaming is "simply" exercising the capacity to manage cohesion. The clearer the dream, the more well formed the cohesion (*Dreaming*, 70).

Focal point

This is a small area of vibrant energy within the energy body. It is what Castaneda refers to as the *assemblage point*. It is the connecting point, the point of entry, for emanations to enter an individual's energy body (*Dreaming*, 6–7). Cohesion results from this interaction, and clarity of perception hinges on how well the emanations are translated. On the positive side, self-reflection engages this process, to allow more energy to enter and to interpret it objectively. On the negative side, this reflection becomes overly focused and calcified—an emanation is isolated and then projected as being more than it is, as being a complete reality.

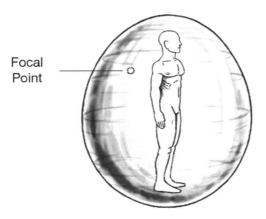

Focal
Point

The Energy Body and Focal Point

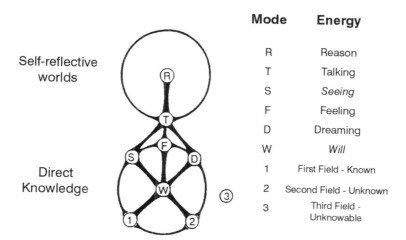

	Mode	Energy
	R	Reason
	T	Talking
	S	*Seeing*
	F	Feeling
	D	Dreaming
	W	*Will*
	1	First Field - Known
	2	Second Field - Unknown
	3	Third Field - Unknowable

Self-reflective worlds

Direct Knowledge

The Eight Cornerstones of Perception. *This diagram represents the organization of perception as viewed in Toltec philosophy. (Diagram from Norbert Classen, Das Wissen der Tolteken, Freiburg, Germany: Hans-Nietsch-Verlag, 2002. Used with permission.)*

Cornerstone	Location[1]	Perception
Reason	Brain	Organizes information from the intellect and five physical senses.
Talking	Brain	Indirect, symbolic assessment of self and environment through translating information from the senses.
Will	Abdomen	Umbilical-like connection with the cosmos; provides control of other cornerstones.
Feeling	Heart	Intuition and affective assessment of self and environment.
Dreaming	Liver	Dreams, dreaming-body states, and nonphysical dimensions may be accessed through this cornerstone.
Seeing	Pancreas	Direct knowledge bypassing the intellect, including perceiving visions and auric fields.
First Energy Field	Genitals	Order, structure, relation, known world.
Second Energy Field	Rectum	Avoid containing human awareness, the unknown.

Within the energy body are different capacities for perception. Their sum and total is what don Juan calls the totality of awareness (*Tales*, 98). I refer to these modes of perception and their organization as *cornerstones,* as they are indeed the support structures of engaging the energy body.

From the chart, notice that reason and *will* form two centers or organization points. Reason organizes thoughts about your environment, your desires and goals, and your worldview. It receives information from the process of talking (to yourself and others). In spite of reason's power, it caters to perceptions on the surface of existence. The more you talk to yourself and create a worldview, the further you remove yourself from total experience. As you verbalize an experience, you symbolize or represent the experience, thus removing yourself from it. As you interpret the symbols, you again remove yourself further from the actual experience. Once and twice removed from complete experience, you perceive only what you have created in thought. This is a great power in itself but it pulls you away from the source of creation, which lies beyond description. Don Juan maintains that as civilization evolved talking and the utilization of reason have eclipsed our other faculties.

Will, one of the renewed faculties, is like an umbilical cord connecting us with creation. As an activating force of nonordinary perceptions, *will* offers an immediate knowing; a direct assessment of the environment that bypasses reflection.

My first experience with *will* occurred one day as I was walking past a U.S. Navy housing complex. As the first twenty-four years of my life were associated with the military, I felt a sense of belonging to it. I entertained thoughts about the Navy and my relation to it. I then felt pressure just below my navel. Something pushed out from the inside and I felt a stream of energy flowing from my abdomen out into the world. It seemed to direct itself toward the housing complex. As I paid attention to this odd, but not uncomfortable sensation, I discovered I could isolate different, very specific feelings. As though the stream of energy were a flashlight scanning a large room, I examined several feelings associated with navy life.

Without conscious deliberation, I settled within a strong feeling that indicated the apartments did not reflect my present life. I then summoned past feelings about Navy life. I noticed my thoughts served as a focus, enabling another part of me to actually produce the feelings of old. Bringing my attention back to the present, my awareness centered itself in *will*, where I was no longer part of the Navy. The housing was part of my world, but I was not a part of the housing. From this experience, I found I could distinguish between reason and *will*.

Will connects with and directs the five remaining avenues of perception. One of these is feeling, an independent mode of perception characterized by various types of feelings. Cultivating feeling enables telepathy and other forms of psychic communication, heightened intuition, and awareness of deeper, more extensive connections with creation. My first encounter with *will* occurred through feeling. As I have not physically been in don Juan's presence since 1978, feeling has enabled periodic communication with him. This communication typically involves receiving a course of action to handle troublesome events. I then use feeling to supplement his recommendations.

Dreaming involves purposefully using the second field for gathering knowledge and awakening the entire energy body. Although dream interpretation is commonly applied to dreaming, another application is developing the dreaming body, or the energy form that defines an out-of-body experience. In this book, I refer to the out-of-body experience as a *dreaming body experience*, or DBE for short. (I will go into DBEs in greater detail a bit later.) During a DBE event, you have the perception of leaving the physical body. But this is only the perception—you've never actually gone out of yourself. You have experienced a shift in cohesion, a change in the location of your focal point, and you are having a dreaming experience. You haven't lost your mind; you've found more of it.

Seeing involves breaking the veils of perception. Having visions, perceiving auric fields, and any form of direct knowing are aspects of *seeing*. According to don Juan, *seeing* results only when you are able to suspend the process of thinking. Whereas dreaming includes a marked tendency to retain subject-object awareness where you perceive a seemingly external environment, with *seeing*, the subject-object awareness disappears as internal and external environments become one.

Seeing relates to a fullness of perception, a unique form of visual-like data. While it may incorporate certain kinds of mental imagery, it is not visualization nor is it random. *Seeing* pertains to ascertaining that which already exists. It also involves perceiving something from a totally different mode than normal, physical perception. You might *see* a luminous vision, a mental image superimposed over a physical image, or another image that presents direct insight into a situation, problem, or event. Visualization, on the other hand, pertains to actively creating mental images. We can also passively entertain mental images without *seeing*.

The first and second energy fields connect only to *will*. These points form a mating, a pair consisting of order and void, known and unknown. Don Juan refers to these points as the *tonal* (toh-na'hl) and the *nagual* (nah-wa'hl) as well as the first and second attentions (*Tales*, 121; *Fire*, 46). The first field reflects order and organization. It allows you to gain awareness of relations between and among the elements of any dimension, physical or nonphysical. Through the selective cueing of what is considered important in forming an inventory, reason arranges the order found in the first field. As valuable as this is, it is a limited, indirect cultivation and formation of what is known about the world. Typically, this process gives you something to talk about and then listens to itself, creating a self-serving loop of information: self-reflection.

It is for this reason that don Juan considers stopping the internal dialogue one of the more important techniques (*Tales*, 34, 233). By interrupting the normal flow of thoughts that uphold your world, you allow new perceptions to surface. This enables you to suspend the constant brain chatter that tells you that "this is thus" and "that is so."

The second energy field pertains to a void that is full. It is the space between bits of matter, and yet it is not. It contains all matter yet is not matter. It also produces an effect of movement, just as the black spaces between individual, still pictures produce the effect of movement as you watch a motion picture. Referring to this as void, space, and effect places it into some kind of order and thus automatically puts it in the domain of the first field. But to get the notion and then the experience that there is another dimension to human awareness requires a little selective cueing, and so the descriptive words help get the idea across.

The cornerstones also have physical locations, which serves to cue a connection between physical and nonphysical energies. I'm sure that, in time, scientific explanations will account for the connections between physical organs and specific modes of perception. In the meantime, we are given the map from Toltecs who have *seen* the correspondence—in the same manner that a CAT scan depicts certain areas of activity in the brain corresponding to certain behaviors.

Often near the surface of the energy body, sometimes within it, is a small star, a piece of the energy body that is brighter than its surroundings. This unobtrusive glow is the focal point. Where it is located corresponds to what is being perceived. For example, when it is on the right side of the luminous body, you experience the first field, physical perceptions. If it is on the left side, you experience the second field, dreaming side of your life. None of these perceptions ever disappear; they are always with you. It is a matter of where you train the focal point to rest, and how you train it to move that governs what you perceive.

By using feeling to explore subtle shifts and movements between moods, physical locations, people, and dreams (for example), you can sense the movement of the focal point. Often excessive fatigue or stress generates a shift of the focal point and a person may experience unusual perceptions such as a spontaneous DBE or *seeing*. With practice and patience, you can learn to control the focal point's movement through directing intent.

There is a natural movement of the focal point from the right to the left side of the energy body during sleep. Ordinary dreams seem vague and shift from scene to scene since you have no control of them. It is not the lack of ability to control the dream, per se, but the inability to steady the focal point that gives a perception of shifting dreams. By stabilizing the focal point, you gain control of the dream. Shift the focal point a little more and you produce a DBE. Shift to a certain point, and you begin to *see*.

The focal point is where consciousness of energy translates into personal awareness. Since we usually maintain a stable reality through life, its movement is often very slight. Nonetheless, influenced by age, culture, associates, indeed all of our experiences, we make minor modifications and changes in its position throughout life. Sufficient experience with nonordinary reality may cause a major movement and re-stabilization; personal reality then changes. Gaining control of the focal point enables a myriad of experiences—all of which are a part of the energy body and hence part of oneself. Taking this a step further, the physical body is one part of the energy body, a small area of the entire energetic structure. You might say the physical body is but one focal point position.

To live as a Toltec requires stabilizing the focal point in an area of the luminous body that reflects nonordinary reality. Although this is a significant accomplishment, it still does not permit freedom. However, finding the point between worlds provides energy that enables you to keep moving the focal point, as you attempt to experience all of the luminous body at once. Don Juan maintains that doing so makes us fully attentive to the third field and thus helps us achieve complete awareness and freedom.

Controlling the focal point may have other benefits as well. During a dream, for instance, I *saw* that moving the focal point relieves tension in the person and, as a result, in the environment. While dreaming, I saw a luminous body relax and achieve a gentle rhythm of energy within it. Since the person no longer tried to hold onto specific perceptions, tension waned. Since any energy body is a part of the light of all creation, the reduction of tension in the self reduces tension in the environment. When this happens reality becomes even more flexible. I intuitively realized that this flexibility could literally alter a course of events whereby humans could then better define their world, their reality. I felt that the evolution of Earth could avoid severe changes if humans could eliminate sufficient tension within themselves. This change would come about by a species-wide change in inventory, a change in the collective focal point.

THE EVOLUTION OF THE ENERGY BODY

Transcendence, as viewed along the lines of the energy body, is mechanical. As the first field relates to the known world, this energy may be considered to be realized energy. In turn, the second field relates to the unknown and so may be considered to be potential. As you tackle transcendence, you learn to handle different energies and use them to establish a foundation from which to explore the unknown. In other words, you use the stability of the first field to intentionally enter, explore, and develop the second field.

You also learn to handle dreaming energies and express them in your physical world. As a result, you expand the first field. That is, you have realized more of your potential. It is by hooking the first and second fields together that you evolve beyond the normal human condition. The more you stretch the first field into the second field, (which is also a way of saying you have expressed more of the second field into the first), the more these terms become meaningless; you have evolved past the conditions they represent. You have broken the spell.

The energy bodies of the old cycle of Toltecs had more of an oblong shape than exists today. Maybe this is why they lost themselves in

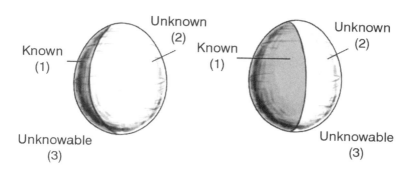

Evolving through the Energy Body. As the first energy field extends into the second field, you become more aware of the complete energy body.

bizarre, and often aberrant, practices. By contrast, the evolution of the human energy body is such that it's becoming more spherical (*Dreaming*, 5–13). Therefore, the new uniformity is automatically producing changes in cohesion, which is automatically changing perception, which is automatically changing behavior. Put another way, a change in uniformity provides automatic shifts of cohesion, producing new connections within and without, thereby enabling new awareness and abilities, engendering new thoughts to access other worlds.

By the time you have hooked the first and second fields together, you have radically transformed the way you view yourself and the world. You have grown into a unified whole where the energy body reaches out to, and connects with, the third energy field. You have then begun to evolve beyond the normal human condition. What you find is, by definition, outside the normal human inventory and social base. At this point, the only thing for certain is that you get to start all over again to fully engage a new level.

CHAKRAS

Another way of viewing and learning to experience the luminous body is through chakras: nonphysical energy centers. Many traditional disciplines indicate there are seven chakras. Some people say there are thirteen. In chapter 5 we'll look at *dreaming gates,* some of which are located in proximity to the chakras, while others are located in the lower regions of the physical body. For now, the main point is to establish a relationship with energetic systems of human anatomy. For this purpose, you'll tap ten chakra energies. Even though there is disagreement on the number of chakras, there is usually agreement on the functions of the first seven. On a mass scale, knowledge of the chakras came to the Western world via Eastern disciplines such as yoga and Hinduism. During the psychedelic days of the 1960s, Eastern philosophies gained many adherents and their beat still resonates today.

Each of the chakras generates a specific energy, and each has its own properties. Developing familiarity with each and balancing one with another, we develop harmony in all spheres that influence the human condition. While all chakras influence perception, the dominant energy center determines what is being perceived. The following chart selectively cues the general physical locations of the chakras in addition to offering their basic landscapes. Note that each chakra resonates with a specific color. The shade of an individual color varies according to the nature of the person. We are the rainbow people, after all, and the chakras are part of our completeness.

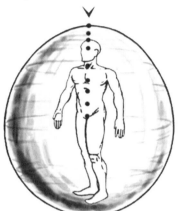

Chakra Locations

Location	Color	Perception
Base of spine	Red	This center relates to physical and biological energy. It carries with it concerns for physical survival. Developed in a balanced manner, its raw, generative power provides energy to move perception to the other chakras.
Abdomen	Orange	Here we find emotional energy. We now have two energies affecting our awareness, thus we feel more animated through this partnership of duality. Some nonordinary systems hold that this area carries sexual energy. Other systems relegate sexual energy to the first center.
Solar Plexus	Yellow	This is mental energy. As such, it provides powers for discrimination between and among the first three chakras. It also relates to control or mastery of the environment.

Location	Color	Perception
Heart	Green	This union/communion energy grants us our first sense of being connected with others and with the environment. This perception of oneness is through relations between and among other life forms.
Base of throat	Light blue	Here we tap communication energy. We also begin directing our intent by using the voice as a vehicle to do so. Many people think that this center carries the initial awareness of God.
Forehead	Dark blue	This psychic energy provides for awareness and command of power through the perception and knowledge of nonphysical orders. In the same manner a physicist learns the natural order of the physical world, the metaphysician learns the natural order of nonphysical realms. Many traditions refer to this as the *third eye,* connoting psychic awareness through visions, telepathy, and other paranormal activities.
Crown of the head	Violet	This is the border separating the natural order of Earth and its inhabitants with other dimensions. Often thought of as the spiritual center, it facilitates our evolution beyond earthy concerns.
Six to eight	Enon	The color enon is a blend of pink, violet, and metallic inches above metallic silver. You probably have seen it on late model automobiles and vans. Auto makers pin many labels on approximations of this color, labels such as "champagne" and "metallic rose." Although we probably have had this chakra with us since time began, we have only recently activated or evolved to it en masse. Partial evidence for this claim is the rise in books, lectures, and seminars dealing with extraterrestrials and nonphysical entities. I regard this chakra as transdimensional energy that provides awareness of and communication with nonphysical entities and extraterrestrial intelligence, be it biological or otherwise.

Location	Color	Perception
One to two feet above the head	White	Located at the very top of the luminous body, this embraces the radiations from which all colors of the visible human light spectrum emanate. Immersed in white light you will soon discover undifferentiated oneness; complete oneness without perceiving any distinctions or relationships whatsoever. Whereas the heart center provides awareness of connections within oneness, here we blissfully acknowledge our wholeness.
Above the light body	Symbol V	This center can't really be called energy because the source of the human energy bandwidth is the white. This non-energy is the unmanifest from which creation springs forth. Some Eastern disciplines refer to it as the Godhead, the originator of God. As it is outside the realm of color, I have only perceived it as the symbol V. This paradoxical perception feels intensely powerful without the usual feelings of energy found in previous centers. It resembles a vacuum filled with everything. It also represents the emanations and environmental influences on perception.

Chakras are aspects of an emanation, a particular bandwidth associated with human consciousness. Each chakra represents a specific cohesion. The chakras run almost in a straight line from the base of the spine to beyond the crown of the head, a linear organization of perception. During the development of this system, India was steeped in culture and was a bastion of civilization. Straight lines were part of the mix. On the other hand, in the Toltec cornerstone chart we have viewed earlier on page 27, notice how the eight cornerstones form a *nonlinear* organization. The Toltecs lived close to nature. As straight lines in nature are uncommon if not rare, the lineage of the Toltecs evolved directly from their experience with life.

There are other distinctions in the way the chakras and cornerstones are organized. Rather than viewing the tenth chakra as the originator of the ninth chakra and the ninth chakra the source of everything else, the first and second fields create a view where there is a mutual bonding between source and creation, both always having existed simultaneously. Whereas the chakras form a linear and hierarchical framework, the cornerstones mold perception into a nonlinear, egalitarian model.

Both provide a way to step outside of ordinary reality and explore nonordinary realities. Yet the chakra system and the eight cornerstones account for similar perceptions. For instance, the tenth chakra correlates with the third field, the sixth chakra to *seeing*, the fourth chakra to feeling, and the second chakra to dreaming. Environmental and cultural influences yield different cohesions, and different cohesions produce different systems. Yet since uniformity is the same, the systems account for similar notions of what can be perceived. I think this is why both systems may be universally applied, as both outline what is natural to humans, but do so from different angles reflected by environmental influences.

To help you get a sense of balancing the chakras, please try the following exercise. Keep in mind that you are stimulating your entire energy body. I have found, from the reports of others, that this is a key exercise in helping produce DBEs.

☀ The Chakra Tune-Up

1. You will work with eight chakras. The ninth chakra comprises all that is of the human domain, and therefore it has its own state of balance. The tenth chakra is way beyond the scope of this exercise and so balance, relating to it, does not even enter the picture. However, after the initial exercise, you may focus your attention in the direction of the ninth and/or tenth chakra, using the tune-up to provide an extra boost of energy to explore those regions of awareness.

2. Down the left side of a blank sheet of paper, list one feature of each chakra, leaving space between each category as you do so. For example, 1-Physical energy; 2-Emotions; 3-Mental abilities; 4-Unity with fellow humans; 5-Communicating with others;

6-Psychic abilities; 7-Spirituality; 8-Extraterrestrial intelligence.

3. Under each category, write one thing you like and one thing you dislike about each. Have fun with this and don't take it too seriously. If you can't think of anything, write down the first thing that enters your thoughts. For instance, you may find it difficult to come up with something you dislike about spirituality. Be liberal about answering. You may not like having to wear a suit and tie to church. You may not enjoy having to drive so far to your weekly meditation meeting. There are no right or wrong answers. In addition, you are not focusing on your dislikes in order to express them. You are becoming more aware of yourself and thus how to better focus your energies. Awareness is knowledge.

4. For each chakra, imagine a sphere of energy. Each sphere should correspond in color with that chakra. For example, the first sphere is red and the second is orange, although the shade of color is your preference. You may also use a form other than a sphere. If visualization is not a strong ability, use whatever form of perception works for you. You might perceive red as a sound, or as a taste, for example. You can also stimulate visualizing red by remembering what a stop sign or a red traffic light looks like.

5. Let the bottom of each sphere represent what you dislike about that energy, and let the top of the sphere represent what you like. You will move from the first chakra to the eighth chakra by placing your attention at the bottom of each sphere (representing what you dislike), and then moving your attention to the top of the sphere (representing what you like). Pause briefly at each point. When you arrive at the top of the eighth chakra, you need no longer concern yourself with likes and dislikes. Now allow your awareness to return, flowing gently back through each chakra to the first chakra.

6. Instead of relating chakra energies to likes and dislikes, now let the bottom of each sphere represent negative polarity and the top represent positive polarity. The positive and negative polarities carry neutral connotations and relate to positive and

negative in the same manner that batteries have positive and negative poles. Place your attention at the negative pole of the first chakra, then the positive pole, and work your way up to the eighth chakra, again pausing at each point. At the top of the eighth chakra, you need no longer concern yourself with polarity. Let your awareness flow gently back through each chakra to the first, paying particular attention to the feeling of energy movement.

7. Shift your focus away from polarity to perceive the movement of energy throughout the charkas, without identifying or labeling the energy. Simply proceed through each chakra, from the first to the eighth. Feel the energy move. Allow your awareness to return gently to the first chakra.

8. At your own pace, cycle energy up and down, through the eight chakras. Do this several times.

9. Now bring your energy to a harmonious state as you feel energy evenly distributed throughout your chakras. You may not sense a cyclic flow of energy as much as you feel peaceful and balanced throughout, perhaps as though you are vibrating. If you do feel a cyclic movement, that's fine. Simply allow the energy to move.

10. During these steps, use your internal, nonverbal dialogue. For example, if you perceive green energy as dim and lackluster, ask it, through thoughts, images, and/or feeling, why this is so. It may reflect a lack of balance in your relationships. Or it may be that you have been working hard in this area and simply need a little rest. Ask about the problem. Ask if you can pull energy from another chakra and give it to the green energy. If one chakra is brighter than the others, ask how you can liven up the others. Strive to feel comfortable with this dialogue as you assess what is happening within you.

The Chakra Tune-Up has a bonus of teaching you a little alchemy. Say you are feeling pretty good and then walk into a room and suddenly feel down. Since you have been working with shifting negative to positive energy, simply remember that shift and perform it. In so doing, you have shifted your focal point.

We'll tackle some Toltec-oriented exercises later. For now, the important point is that by exercising the cornerstones and chakras you automatically develop more awareness. Doing so is quite compatible as they are both energy-based systems. And we're talking about becoming more aware, not necessarily becoming more "Toltec." You can use your newfound abilities to develop your intellect, your emotional intelligence, and your psychic prowess. Just remember the idea is to awaken your energy body, not use your power for duplicity or greed. By managing your various energies well, you step further into the unknown. At the same time, you build more of the known.

3

Domains of Dreaming

Land of Dreams

Corn swirling in the cool wind,
babbling brooks with white glowing water.
Mystical stones of old Celtic times,
meadows of magenta red poppies.
Forests and woods with wonderful ancient trees,
animal homes in the grassy and mossy grounds.
Children playing and running about,
cows and chickens making farmlike sounds.
Castles and rocks,
climbing mountains to reach the sun.
Fish in the nice and peaceful seas.

Don Juan says there are three ways the energy body deals with energy (*Dreaming*, 31). One is to perceive, or *see*, the flow of energy. Another is to use it as a boost into other worlds, or nonordinary dreaming. And the third is to perceive our ordinary world. This can also be mixed and matched so that you can use it to *see* conditions of energy in your daily world. You can *see* while having a DBE, or any other form of dreaming for that matter. At this level of dreaming, your senses are heightened and you've temporarily removed yourself from the stress of the physical world. This frees up a significant amount of energy, allowing you to exercise *seeing*. Then, in a traditional shamanic maneuver, you bring home what you learned in dreaming in order to practically apply it to all aspects of your life.

You can also take the energy gained from radical explorations of the cosmos and bring it home to boost your sense of daily life, to enter into heightened awareness. Daily life is a dream, after all, so why not deal with it as such? Due to our social agreements, we've standardized cohesion, a shared cohesion that becomes quite fixated much to the detriment of the species and the planet. And it is important to note that these agreements may be of the ordinary or nonordinary kind. While an energetic reality itself is much more vibrant, fluid, and majestic than the ordinary material world, it is built of an inventory and so may be the means of captivity or liberation, a dream of bondage or of completeness.

After I had left Tucson and my physical encounters with don Juan, I was researching a magazine article on out-of-body experiences (OBE), when I discovered the Monroe Institute, located in the foothills of the Blue Ridge Mountains of Virginia. The Institute was founded by Robert Monroe, author of a classic book on out-of-body experiences, *Journeys Out of the Body*.[1] I discovered that the Monroe Institute had pioneered a technology using sound to assist in balancing electrical brainwaves. This results in a sustained focus of attention, which is one effect of meditation. My initiation into the Institute's work was by attending a six-day, in-residence seminar. During it, I fell headlong into an unexpected journey that later included time in the Institute's dream-research laboratory.

A few months after my introduction to the Institute, I began working for the Association for Research and Enlightenment in Virginia Beach, Virginia. (As mentioned earlier, the Association for Research and Enlightenment—or A.R.E. for short—is the sister organization of the Edgar Cayce Foundation.) One of the more interesting events was discovering that Edgar Cayce had also dealt with sophisticated levels of dreaming, including *astral projection*, which is often considered to be an OBE. (As indicated earlier, for the purposes of this work, I'll use the term *dreaming-body experience*, or DBE, to indicate an OBE.)

DBE is an advanced technique that provides insight and control of the second energy field. Often people define a DBE as a dream, a mental flight of consciousness, or another form of psychic phenomena. However, in keeping with the literature that defines a classic DBE, I view dreams and mental projections as *other-than-physical-body experiences*. DBE is one form of the other-than-physical-body experience, and it has three common features.

First, consciousness is exteriorized away from the physical body. Once this has been experienced, you can entertain no doubt that consciousness can exist outside your physical body. Through DBE, you may view your physical body from your bedroom ceiling or from across a room.

Second, this nonphysical perspective has form of some kind. This form is the dreaming body. It might resemble your physical body where you experience arms, legs, shoulders, etc. Or it might be a sphere of light or some other form, such as an animal. If you choose, you may also replicate your physical senses: you can see, hear, smell, touch, and taste.

Third, the form is animated and has emotions. DBE is not dry in the sense of just being aware. It carries the capacity for different kinds of movement, feelings, and emotions.

Since the dreaming body has form and emotions, you can interact with your surroundings as you would from your physical body. Indeed, the similarities of perception with the physical body, plus the enhanced capabilities of the dreaming body, make DBE a practical method to better understand perception. Replicating the physical senses serves as a bridge between physical and nonphysical perception, preventing the experience from becoming too removed from the ordinary. The enhanced abilities during a DBE—such as transcending ordinary time and space—accelerate learning by providing varied experiences from which to measure and to comprehend awareness.

As part of my affiliation with the Monroe Institute, I talked and corresponded with people all around the world about DBE, wherein I found a variety of explanations regarding DBE. One view states that the dreaming body already exists and remains continually active; that a DBE is a shift in awareness from the physical to a nonphysical body. Another view states that we exist everywhere at once, and training is required to focus attention in different ways. The physical body and the dreaming body are seen as two of many manifestations within overall awareness. Another view maintains that exercises are necessary to create a non-physical body, which then leaves the physical body.

One view maintains that DBE is an actual separation from the physical body, while another view holds that the transition and separation are illusory, that it's a matter of refocusing attention. And yet another view maintains that DBE is an electrochemical reaction and all experience occurs solely within the brain, an interesting hallucination at best.

From these discussions with others about DBEs, I found that regardless of cultural upbringing or explanations about DBE, many of the actual DBE experiences are similar. For instance, I heard many stories of spontaneous DBEs, where the dreaming body hovers on the ceiling of the bedroom, looking down on and observing a sleeping physical body. The surprise at viewing the physical body from a distance typically jolts the nonphysical body back into the physical body. People also reported the ability to glide through walls and ceilings, and view their neighborhood almost as though they were in their physical bodies. These common experiences point to DBE as a mode of perception natural to the human species.

I have also learned that almost anything can bring about a DBE. Besides a near-death experience, fatigue, stress, despair, and illness can alter normal processes, allowing the perception of a separation between physical and nonphysical energies. A DBE may also result from joy, euphoria, or ecstasy.

By definition, spontaneous DBEs occur randomly, without notice or an intent to bring them about. Spontaneous DBEs provide interesting stories and often leave lasting impressions. They also offer clues regarding how to purposefully experience dreaming. In fact, circumstances surrounding a spontaneous DBE often closely match circumstances surrounding a deliberate DBE. For example, an unusually deep meditation might trigger a spontaneous or a sought-after DBE, the principal difference being that the person who had a deliberate DBE incorporated the intent to have one within the meditation. For this person, DBEs occur regularly, not randomly. Later in this book, in chapter 11, we will go into DBE's in greater detail, particularly how to activate the potential to experience them.

The currents of my life dictated that I leave the A.R.E. and return to the mountains where I eventually became employed at the Monroe Institute. As in Vietnam, a force seemingly outside of, or beyond, my conscious self determined what lay in store for me. But before I left for the hills, I was given an unexpected gift of three sessions in a flotation tank. The gift came from a man who was on his deathbed.

Floating has gained popularity as a result of its many benefits, including relaxation, its ability to enhance problem solving, and its ability to enable the general exploration of consciousness. A float tank was once called a "sensory deprivation chamber." It was invented by John Lilly, M.D., the man who pioneered communication with dolphins and who also has a list of medical technology inventions to his credit.[2]

The proprietor of the float tank patiently explained the procedure. She told me I would be alone in a completely dark environment, suspended in water saturated with several hundred pounds of Epsom salts. The salts provide buoyancy, to keep me floating on the surface of the warm water. A good tip, she said, is not to worry about your head sinking. If you do, you tend to try to hold it up, causing tension in the neck muscles.

For each session, I undressed, showered, and then crawled through a small hatch, pulling it closed behind me, shutting out all light. I slipped into silky, sensuous water. I lay back, delighting in the odd sensation of floating effortlessly.

For the first session, I had two things on my mind before entering the tank. In other words, my intent was already loaded. The storyline of the movie *Altered States* was loosely based on John Lilly's explorations, and part of the movie's plot consisted of him changing his physical form into that of a prehistoric humanoid. I wanted to know how easy such a transmutation might be within this technological dream environment. Second, I wanted to see if I could separate my physical and nonphysical consciousness and have a DBE.

Shortly into the session, I lost all physical sensations. I then gained the subjective awareness of being a five-foot lizard emerging from the water onto a shoreline. Through the lizard's eyes, I saw a tropical beach lined with palm trees. I felt bombarded with data about the evolution of consciousness, symbolized by man as one focus of perception within all consciousness. The information was coming so fast I could hardly catch any of it. I also felt exceedingly aware of my lizard body and the environment. I soon realized a profound respect for the native intelligence and awareness of lizards. Never before had I instinctively sensed the environment with such clarity. As a lizard, I crawled out of the water a little more and then returned to the awareness of my physical body as I tried to analyze the experience.

Prior to this, during a few spontaneous DBEs, I had experienced shifts in perception from my human body to that of animals, not an uncommon dreaming experience for many people. This shift into lizardness, as it were, occurred with far less effort and with far greater control. The forty-five minute session ended just as I began thinking about out-of-body travel.

When pursuing a nonordinary reality, often a natural part of growth is becoming aware of phenomena such as DBEs and other dimensions such as those housing extraterrestrials, faeries, or whatever and whomever. From one perspective, it's a matter of perceiving that which is there already. Edgar Cayce, Robert Monroe, and don Juan all maintain that we regularly have other-than-physical body experiences during sleep. So as we develop awareness, we notice more of what we're already up to—including dreaming. This means that the essential method of developing dream states is developing awareness. With its versatile applications, practicing dreaming then becomes a tool to further develop awareness.

Ordinary dreaming has never captured my interest but DBEs have. However, en route to DBEs, my interest in other types of dreams widened as I discovered their capacities and levels of progression. Ordinary dreams became vivid, full of color and life. Achieving a degree of comfort with these, I began to have instructional dreams where the dream clearly imparted some kind of knowledge. Following these dreams, I would enter what's called a lucid dream and, after the lucid dream had firmly been established, a DBE would occur. With time and practice, the DBEs developed into occasional bilocations where I would be awake in two environments simultaneously.

Before tapping the vivid-dream stage, though, I first had to *remember* my dreams. Before this, I had to be aware of falling asleep. I realized that each evening I unwittingly intended to go to sleep rather than to be aware of dreaming. Instead of taking time to meditate, for instance, I would invariably roll over on my side, which was the signal to go to sleep. I realized that sleep entails a process of "falling off," and the work now involved maintaining awareness. To change habits, I would lie on my back and gaze at the middle of my forehead with my eyes closed. I programmed myself, as it were, with the suggestion: "enter your dreams to have a DBE." This led to pre-sleep experiences of seeing sparkles of light in deep darkness, sinking feelings, and an infusion of energy. It turns out that when I maintained an emotionally balanced, flowing life, the frequency and intensity of my dreaming increased.

This growth did not reflect a definite step-by-step process wherein DBEs always followed lucid dreams, which always followed vague dreams. I might have a DBE one night and a vague dream the next night. For this reason, the information here is not chronological; rather it is presented by topic in order to provide a better sense of what dreaming offers both from a practical and an adventurous standpoint. In looking at varieties of ordinary and nonordinary dreaming, we'll also touch on applying nonordinary dreaming to waking consciousness and, in later chapters, we'll explore this more fully. Dreaming, after all, is the skill of engaging awareness head on.

TYPES OF DREAMING

Vivid Dreaming

There are many things to consider when discussing the elements of a *vivid* dream, however, a key feature of a vivid dream is how much it distracts from the goal of a DBE. For example, during one vivid dream I found myself suspended in a matrix of objects that were equidistant from each other. Some of the objects were large metallic spheres, others were pyramids, and others were cubes. Although not visually apparent, I sensed each object was tethered to the objects surrounding it. Intrigued by the precision of the design, I lost all awareness that this was a dream and thus lost track of my goal to stay focused on dreaming itself, rather than on the dream's content.

Another experience demonstrated the value of *remembering* dreams. Years ago I usually drank a beer with lunch. At the time, I often wondered about the effects of alcohol on dreaming. Sometimes even one beer dulled my perception; other times it seemed to stimulate dream activity. One night I dreamed of a huge bottle of beer blocking the road I was driving on. The connection was obvious and I reduced my consumption, which seemed to assist dreaming.

Other vivid dreams readily lent themselves to interpretation. In one I was a submarine. While submerged, I scraped along the hull of an aircraft carrier. As I did, I stirred to life within the dream, although I did not take the dream to another level. Upon waking, I felt that the carrier represented power, and the submarine represented my subconscious. I had symbolically connected with the goal of tapping deeper levels of myself in order to develop personal power.

Often a vivid dream might have no meaning other than relating to and processing the events of daily life. For example, while considering which university courses I would take at school the following semester, I dreamed of asking a professor if she was going to teach magazine feature writing. She said yes. Although I did not take the course that semester, I later learned that she *did* teach it and I subsequently took the course. In another dream, a woman tried to guess my age; the prior evening I had discussed age, with friends, over dinner.

On another occasion, during a time when I was under stress and felt rushed with a variety of projects, I dreamed that I was driving my fourteen-year-old car on a bridge over a large body of water. The bridge kept rising higher and higher. The temperature gauge indicated my car's engine was hot but not overheated. I then noticed that the road was slick from rain, and my car was not noted for its traction. The steepness of the bridge further increased and I felt anxious about the car stalling and rolling backward. Just as I became aware of all of these adverse elements simultaneously, the bridge rose straight up, dissolved, and I woke up. These dreams reflected daily issues and tensions and serve to indicate the effect daily life has on dreaming and vice versa.

Some vivid dreams are exceedingly graphic, having extraordinary color, depth, and clarity. Often these, too, related to specific events in my daily life. In one dream I saw the transmission on my car leaking. The next day I noticed fluid on the ground under the transmission. Taking my car to a garage I found I had to have the seals replaced. Although it is quite possible that I had physically seen transmission fluid on the ground earlier without paying conscious attention to it, the dream brought the problem to my attention.

Other vivid dreams seemingly foretold events, with mixed results. In waking consciousness, I had finished an article, "On My Way to the Moon," which dealt with some of my DBEs. In order to gain exposure, I sent it to a magazine that had never published my work. The editor acknowledged receipt and his interest in the article. During one dream I talked with that editor. In the dream, he told me he had accepted the article and payment would be in the mail. In my physical life, he later rejected the article. This dampened my spirits regarding the viability of precognitive dreams. However, I also wondered if the dream might have foretold acceptance by another magazine and I had merely crossed my signals.

Seven months later I dreamed that my DBE article was in another magazine. The next day I printed two copies of the "Moon" article and sent them off to magazines that had previously published my material. One magazine rejected it, saying they were heading in new, more mainstream directions. The other magazine accepted it for publication.

During vivid dreaming, I exercised no control. I just sat back and watched the scenes unfold. Like watching a 3-D, stereophonic movie, the unusual stimulation of a heightened dream occupied my attention so that I would not remember to go beyond this level. As if the vividness were not enough of a problem, often nonsensical scenarios left me at a loss. For instance, in one vivid dream the novelty of seeing large insects flying over marching Australian sailors disrupted my concentration. In another dream, I tried to rinse two black ladybugs down a kitchen sink, but they hung on fiercely as their legs turned into human hands.

In another vivid dream, I was with a cowboy in the old West. We saw a rattlesnake and he tried to throw his leather glove over it. He missed. The snake prepared to strike, but since I was paying attention it did not. The cowboy then grabbed the snake in his right hand and walked off. Waking, I felt that the snake represented feminine energy, which I needed to cultivate to develop dreaming. I needed to relax more, assume a more open stance, and try not to control everything in my life. Most importantly, I needed to feel and intuit my surroundings—not blindly "strike out."

Lucid Dreaming

The common definition of a *lucid* dream is knowing that you're dreaming while you're dreaming.[3] As we have discussed, vivid dreams usually shift, going from one dream to another to another. Just as you think you have a handle on what's happening, the dream alters course. However, in lucid dreaming, you the dreamer are able to control the dream.

There is a Toltec technique that allows you to be in charge of your dream instead of the dream running the show; it enables you, the dreamer, to turn a vivid dream into a lucid dream. The technique consists of locating your hands, in your dream. If you are able to do this successfully, you have "woken" within the dream. The environment of a lucid dream can still shift, but you control the shift. You can turn a monster into a door, or a tree into an airplane, simply by intending this to happen. In this level of dreaming, shapes are typically sharp and clear, and colors vibrant and deep. Lucid dreaming requires more focus than vivid dreaming does. The task of finding your hands, then, provides a suitable exercise for control (*Dreaming*, 21). (You will learn how to find your hands in the last chapter of this book.)

As before, sometimes I could find my hands in a dream but to no avail. For instance, during a nap I dreamed I was driving a car, a friend was in the passenger seat. I felt tugging on my hands from someone who was not visible in the dream; they were saying, "Come on." Because I made no conscious connection with finding my hands, I missed this clue. Other times I wondered if I was doing the exercise correctly and realized I had to become unconcerned about the results of my actions insofar as what others might think or say about my actions. This theme was reinforced when, during a nap, I sensed that each action I undertook during the day either detracted from or enhanced my potential to be successful, making it necessary to stay focused on and act according to my own goals.

In the early stages of my dream experimentation, reaching the border of lucid dreaming brought on feelings of panic and fear. The energy associated with entering a dream was exhilarating and terrifying at the same time. For several years, whenever I roused myself to shift from a vivid dream to a lucid one, I would suddenly find myself swimming in the ocean. My fears about the unknown would surface and I would then see a shark in the distance. As my emotions careened out of control, the shark would swim toward me. I would react with more fear, not yet having the knowledge that I could *intend* for the shark to disappear. Invariably, the shark would swim closer, come up to me from behind, and attack me. Just as its jaws closed around my legs, I would wake up.

Frustrated and fearful of developing lucid dreams, I tried to interpret this repeated occurrence. I realized that the water represented my emotions. I later learned that water was a standard dream symbol for emotions. When I thought about how I viewed sharks, I realized they lack intelligence: they eat license plates and attack their own kind. I also realized I had the utmost respect for them. They have been around a long, long time with only minor evolutionary changes. They are great works of art.

Their stupidity, on the other hand, echoed my unwillingness to deal with my emotions. I would go into an emotional panic when I didn't possess my emotional wits. At the same time, I had survived many unusual circumstances, so perhaps there *was* hope for me! I applied this interpretation by trying to recognize and allow my emotions latitude, even if I couldn't master them. This resulted in a marked decrease of sharks attacking me while I was dreaming. The dream attacks ended for good after I ate a shark fillet while at dinner with some friends.

A few times I found my hands in a dream but forgot why I had been looking for them in the first place, which prevented the dream from going lucid. And going lucid did not necessarily mean having revelatory experiences—the experiences might only be curiously bizarre. For instance, I once dreamed I was driving along a California country road with my real-life girlfriend in the passenger seat. I was cruising at fifty-five miles an hour and holding her hand. A man on a skateboard passed us on the left side of my car. He hooted and hollered. This jarred me into realizing that I was dreaming and I entered a lucid state. Unexpectedly, the scene remained the same. I reasoned that the guy couldn't pass me on a skateboard; it violated physical laws. He slowed down and I passed him. I then reminded myself not to make hard-and-fast rules, especially when dreaming. He whizzed by me again and disappeared.

The dream became freaky, almost nightmarish as I felt myself losing my awareness that I was dreaming. The dream deteriorated further when I wildly thought that terror must be waiting ahead. I then brought myself back with the understanding that the subtle fluctuations of my mind were creating this dream. While still in the same dream, part of me wished to see death. A motorcycle pulled along the left side of the car and then kept pace with my speed. The driver wore a hood. I looked at the driver and, as he turned to me, I saw a fleshless skull under the hood. With a long-stem rose clenched in its teeth, it smiled. I thought that this was great entertainment and I woke up.

Lucid dreams mostly interest me in that they border DBE. Working through vivid and lucid dreams provides a natural avenue to this more refined dreaming state. Not that there is necessarily an inherent advantage, but DBEs strike me as more adventuresome, and more stable. If there is a single distinction between dreams and DBEs, it is that whereas dreamscapes shift, the DBE environment remains stable. The elements in the terrain of awareness sustain themselves. It is easy to change the environment through travel from place A to place B, but it is as difficult to change one thing into something else during a DBE as it is to change a house into something else in physical consciousness. For this to happen, the solidity of the entire dream must change to become a distinctly new dream, not unlike going from New York City to Los Angeles in waking life. For this reason, a DBE, to me, offers clearer and more stable information. With precise control, an object or situation under scrutiny isn't subject to moods or wishful thinking, things that often influence other intuitive or psychic abilities.

THE DREAMING BODY

By stabilizing a lucid dream you may enter a DBE. Stabilizing your dream is done by focusing on and maintaining awareness of the overall environment in your lucid dream. By sustaining this awareness, you create a focus to your lucid dream that will then allow the lucid dream to move on to its next natural stage: that of a DBE. Many of my biases regarding dreams and DBEs came directly from don Juan. He thinks that the effective development of dreaming requires one to bypass dreams en route to a DBE. DBEs, he maintains, represent the first full stage of success in dreaming. He fully appreciated the value of other aspects of dreaming but partly out of a need to grow beyond dreams and partly out of the necessity to create that need in his students, he hammered away at the gift of realizing greater and greater levels of awareness.

A classic DBE contains the perception of having a body, a form of some kind, which, as we have discussed earlier, is known to the Toltecs as the dreaming body. Whether the form is a replica of your physical body, a sphere of light, an animal, or another form, perceiving the environment from the perspective of this second body—and not from the physical body—is what constitutes a DBE. Another feature of a DBE is the ability to perceive actual events. During a DBE it is possible to perceive something just as though you perceived it from the vantage point of your physical body. Many times people float about their bedroom during a nighttime DBE while their physical body sleeps. Often the surprise of seeing their physical body jolts them back into it. A third aspect is that the dreaming body has feeling and emotion. So a DBE is characterized as consciousness exteriorized from the physical body, as having form, and as having emotion.

The dreaming body can also be projected to distant locations. Robert Monroe provides evidence for this. During a DBE he reported that he visited a friend and pinched her before he returned to his body. Three days later he talked with her and discovered she had a bruise where he had pinched her.

Much of the current press given to DBEs stems from people having had a near-death experience (NDE), where the physical body undergoes severe, close-to-dying trauma. Often during a NDE, a person has a DBE and sees rescue attempts or even surgery from a point of view that is above the physical drama. However, in a rigorous, scientific look at DBE, psychiatrists Glen Gabbard and Stuart Twemlow report in their book, *With the Eyes of the Mind*, that, in their studies, almost 80 percent of spontaneous DBEs (they use the term "OBE") occurred during states of deep mental and physical relaxation. Across the board, NDEs accounted for less than 15 percent of all reported cases, with the remaining 5 percent or so occurring from fatigue, stress, or drug use. Ninety-four percent found a DBE more real than a dream. Depending on the study, 86 to 95 percent of those having a DBE wanted to have another.[4]

I think profound relaxation enables DBEs because people manage to become sufficiently removed from the tensions of their own habits, which allows a very natural shift from physical to nonphysical perception. They loosen their grip on physical perception to such a degree that their nonphysical perception—the stuff dreams are made of—surfaces with enough clarity to produce the DBE.

On occasion dreams may precede a DBE, however, this progression is not always evident. For example, often I just find myself outside of my physical body, flying over treetops or playing in the clouds. Just as often, though, I can acknowledge the onset of a DBE as I work my way through a dream. Once, when I felt unusually connected to the physical environment in the dream I was having, I became aware of the fact that I was dreaming. It was as if physical laws of gravity and temperature were stronger than normal. Recognizing the dream, I left my body as a sphere of blue light. I traveled to an indoor pistol range where my first thought was to enter an empty booth for some target practice. Remembering I was in my dreaming body, I hovered about the range, watching others shoot. With a calm suddenness, I scrutinized the situation, or, rather, knowledge about the situation broke like a wave within me. I knew that by breaking my routine of dreaming, I had remembered my DBE. Blended into my attitude were the components of accepting and participating in the experience, coupled with my rejection of what was occurring. This enabled presence of mind.

In addition, for the first time in a long time I felt casual about being around firearms. Ever since my return from Vietnam, I had held a fascinating disdain for them. Now I felt like the fever had broken and I was no longer tied to that fixation. Failures of attempts to have a DBE also produced significant results. Once, just prior to leaving my body, I woke to the awareness that I must modify my diet. I felt that during the previous day I had eaten too much butter, the day before that too much sugar. Another time I felt ripples of energy along my spine while I was awake. I brought them to a standing wave where energy was evenly distributed throughout my entire physical body. While the energy was too diffuse to enter a DBE, I felt that by developing and connecting solidly with my power predilections, I would accumulate more energy to apply to DBEs.

I later recognized vibrations as something that often signaled the transition between a waking or dreaming state to that of a DBE. For instance, during a dream I saw a tornado. As it came toward me, I started shaking from its force, which then became an awareness of vibrations associated with exiting the physical body. I consciously realized I was heading from a dream to a DBE as I made this shift. About a half foot out, I started thinking about the tornado, since I'd dreamed of them before. I thought, *This is the real Wizard of Oz* and, due to my ensuing laughter, I re-oriented to my body.

Sound energy also plays a role in these transitions between different states. While lounging around my house one afternoon, I heard a sound resembling a freight train. The noise increased and it seemed like an invisible train was hurling through the living room. The vibration along my spine began and I gained control of it by moving it up and down through my body and then evenly distributing it through my body. I then began to lift out. I got out about six inches and stumbled at discovering this new, audio aspect of a DBE. Returning to my body, I was both elated because I had not gotten spooked, and deflated because I had lost my nonattachment by succumbing to the excitement of the novel experience.

Here's another example: Ever since childhood, I have wanted to visit the moon. The one academic study I took to as a boy was astronomy. I avoided history and mathematics and, aside from astronomy books written for children, I typically enjoyed *The Flash* and other science-fiction comic books. Going to the moon appealed to me; it was a natural step in my overall desire to head elsewhere. As an adult, I often tried to set up a DBE to go the moon by gathering mental and emotional energy to go there. I always got sidetracked, ending up almost anywhere *but* the moon. However, with patience, wishes come true.

Lying on my back on my living room floor one day, I was dreamily dozing when I abruptly entered a DBE. I had no sensation of leaving my physical body. I sort of bounced out of it without any indication, other than knowing I was now out-of-body and in deep space. Upon recognizing this, I thought of the moon and immediately found myself there. As a rule, during a DBE my senses are heightened and extremely keen and this time was no exception—the moon was breathtaking! The soft dirt shimmered as though it was magical dust. Light reflected off the smallest rock. The moon radiated abundant energy and I found it a unique form of life unto itself. The surprise of making it to the moon bounced me back into my physical body. I would have liked to have stayed longer, but I was graciously left with a moon-size piece of knowledge: desires manifest regardless of the time it takes.

This knowledge engulfed the excitement of having visited the moon. Although I had experienced a life-long dream, learning about the inner-most forces that guide perception made the moon trip itself seem like a child's wish, a child's game. But I also knew that my childhood wish was largely responsible for the adventure and growth in my life.

Bilocation

An advanced form of DBE is remaining awake in two environments simultaneously. Often referred to as *bilocation*, the person stays physically awake during a DBE and can easily shift perception back and forth between the dreaming body and the environment of the physical body. My first recognizable DBE was a bilocation.

I was in the Superstition Mountains, just outside of Phoenix, Arizona. The previous day, two friends and I had left my truck at the end of a dirt road and had hiked all afternoon and late into the night. Ready for sleep, we camped in a high-altitude, desert meadow. My friends had sleeping bags but I was traveling lightly and had only a blanket. I stayed warm by burning branches and dry cow dung. We began hiking as the sun rose. By late morning we came across an empty cabin in the midst of an apple orchard. I stayed close to the cabin all day; I knew that when night fell it would be colder than the previous night and I welcomed the shelter.

After dark, while standing in front of the cabin's fireplace mantel admiring its craftsmanship, I lost all sense of the cabin and suddenly found myself flying over treetops, flying with great speed. My perception shifted and I then became aware of standing in front of mantelpiece again. Then I shifted awareness back into the night where I was again flying over the trees. I felt totally in one place or the other; when I flew, my physical body seemed a memory and, likewise, when I perceived myself in front of the mantel, I was no longer aware of flying, but knew I had been doing it. This shift occurred three times.

The anomaly of this situation was that it was the one and only time I had ingested the psychotropic cactus, peyote. About an hour before bilocating I had eaten five or six dried, twisted, brown peyote buttons. I ate the peyote while sitting alone next to a tree in the orchard. I vomited and knew that this indicated I had eaten the proper amount for my constitution. I walked into the cabin and the bilocation began.

Don Juan has expressed his admiration for this cactus, believing it to be the home of an entity known as *mescalito*, mescaline being the principle mind-altering agent of the cactus. He thinks that the energy boost mescalito supplies offers valuable lessons (*Teachings*, 100–119). Don Juan only prescribes peyote, however, if his apprentices need to experience a radical reorientation of perception to drive home the point that there is more to us than we think. However, he also thinks drugs warp personal energy and should be used with caution and reverence, and only when meditative exercises fail. He never suggested that I take peyote. I tried it solely out of curiosity, and continue to have no desire to take it again.

During another bilocation I sat in a restaurant. I really didn't want to be there and wasn't very hungry. But I had been pressured into accepting the lunch invitation, so there I was. Fortunately, the two women I accompanied kept each other occupied as I daydreamed. I suddenly became aware of two entities of light near our table. Their luminous bodies resembled the egg-shaped light bodies of humans, but I felt like these beings were not physical and resided in another dimension. Since I had been contemplating a romantic interest with one of the women at the table, I asked the entities about sex. The light within their bodies shifted as though a wave of current rippled through them. In my head I heard that they didn't want to talk about it and I was on my own with that subject. When I asked what the two luminous beings wanted to discuss, their images vanished.

Taking a brief walk after lunch, I felt disoriented but was able to avoid walking into telephone poles along the sidewalk. During the walk, I realized that the only thing that separated me—as a physical being in life—from them as nonphysical beings in their version of existence, was a very specific feeling. This feeling assisted in my being able to focus my perception on the various aspects known as *life*.

Don Juan asserts that the dreaming body can evolve and perform maneuvers more extraordinary than bilocation—that it can develop to where the dreamer can project it to a location and be seen by others who are not out-of-body. He says the dreaming body can't eat or bring back physical objects, but can gather information and interact with people as though it were physical. This ability develops the knowledge that physical matter is thought, a portion of the mind.

Don Juan teaches that controlling thought at that level enables a total transference of physical matter into a nonphysical dimension and back; more akin to teleportation. I believe he demonstrated that capacity when he entered or exited the physical dimension. My rational memory would see him walking to me from a distance. Reason can't acknowledge something outside of its domain and so provides its interpretation of the event. My dreaming memory would *see* him descending from a field of light, a natural terrain or environment of nonphysical dimensions. When the two intersected, I saw him as a physical person.

Third-Level Dreaming

A few times I have had a third-level DBE. It was as though I had a DBE from a DBE. A distinguishing characteristic of this third type of projection is the absence of form. Awareness is focused at a point, and the point shifts perspective, but the awareness itself does not have substance. My first experience with this occurred in the laboratory at the Monroe Institute. Another time it occurred during an afternoon meditation wherein I experienced images of flying upside down over a meadow in a mountain range. I transferred my attention to the flight and entered a DBE. Arching my back, I looped up and back and started flying right side up. Leveling out, I noticed I could watch my dreaming body fly from a perspective above it. I could also shift my perception from that point to see my physical body rest in my apartment. I discovered that I could also watch both bodies simultaneously.

The next chapter presents other aspects and applications of dreaming, such as dreaming with others and visits to inter- and extra-dimensional worlds. Dreaming is a land of potential, a no-money-down virtual reality technology. Anything can happen and often does! Ordinary reality is but one dream, as is nonordinary reality. As you go about your waking and sleeping lives, there are dreams within dreams. Indeed, it's *all* a dream.

4

Applications of Dreaming

Storyteller

Old wrinkled man,
Sitting on a carved stone.
Children gazing into his eyes,
Seeing pictures within his mind.
Myths and legends he's to tell,
His special words speak his stories.
You get trapped in his voice,
From his force.

Domains of dreaming, such as vivid, lucid, and DBEs, are the broad-stroke abilities that dreaming provides. Dreaming also offers many applications. For instance, dreaming is our immediate access to the energies of this and other worlds. It's also our birthright, a faculty of perception given to us as a function of how we're created. As such, it's a direct avenue to creativity and learning. Let's explore some other aspects of dreaming now.

Instructional Dreaming

No matter what type of dream I was having (vivid, lucid, or a DBE), there were direct and specific lessons found in all phases or levels of dreaming. For example, in one dream I clearly distinguished differences between physical and nonphysical senses. The nonphysical perceptions were sharp and independent of the physical senses. I sensed environments and dream-world entities, although I did not fully interact within them. From this, I drew knowledge that awareness is not contingent upon the physical senses. I learned that nonphysical environments could sustain meaningful experience, or their equivalent of physical life.

I would also stay in dream states for prolonged periods. Some dream research I had done indicated that dreams last for a very short time, perhaps only minutes. Other research indicated that dreams occur in ninety-minute cycles and may be quite prolonged. I discovered I could remain in a dreaming state for twenty hours or longer if I had no commitments such as having to go to work. I took breaks only to go the bathroom or to eat, and found that, after having done so, I could then resume dreaming with very little effort; I only had to refocus on dreaming. I would then lose awareness of my physical body. However, if I wanted to, I could focus on my physical body from the viewpoint of the dream. I sensed my physical body, without feeling my consciousness centered within it.

I also received instruction on morals and ethics. In one dream, I perceived an unidentified bundle of energy. Unraveling the energy, I intuitively perceived that dream interpretation is often based on good and evil (positive and negative). In other words, dreams can reveal certain things one should or should not do. A shift, however, to an unbiased or non-interpretational experience results in a supraconceptual state. This means that the dreamer can go beyond symbolic meaning to acknowledge without judgment, and possibly participate in, whatever is at hand.

After this particular dream, I reflected on don Juan's assertion that perception grows as layers of interpretation are explored and then done away with. He maintained that first there is an interpretive split between good and evil. We thus view circumstances in terms of good and evil. Expanding awareness, we shift so that we are able to view events as being either positive or negative, more like an algebra equation than from the emotional biases of good and evil. We then perceive from the vantage point that everything is mind, and any interpretation stems from our relation to the circumstances.

Highlighting this awareness, I dreamed that I turned into a tornado. When I grew concerned about people and property, I shifted back to my human perspective. I then felt it was okay to merge with the tornado again. It rose high into the sky, raging with a controlled and deliberate fury that shattered everything it in vicinity. A man on the ground shot into the tornado with a rifle. I just laughed this off, knowing the bullet had no effect. I shifted back to myself and worried that the bullet might spin off the tornado and hit someone. I abruptly shifted back to the tornado, watching it tear houses to bits and easily uproot large trees. I then knew that this was okay. I was nature. There was no moral distinction. This dream served another purpose in that it reminded me to just be myself, be natural, and accept who I am.

Some years ago, there was a television miniseries called *The Winds of War*. During one episode, the idea of presence of mind was brought up. A few days later, during a dream, I wondered what that actually meant, and my dream then shifted to a dream of Vietnam. I was in a small, remote outpost under attack by North Vietnamese regulars, the well-trained, professional army of North Vietnam. During the siege, I learned that presence of mind meant acting with deliberation and strength in the midst of death.

Enraptured by learning something, I usually got caught up in these dreams. If I tried to act by my own volition, I would feel sucked into the respective event and lose a sense of myself. I realized that I had to remain relaxed to stay in control. This would automatically allow my intent to merge with the dream, elevating it to a new level. If I could maintain this intent, a DBE would often ensue.

In one incident, I drifted from a wakeful meditation into an easy sleep where I had a dream that I don't remember and didn't care to log in my diary. However, I did realize it was a dream, and as I did my awareness shifted to a DBE. I didn't feel my consciousness leave my physical body. As often occurred, I found myself outside of it, awake and hovering over the streets of Tucson. I discovered that I could either fly about town as if I were the wind, or I could sit in the sky as though I were suspended in a reclining chair. It still seemed like I had a body of sorts; I felt as though I had arms, legs, a head, a torso. All the while, I intuitively knew that my physical body slept a few blocks away in my sixteenth-floor apartment.

Another example: While I was sitting in my imaginary chair, I soon realized I could alter my perception of time as measured by the city traffic some two hundred feet below. I could watch the cars zipping about town as though they were in a Keystone Kop film, or I could watch them crawling about town as though in slow-motion. I did not effect the traffic itself, just my relation to it. Only my perception of time had changed. After playing with this ability for a short time and learning about the flexibility of time, I returned to my sleeping body and allowed it to continue sleeping.

Tutorial Dreaming

Hand-in-hand with instructional dreaming is the kind where another person or being of some kind provides the lesson. For instance, during an afternoon nap, I dreamed I conversed with someone I couldn't see. The conversation seemed ordinary in all other respects. Evidently, I assumed this entity had knowledge about consciousness. I asked a general question regarding the development of perception. "First, it is the greatest of pursuits," came the disembodied reply. "Second, due to the complexity—and possibly ambiguous nature—of the quest, a specific goal is useful."

From this I understood that I needed reasons why I wanted to explore specific avenues of perception. Why did I want to have DBEs? How would I apply knowledge of other realms? Not only would having objectives focus energy and generate momentum for any goal, it would help keep my perception clear and polished so I would not succumb to doubts.

In another dream, don Juan stood next to me. We discussed DBEs. I became aware of a muffled noise in the background, almost like the drone of a small, distant airplane. I raised my arms to take off as though my arms would turn into wings. The noise increased to a growl. But I couldn't take off! I asked don Juan why this was so. He showed me an image of my father and said I was always trying to please him and everybody else, thereby losing a sense of my life and my own personal power.

I also dreamed of Castaneda. In one dream of him, I was by myself contemplating landscapes of awareness, the varied aspects that make up regions of consciousness. Castaneda appeared out of nowhere. As I turned my attention to him, a moth fluttered about the right side of my body. The moth grew huge and beat its wings on my neck. I grew nervous. Castaneda made a note to himself about Virginia Beach, as though he must visit. The moth then bit the left side of my neck and I woke up. In his book *Tales of Power*, Castaneda reports similar encounters with moths, or rather an energy that appeared as a moth. He used them to symbolize knowledge (*Tales*, 25). In this dream, I had been on the brink of tapping the knowledge of how to transport my awareness directly to an individual, but lost track as "knowledge" flapped about me.

In another dream I felt intense pressure in my chest as though I was having a heart attack. I heard Castaneda tell me to exhale through my mouth to relieve the pressure. He then told me to stop, so I wouldn't release too much pressure. I physically awoke and saw images of three men kneeling over me. One was Indian, two were Caucasian. Their bodies were of light and not of physical matter. As two of them lifted my nonphysical body out of my physical body, I became aware of being held near the edge of a cliff. The two men threw me over the edge and, as I fell, my awareness returned to my physical body. This event simulated Castaneda's descriptive account of the end of his apprenticeship with don Juan (*Tales*, 294–95; *Second Ring*, 1–2). (I must emphasize, however, that there is no evidence that Castaneda, himself, consciously or otherwise, intended these dream-time visits or that I actually was dealing with him. There are, after all, many nuances that spark dreams.)

There were other times that I awoke to find a light-bodied person in my room. For instance, I woke early one morning to an unusual sensation in my abdomen. I saw a Mexican-looking woman standing next to my bed; she appeared short, homely, and natural as though she were a country peasant and relaxed in the role. She held a long, thin tube—flanged where she placed her mouth, and narrow at the other end—which rested on my belly. My fear jolted me and she faded. I used feeling to try to make sense out of the situation. My intuition indicated that she was friendly, an assistant of don Juan's who stimulated my *will* by using an old-style, Toltec technique. That entire day I felt out of touch with my normal self, as though I didn't want to deal with the physical world, but wanted to return to dreaming.

One afternoon as I dozed on the floor of my mother's den, I became distinctly aware of shifting from wakefulness to sleep to a dream to a DBE and back again, retracing the steps then going through the cycle again. My mother walked past and I felt she wanted to wake me but I sent out "do not disturb" energy and she let me be. (I asked her about this the next day and she said she wanted to ask me something but decided not to, since she felt I wanted to be left alone.) I briefly stayed in each level of dreaming until the third cycle. I then stayed in a DBE where I met an entity who talked to rows of plants that were trimmed to look like humans. These plants were similar to the hedges at Disney World that are trimmed to look like Disney characters. I asked this man his name and felt that his response was "Ansel," but he paid no attention to me as he lectured to the plants, which were lined up in military fashion. He sounded programmed to say only certain things and I thought he must be some kind of computer.

Just as I got fed up with him for ignoring me, and started to bring my consciousness back to my physical body, he whirled around and asked me what I wanted. Startled, I roused slightly from sleep. Still lying on the floor, I felt like I might levitate and start hopping uncontrollably about the house. I felt concerned about my mother witnessing this, and I suppressed all my energy, trying to return all of it to the physical. As I did, out of nowhere I heard Ansel's booming voice, "Are you still concerned with people?" This shocked me further, and I fully woke.

Sexual Dreaming

During a DBE, I flew as a sphere of light. Another dreaming body that seemed feminine came toward me and I felt strongly attracted to it. Our energies touched and exquisite flashes of electricity consumed me. Our light bodies merged smoothly until we became one. Ecstasy.

One of the more frequent questions at DBE lectures concerns the possibility of having *astral sex* during a DBE. For most people, sexual dreams are common and actively seeking a special liaison while having a DBE and being away from everyday ethical constraints proves titillating to many. Sexually related activity can happen during a DBE but we probably need a new term to go along with astral sex, as it may not be sexual at all. It resembles sex in many ways: eroticism, heightened awareness of body or form, and orgasm-like experiences may all be present, but more than sex, this kind of an experience is a merging of two individual entities, often to a point of rapture. Fully entering and experiencing another being transcends sex. Sexual feelings are only a small part of that merger and may not even be present, but since they most relate to the physical act in terms of technique and heightened feelings, the experience carries sexual connotations.

Moreover, not all meetings between light bodies simulate sexual energy. This merging may also occur where the participants feel more understanding of the other, without relation to sex. When sexual feelings are aroused, however, the intensity of the experience mounts, as it does with physical sex. Time seems irrelevant and two beings can remain together for five seconds or five hours.

Specific-Goal Dreaming

In addition to learning the varieties of dreaming, I discovered that it is possible to engage dreaming for specific purposes; that it has practical applications for whatever pursuit interests you. Several years ago I had a vivid dream wherein I looked at some written material. I zoomed in and saw music notes and lyrics penned neatly across the page. I felt that these were mine and had always been mine. My surprise at this realization caused the page to blur and then vanish. Later, when studying journalism in college and then writing magazine articles professionally, I would "find" paragraphs and entire articles through dreaming. Sometimes I would mentally see the words already written; other times I would become aware of a mass of energy and I would write intuitively, as though the article was an entity that would visit me, wait for me to write it, and then leave.

This can be expanded to tackle virtually any endeavor, as dreaming opens the door to investigate the parts or the whole of the human experience.

Dreaming Awake

The internationally recognized therapist Arnold Mindell refers to *dreaming awake* as having a twenty-four-hour lucid dream.[1] It consists of orienting yourself to your daily life as though it were a dream. You then feel connected to your world in a more heightened, expansive manner. For this reason, dreaming awake has also been called *heightened awareness*. Personally, I have found dreaming awake to be the single, most effective exercise in opening the door to other forms of dreaming. Later chapters more fully explore dreaming awake.

THE INORGANIC WORLD

Referring back to dreaming level two, don Juan says that the inorganic world is a testing ground where you learn how to handle power, the toughest obstacle of all the stages. Castaneda, for example, was tempted by inorganic beings to learn telekinesis. All he had to do was sign over his soul, so to speak. Fortunately, he resisted (*Dreaming*, 115).

On occasion, during dreaming, I have entered the world of inorganic beings. Consistent with don Juan's teachings, I found that these creatures live in, or perhaps actually are, a labyrinth of tunnels. Once, I was at a spot where I could head in the direction of any one of several tunnels that were before me. I picked the larger tunnel, and just as I entered it, I met a group of beings. Their appearance was not solid. Their bodies shifted about. At times they looked ghastly and ghostly, other times thin-framed, almost humanoid. And yet at other times they seemed waiflike, like an image that can never be brought into focus. As soon as I noticed them, they came toward me and hovered about my body, asking me what I wanted. I felt simultaneously interested, entertained, and repelled. I then felt don Juan's energy, and remembered his admonition to be very careful in this land. So I left the tunnel, which ended my dreaming.

Getting back to the idea of the inorganic world being a testing ground, in the inorganic world you can learn to shape your dreamscapes at will. This is not unlike learning to do this in lucid dreaming, and actually a case could be made that visits to the inorganic world occur in lucid dreams. In any event, by fooling around with this ability, you either get to point where it is no fun to determine the outcome of your adventures, or you get lost in controlling your world.

In terms of power as an obstacle, if you can't let go you're experiencing the illusion of control. In fact, you're not controlling anything. You're actually not awakening anything deeper than this level within your energy body. Therefore, one attitude to help you handle power is to consider daily life as a lucid dream. And to grow beyond this level, you need to let *life* reign, not your self-reflection. Even if life itself is a huge projection of such reflection, to find freedom you must grow beyond the limits of each level of projection.

ELEMENTAL SPIRITS

What might be another class of inorganic beings are those species that comprise the elemental worlds. Or, since they have a connection to our organic world, perhaps they are not inorganic. I don't know yet. At any rate, encounters with these creatures often occur when one is dreaming awake.

It is my understanding that these entities hover around elements of nature, such as trees, rivers, and animals. I first encountered one several years ago in my apartment in Florida. It was one-foot high, stocky like a blacksmith, and dressed in medium brown knickers, a forest green jacket, and a green, stove-pipe hat. As I rounded a corner into my dining area, I saw it on the dining table. Shocked, I withdrew. When I peeked around the corner, it was gone.

A few years later, during the days when I lived like a stray dog in the mountains of Virginia, I had several similar encounters. Some of these occurred during or near the time that I took my in-residence seminar at the Monroe Institute. I didn't have to be plugged into the Institute's sound technology for these encounters to happen. One day, just prior to the seminar, I was out for a walk. I saw an entity about eight inches high, with wings expanded to approximately ten inches. The otherwise human-shaped figure felt feminine. Specks of light danced off her five-point wand. She said, "We'll be with you."

Later in the program, I visited the winged elemental during a taped exercise where I saw that a creek was her natural abode. She was a "waterhole spirit," or so I figured. Two days after the program, I met her again as I walked home from visiting friends. Crossing a small bridge, on a hunch I stopped and looked at the flowing creek. At the edge of the water I saw her. She flew to my right shoulder. Through feeling, she said that her name was Xena. She said I should tell people about her and her relationship to nature.

When humans cut down vegetation, she said, the elementals' home is removed from our world. Humans don't destroy the elementals, but we destroy our connection to—and thus our ability to perceive—them. A week later I stopped at the creek again and Xena showed me her home. Superimposed over the bank of the creek, I saw a network of small caves. I knew that in my current physical reality the bank was solid, that it did not have these tunnels. However, I also became aware of *her* world, a world that coexists with ours—if we give it a chance to.

Some years later I was giving a workshop in Ireland. The idea of the workshop was to use the myth of the ancient culture in combination with the land itself to explore the elemental world. There were a dozen of us traipsing about the area, visiting windmills and shops, as well as trees and rivers. A key lesson was to elicit otherworldly experiences within the context of ordinary living. Everyone had at least one encounter and communication with the elemental world. Some even talked and danced with witches that hovered about in a dream world. Others saw faeries and gnomes. Everyone had entered the state of dreaming awake and perceived some type of creature that existed in an emanation of the second field. All were sure their encounters were legitimate.

EXTRATERRESTRIALS

While dreaming, I've encountered other entities that I categorize as extra-terrestrials (ETs), or entities associated with physical planets other than Earth. Many of my experiences occurred while in the dream-research lab at the Monroe Institute. At that time, the common term for the experiences was *channeling*. I have since come to understand this as a different dynamic, albeit dreaming related. (Complete transcripts of these sessions may be found in my book, *Traveling with Power*.)

About a half year before my ET saga at the Monroe Institute, I dreamed I was by the seashore reading a book. A half mile down the beach, a fishing pier extended into the ocean. I noticed two green spheres of energy in the sand about ten feet away; one bright sphere and one dull sphere. I focused on the bright one, and for some reason I wished for fire. I looked across the road and a football stadium burst into flames. I ran at tremendous speed for a fire alarm. When I realized my actions, I grew sluggish, barely able to move. I managed to arrive at an alarm and pulled it. A man talking into a nearby phone told me to shut it off since he only wanted two units to respond to the fire. Into the phone he said, "There is a green man here." I asked what a green man was and his reply was that it was a concerned and helpful citizen.

I walked back to get the book I had left on the beach. A boat sped toward me and I felt anxious that it would leave the water and travel onto the sand, and I might not get out of the way in time. As I intended the boat to stop, the dream turned lucid but I didn't try to control the dream any further than I already had. A large flying saucer then appeared over the pier. It began to tumble and twirl out of control and crashed into people on the pier who were trying to escape the fire. I woke up trembling slightly, feeling that ETs are real.

I later dreamed I met an attractive woman. She told me she was an alien and would show me her natural form. The area around her left eye began to shift and she went into a closet to change. I started laughing, wondering how grotesque she'd be. The door opened and I saw a large lump of white light. The dream ended and I slept for thirteen hours.

In another dream I looked at three humans from an ET's perspective, as though I was one of them. I could only think how primitive humans looked. In yet another dream, a man I didn't know and I were picked up by a small, metallic, flying saucer. I felt like I had no choice but to enter the craft. We left Earth's atmosphere and rolled over, inverting the saucer. I heard a rush of energy similar to the psychic transition that one makes when entering a DBE, but I didn't make the connection. I pushed myself into forgetting the dream in order to escape my captors.

Another ET-DBE occurred when I projected to Mars during a third-level DBE. Although the terrain was stark and barren, I found the planet inhabited by nonphysical beings, some of which resembled the blue spheres of light in the film *The Martian Chronicles*. Others looked like triangles, squares, and other geometric forms. Telepathically, they expressed concern that humans couldn't perceive them. They felt endangered by the likelihood of a reckless space exploration program that didn't consider and plan for alternate forms of intelligence.

This series of dreams culminated when I dreamed of an ET showing me their version of an electromagnetic device I had been toying with. For about a year I had been exploring the feasibility of a technology that would stimulate and enhance human perception, and possibly promote physical healing. The equipment necessary to build a prototype for this device would fill a large room, as was the case with the development of the first computers. In the dream, an ET extended his arm, which held a device measuring three feet long by four inches wide. I intuitively knew that this was the same technology that I was working on, only a more advanced version of it. It seemed that the ETs had a personal computer model.

I had had all of these dream experiences with ETs, but then I encountered the real thing. One summer day at the Monroe Institute I was walking down a dirt road near the lab, heading toward a cluster of barns. The sky had few clouds and, although hazy, was generally clear. As I looked up into it, I noticed an unusual light a few hundred yards up. It was almost the same kind of light you might experience upon standing up too quickly, where light swirls in front of your eyes. Yet the light remained in the same location, regardless of how I moved or where I looked.

I then saw a curved metallic object seeming to come out of the light. The object grew until I saw what was perhaps a full quarter panel of a circular, metallic disc about fifty feet wide. Light surrounded the disc and looked like an entrance point from another dimension. That was the thought I had. Mentally, I grew very detached. But my physical body reflected my emotional reaction; I felt nervous tremors and great agitation. When this agitation reached a certain level, the disc reversed its direction and disappeared along with the sparkling light.

This experience illustrates the concept of biocognitive interface: the idea that the more you become intellectually or psychically familiar with something previously unknown to you, the more it will begin to manifest in your physical reality. I had become familiar with ETS as a result of my dream experiences with them, and then they manifested on my physical plane. As a consequence of this very real experience with the flying saucer, I no longer had the luxury of believing that my lab interactions with ETs were the result of simple imagination. Moreover, such an experience can jar, or even demolish, our sense of reality. Even if we are open to ETs, our education and enculturation not only try to override their possibility, but often refute it as outlandish, thereby creating barriers in our awareness. Perceiving the saucer, I received a rather harsh jolt that tore away a view of the world that I had been unwittingly cultivating for a lifetime.

As stated above, this experience also validated the concept of biocognitive interface. Primarily from these sessions, I had grown relaxed in my thinking about ETs. I had also calmed my emotions somewhat, enabling the physical sighting to occur. Evidently, I had not calmed my emotions sufficiently, nor had I integrated those perceptions at the physical level. Like a link in a chain, my growing and keen distress separated the connection between my intellect, emotions, and physical body, which ended the encounter.

Don Juan says the overriding impact of the inorganic world is that it demolishes one's reason. Maybe contact with other kinds of intelligent life that is out of this world has the same effect. If this is true, perhaps we can bypass the seductions of the inorganic world and visit ETs, to accomplish the same result.

It might also be a good way to learn Toltec-like lessons. For instance, several ETs once pulled me into a DBE. Now there's a barn burner for you. It definitely shakes a reasonably well put together world to its foundation, leaving you wondering what reality is in the first place. To get on with the quest, though, such experiences are necessary in order to turn mental concepts into knowledge. That is, you can talk about DBEs all day long but until you thoroughly experience and integrate them, your knowledge remains just talk.

Dreaming level six, or teleportation, which I will discuss in greater detail later, is where you turn your body into a time machine. You pull yourself out of the normal flow of time and pop off to distances that it would take hours to walk or drive to. Theoretically, you pull yourself out of the first field, enter the second field, travel, and then return to the first field. All in the blink of an eye.

As humans evolve, perhaps the eighth chakra will become the crown chakra. As a result, we will become an entirely new species. We'll look different, act differently, think differently—the whole nine yards. Maybe our eyes will be larger, like the eyes of the ETs we see in movies. If so, maybe we'll see new colors, like Enon, the color of the eighth chakra. And surely we'll see this color on the outer edge of rainbows. Move over, Dorothy!

All of this is in the works, or should I say in the workings? Indeed, it is all part of the ever-present scheme of the universe. Stepping outside of normal time, we find that it's all happening right now, even if we aren't aware of it. Enon, for example, is already part of rainbows. Our eyes just haven't evolved to the point of being able to handle that frequency, at least on a physical level. So perhaps dreaming also gives us a glimpse of our future selves—ourselves as ETs.

THE MECHANICS OF OTHER APPLICATIONS OF DREAMING

The mechanics behind having these types of experiences are as follows: In relation to our physical world, elementals and other inorganic beings exist in the second field. ETs probably exist in such a manner as well and there are probably those that also exist in the physical, first field. By expanding your awareness into the second field and thus making more of your personal first field aware, you access their dimension. At some point, the second field becomes integrated with the first field and dreaming awake ensues.

If a sufficient number of people expanded their awareness, we would incorporate the existence of ETs and other elements of the inorganic world into our inventory, our reality. Perceiving elementals or ETs and the respective interdimensional connection is then a reflection of the shift and re-stabilization of the focal point, characterized by the formation of a new, stable cohesion.

NEAR-DEATH EXPERIENCES

Experiences with white light and meetings with inhabitants of that energy are often part and parcel of a near-death experience (NDE). This is where don Juan takes exception to the normal interpretation, however. People who experience a NDE typically say they've met God, talked with Jesus, experienced unconditional love, and/or felt totally complete. Don Juan says these people feel complete because they've met the *human mold*, the embodiment of "all that is human." I think that this mold is centered at the top of each person's energy body. In collaboration with the powers that be, it is like a Jell-o mold that stamps out our neat little, uniform energy bodies. So by fully touching it, how could one not feel complete? But that doesn't mean it is God, perhaps it's just one emanation of God's highest power.

We have discussed tunnels earlier in that they are associated with inorganic and faery worlds. However, they are also a common element in a classic NDE such as when one travels through a tunnel to a white light or to meet deceased relatives.[2] Perhaps tunnels are avenues of perception, rather than concrete formations. Maybe they are a perceptual effect of being able to channel awareness along specific paths. The ability to form and channel energy then produces the perception of tunnels.

In dreaming states, a person often enters heightened awareness. Because of this, there is no struggle to produce rarified perceptions, as these occur as an integral part of the respective experience, be it a NDE, a DBE, or an encounter with an ET; all of which are in the fabric of dreaming.

I had my first NDE when I was approximately eight years old; the near-drowning incident relayed in the early pages of this book. I've had a few more since. Two of them were clinically induced while I was in the research lab at the Monroe Institute; the protocol of the session was to use a sound-based technology to change brainwave activity.[3] In this case, we used a sound pattern of 1.5hz, which is close to being clinically brain dead.

Shortly into the session, I vaguely had the sense of being in the air above the lab and looking down. I then felt ET energy but there was something beyond that. Placing all of my attention toward that "something," I found myself in a tunnel with white light at the end of it. I became concerned as I had recently seen the film *Poltergeist*. In it, a psychic tried to retrieve a girl from another dimension. In so doing, she yelled to the girl's parents, "Don't let her go into the white light, you'll never get her back!" So here I was, yelling in my head, *Don't let me go into the white light, you'll never get me back!* I jumped in anyway. Dreamers, go figure!

I experienced the tunnel as a vortex with the end of it vanishing in the distance. I sensed that the white light consisted of a uniform and consistent field of energy of indescribable proportions. Exiting the tunnel, I saw a huge ball of white light. Although I sensed it in impersonal terms, because of the level of vulnerability invoked in me and the intimacy associated with the situation, I could understand why it might be thought of as a tremendous light being or entity, as something rather caring and personal.

Approaching the light, I perceived it as pure energy. Entering it, I felt it could be used for one's own purpose, that it was passive and its values neutral. I then briefly entered and traveled all the way through the light. Exiting and looking back, I found that everything was reversed: a mirror image of the physical universe that I knew in my daily life. My mind recoiled at the scope of this awareness and it was at that point that I returned to normal consciousness.

DREAMING WITH OTHERS

I have often heard stories about purposely meeting another person during dreaming, typically while dreaming awake. In *The Second Ring of Power* and *The Eagle's Gift*, Castaneda also offers accounts of hooking up with others. But I only pursued the matter after a small bit of evidence suggested that I had helped someone into a DBE.

This person was Susan, a psychotherapist from New England. We had met at a Monroe Institute seminar and maintained communication. She and I decided to see if I could influence her during a laboratory session that she was going to undergo at the institute. Making plans for our experiment, she said she would be in the sensory deprivation booth in the lab the following day at 9:30 a.m. At the time, I lived about 900 miles away.

Resting in a reclining chair in my living room the next morning, I relaxed and focused my attention within the lab where I had spent many hours. My awareness shifted to a small, dark room and I knew I was in the booth at the lab. I felt Susan's presence and, slightly straining my vision, I could see a vague outline of her on the waterbed. I merged with her energy and focused my efforts on helping her enter dreaming, preferably a DBE. My perception then left the booth and hovered about six feet outside of it, roughly ten feet off the floor. I noticed a bundle of energy next to me. It felt like Susan. The energy moved like a plastic bag filled with water, as though it tried to maintain a spherical shape but couldn't. As it shifted, dense blue and white lights pulsed through the otherwise clear, soft white light.

Susan later told me that early in the session she perceived herself flanked by light beings. She also had a mental image of my physical body and felt as though I was present. Susan then felt as though she were floating and said I held her, offering support for her journey.

A few months later I tried this with Tom, a psychologist who lived about sixty miles away from me. One night at 11:00 p.m., I attempted to influence his perception from a distance. Through the same technique of relaxing and focusing my dreaming on him, I soon felt a connection. I saw his feet and head. I also saw flashes of red, blue, and yellow light throughout him. I tugged at his dreaming body at the feet and later pried at the chakra at the top of his head. I then went under his body and pushed up on his dreaming body. Not getting anywhere, I scanned his energy, trying to diagnosis the difficulty. I felt he lacked confidence that he could have a DBE on his own. I had an image that his perception of himself locked himself within himself. This prevented a flow of energy throughout his being. Talking with him the next day, he said he felt tremendous energy pouring into him at the time of the dreaming encounter and confirmed my feelings about his lack of confidence.

A few weeks later, Tom and I scheduled another nonphysical session for 11:00 p.m. The experience was much like the first session. However, a couple hours later, Tom woke up, thinking I had returned. He relaxed and tried to sense my instructions. He later says that this time I did something different. Instead of working on his head, feet, and back, I shifted his energy to the left and then to the right. As I manipulated his energy, his dreaming body slowly separated from his physical body. He said our dreaming bodies congratulated each other on this success. He then floated out of his bedroom into the living room. Excited, he returned to his physical body.

Comparing notes the next day, I told him that during his DBE I was sound asleep, not having slept that deeply for almost a year. We conjectured that I had to remove my conscious mind from the effort in order to bypass my normal technique and employ another method. The experience taught me to relax more and try to deal with the moment at hand without preconceptions. It offered Tom support that he could have DBE on his own, since I was not consciously manipulating his energy at that time. It also offered convincing evidence that we do travel in dreaming without conscious awareness of doing so.

About six weeks after Tom's DBE, we scheduled a session when he would be on an airplane flying from Florida to Arizona. At the selected time, I located his emotional identity. (We all have a certain feeling, which separates us from others. By focusing on this aspect of a person's identity, you can send your nonphysical energy directly to them regardless of their physical location.) Within several minutes I became aware of myself as oblong energy floating in the coach section of an airliner. I immediately saw Tom. He sat on the right side of the fuselage and had three seats to himself. He looked in my direction as though he was aware of my presence.

A dark-haired flight attendant passed me and I turned to follow her into the first-class section. I returned to coach and looked around. Since Tom appeared busy I didn't approach him. Just before leaving, I felt the airplane start to jostle about. I had the thought that it must have entered a storm. I returned directly to my physical body from the cabin of the plane and made note of the time.

Comparing notes a few days later, Tom said that even though the airplane was almost full, he had three seats to himself on the right side. He mentioned that he had perceived a mental image of me sometime during his flight but didn't pursue this further because he was busy with work. When I asked him about the bumpy ride, he said that at the time I mentioned, the plane was descending into Houston and had entered a storm. He said he didn't remember the color of the flight attendant's hair.

The true goal of dreaming, says don Juan, is to perfect the energy body (*Dreaming*, 42). Remember, the goal is not to simply enter mind-boggling worlds. The primary goal is to use these experiences to evolve your energy into a natural field, and remain in heightened awareness. The training is to become a seer, not a wizard. It just so happens that a wizardly lifestyle may be part of a Toltec path, but the path is also that of the seer.

A perfected energy body, then, contains energy that is perfectly matched with the Eagle's emanations. One effect is that you are simultaneously totally here, totally an individual, and totally not here, totally part of all that is around you. This is what I *saw* in don Juan. His energy body delicately and exquisitely matched the fibers of light that were outside of him. He had learned to *be*, completely.

5

Dreaming Levels of Awareness

The Dreamer

My journey begins:
trees rustling all around me,
whispers of the wind,
trickling water in the river,
crystals shining in the sun,
with flashing colors from my rainbow.
The smoke disappears.
I carry with me my dreaming bag;
it reminds me that I'm sleeping in my bed.
Rain drops fall upon me
like pearls of the ocean.

You might say that Toltecs have created the dream of a land where the inhabitants' primary concern is that of developing perception. Walking around its shores, you witness a host of marvels like teleportation and talks with otherworldly entities. As you travel inland, you discover a wealth of insight regarding the nature of awareness itself. This unusual dream offers marked contrasts with the sights you may be accustomed to. Just like a regular dream, these sights and sounds often shift of their own accord and play with your sensibilities. This makes the task of exploring harder but yields the rich rewards of measuring one dream with another. By doing so, you free yourself from the constraints of the dream and begin controlling the dream. You may then slip in between different dreams of reality to arrive at the core of perception.

To groom these levels of awareness, Toltecs frequently uses elements in nature to get the point across. By using water, for example, you may hook your perception to different aspects of the first and second energy fields. The quality of wetness is a first-field property of water; this quality can be perceived through the physical senses. Thus, describing energy as wet builds understanding concerning what the first field embodies. We are aware of the wetness of water in drinking, swimming, and putting out fires, for instance.

The quality of motion is a second-field feature of water. There is a peculiar motion—a sense of matter—that can be detected through a portion of feeling that is not normally used. It is done with the entire body, highlighting the direct characteristics of feeling as it relates to perception. Latching on to this movement acts as a catalyst, enabling you to move perception along atypical routes, such as into dimensions other than physical reality. Castaneda presents perspectives on separating natural elements in order to stimulate such awareness (*Fire*, 92–93).

Examining something through two levels of attention provides additional (and often seemingly opposing) points of reference. While studying the second field I learned that perception automatically seeks what is described; in the case of water, hooking on to its flowing motion is used to shift the focal point deeper into the second field. By having this pointed out, it makes the ability a learnable goal. This selective cueing process is the foundation for building inventories. Again, by selecting what's important, then cueing it up in consciousness, an inventory is built. This becomes the reality built over time as one generation signals to the next what reality is made of.

It turns out that separating the properties of water in two is like triangulating an object in order to obtain a better fix on it. For example, say a ship floundering at sea broadcasts a distress signal. This signal automatically triggers an alarm in ports that monitor the international distress frequency. If a ship in trouble off the Virginia coast sends a distress signal, a computer in Norfolk receives it, thereby activating an alarm; a computer lets you know that the signal is strongest from the east. That's great information but doesn't say anything about how far away the ship is.

Another computer in New York tracks the signal and finds it is strongest from the southeast. Two straight lines drawn from Norfolk and New York in the directions of the strongest signals will intersect, indicating the location of the ship. Norfolk, the closer port, then knows that the ship is so many miles due east and can dispatch a rescue vessel.

Triangulation is the act of perceiving something from two separate angles. Separating water in two allows you to perceive it from two distinct angles, enabling a better understanding and use of it. In the same manner, studying the second field in relation to the first field provides an additional reference for studying reality itself. Not only do you experience different ways of accumulating information but, by learning that perception automatically looks for whatever is described, you loosen the grip of ordinary reality and set the stage to be able to glimpse something beyond.

Another way of approaching this split of awareness is by reversing the figure and ground of images. Once don Juan instructed me to gather

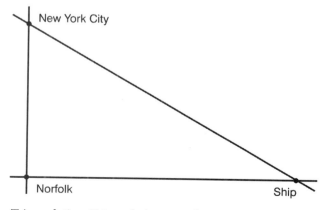

Triangulation. Triangulation provides a clearer, more accurate representation of what is perceived.

leaves into a pile and then reverse the figure-ground relationship between leaves and shadows, and then immerse myself in the shadows. In other words, when we see a pile of leaves we typically focus on the leaves rather than on the shadows. The leaves are the "figure" and the shadows are the "ground." Typically this arrangement has been selectively cued to us as being the more meaningful way to look at something. To break this habit, don Juan wanted me to reverse my focus just to exercise my perception, if for no other reason. Remember, though, exercising the first and second fields is intended to drive perception toward the third field. As an exercise, ask yourself: What is the reality? The vase, the faces, the entire graphic, the page, the book, the room, the city? Reality, or at least the perception of it, is an ever-expanding dream.

Don Juan maintains that tapping the third field delivers a person to a state of *being*, an experience of equilibrium where one prefers to experience life rather than to create views of it. The heart of the matter is the ability to control perception. To facilitate this, he teaches that viewing the world from a completely different perspective other than from one's normal reference point creates a split in awareness.

With this approach, don Juan structured his teachings to create a radically different worldview, a nonordinary reality based on the Toltec tradition. By learning to balance this worldview with the ordinary worldview as reflected by contemporary society, I learned how to go between them to a place where both existed and did not exist at the same time.

This is an important consideration. In effect, we're dealing with two

Figure-Ground Reversal. From one perspective, the white vase is the figure and the black faces looking at each other form the ground. Shift perspective and the faces become the figure with the vase as the ground.

models or inventories *about* reality, models which often become confused as *being reality*. In ordinary reality, we primarily feed our awareness with information derived from the five physical senses. Reason organizes this information and creates a view of reality. While this reality is valid, it is limited. When compared to a normal day filled with commonplace concerns, dealing with entities from other dimensions, superhuman feats of agility and endurance, and travels into dimensions beyond physical time and space, what's real and what's not becomes a little clearer, (or maybe less so depending on your point of view!). The key point here is that don Juan "simply" uses nonordinary reality as a means to break free from the boundaries of *all* realities, not to create more boundaries. Once you firmly recognize the process and effect of models about reality, any given number of doors will open to you.

Once these types of boundaries are transcended, the person enters another realm, the realm don Juan refers to as the *person of knowledge*. This person has grown beyond the need for a system, that is, beyond method. His or her sole interest is the continued exploration and development of perception, to expand awareness beyond the forms of convention and thereby awaken completely.

The state of *being* is a defining characteristic of having arrived at this level of awareness. This, to don Juan, is the purpose of any system of consciousness development: the complete awakening of all that is natural to our being, which includes the energy body. From this perspective, again, *being* occurs when one has developed their first and second fields. That is to say, Toltec teachings not only describe a reality beyond the ordinary, but offer the means to experience it for the purpose of going beyond it, to live a life well beyond ordinary and nonordinary realms. Castaneda's books offer valuable information for this pursuit, and the possibility of engaging such an adventure and learning from it applies to all humans, simply due to the way humans are created: we all have a physical body and an energy body.

As energy-body perceivers, learning is what we humans do naturally. From many educational perspectives, and certainly from a Toltec point of view, learning is measured by changes in behavior—be they intellectual, emotional, physical, or psychic. The stages along a Toltec path reflect multi-level changes, not only how and what we think, and how we look at the world, but how we participate with it as well. As we increase our learning skills, we evolve. Therefore, learning indicates an increased ability to do, to act.

A good philosophy requires that you learn for mastery, that you fully engage self-motivated learning to become secure within your own right. The structure of a system is to help you get to the essence of your quest. Learning Toltec practices and views, for instance, supports stepping away from its structure to make a leap beyond its form; indeed, it consists of learning beyond all known boundary markers. To make this kind of leap requires a series of strong steps, with each step furthering your ability to learn. So this is where the levels of dreaming and the stages of evolution come in. In themselves, they help one transcend current cohesions, current ways of looking at the world.

The dramatic shifts in cohesion that dreaming supplies give you more to witness, experience, *see*, and consider. And, once again, this speeds your evolution when handled properly. Otherwise, you may lose yourself in your adventures.

Keep in mind that hooking your dreaming into a variety of practical applications stretches and stabilizes your awareness throughout your energy body by blending the first and second fields, and so speeds up your evolution. What "practical" means to you is something for you to figure out. To me, writing is very practical. But how about building a machine that teleports people? That's a pretty wild idea, and may not seem very practical by today's standards. But if you could learn how to teleport your awareness, couldn't that knowledge then be expressed in the physical world through some type of technology? Isn't technology the projection of innate capacities of consciousness—dreams come true?

Accelerating your evolution, then, is what dreaming is all about. However, just plugging yourself in to the fast track may prove damaging. You might succumb to power, or maybe you'll get lost in the second field just like the old-cycle Toltecs. Preventing these maladies is where tracking skills save the day. Through *nonpatterning*, or what don Juan calls *not-doing*, for instance, you can suspend movement and, as a result, remove yourself from your fast-track momentum (*Journey*, 219–39). You may then give yourself a breather to make sure you're oriented properly. Or, by using a model of dreaming levels to measure your steps, you generate more strength of mind and peace of heart. This is all part of the preparation that will continue to be addressed later. Right now, you're getting comfortable with what dreaming is and what it can be used for.

Since dreaming places you in heightened awareness, you can also learn from your journeys more readily. By stepping outside of the first field, you're not subject to its pushes and pulls. As a result, perception is more fluid, flexible, and free. For example, you may enter dreaming to learn advanced *seeing* practices, such as *seeing* the Eagle's emanations. Toltecs of old did this in order not to experience spontaneous combustion. It seems like tapping the amount of energy in an emanation through the physical body alone, without first building a suitable cohesion, can be dangerous (*Fire*, 183).

Therefore, just like computer software speeds up calculations, dreaming can bestow huge amounts of experience, and then help you to compare and contrast those experiences. Over time, dreaming can also help you generate wisdom. And all of this combined is what helps you beat the rap of falling into disrepair and despair.

Over the centuries, Toltecs have produced a map of dreaming cohesions. These cohesions may also be considered levels of, or degrees of, competency with dreaming. Each level is a leap of perception and, while not to be taken lightly, should be approached with complete abandon. The following is a brief outline of these levels, with a few modifications based on personal experience.

DREAMING LEVELS

Entering a level of dreaming is changing the energy body to the vibration of that cohesion, bringing it into phase, so to speak, with personal awareness. You then produce the perception of that order, and some of the experiences available from within that cohesion. In addition, each level represents a greater degree of heightened awareness. Therefore, success hinges on how much personal power you have. Whatever you perceive is based on the interplay between uniformity and cohesion, the key attributes of perception (*Dreaming*, 40). As these levels reflect more awareness and more self, world, and cosmos, you might also say that these are steps to access more of what God is dreaming.

Finding success means that you've integrated within your energy body the various energies of a complete cohesion. Just as there are a variety of energies associated with a skill in your daily world, the same applies to dreaming. The practices for this consolidation of a dreaming level are entering a new cohesion, traveling within it, and then hooking into your daily world. Indeed, notice that odd-numbered levels deal with entering a new domain, and even-numbered levels deal with stabilizing, or learning to handle, that domain. All the while, the quest is to blend the first and second fields, the physical and dreaming energies.

In *The Art of Dreaming*, don Juan mentions seven dreaming levels, or *gates*. Castaneda, however, ends his dissertation at the fourth stage. Putting pieces of the puzzle together, in my book *On the Toltec Path* I first conjectured about what I think the remaining three gates consist of and, over time, I have found that this schematic holds water. In addition to these, I offer personal considerations about two more levels. They're based on a continued exploration of don Juan's map for burning with the *Fire from*

A Shift in Cohesion Produces a Shift in the Focal Point. As your energy pattern changes, your focal point also shifts. Seeing focal point shifts is a way to measure shifts in cohesion. Dreaming is about producing these shifts.

Within, as well as recapitulating the effects don Juan had on my energy body. I'm not saying I'm right. I am saying that it is expected that each generation will attempt to add to the body of knowledge. Toltecs are no different than academicians in this regard.

Level One: Entering Dreaming

What separates ordinary vivid dreams from lucid dreams is that in lucid dreaming you're awake. Experiencing vivid dreams is like watching a movie, while lucid dreaming is actually stepping into the movie, being a part of it. Just because you enter a "sleep" cohesion doesn't mean you can't be awake. We've just learned that we're supposed to shut down awareness when we go to sleep. But sleep is a natural way to shift into dreaming, and a way to strengthen cohesion-shifting muscles. However, your dreams will remain in the land of ordinariness if you don't apply intent. That is, unless you intend to enter dreaming, you're not bringing your personal power into focus. As a result, you'll experience difficulty in breaking the barrier of becoming awake within your dreams.

As you slide off to sleep and your cohesion begins to shift, anything you have been holding on to may enter your awareness. Since this includes your fears and concerns, you might want to turn off the show. On the very threshold of dreaming, it is quite common for people to turn away, and intend sleep. Therefore, overcome this by facing up to whatever you're experiencing.

There is a point, a very narrow margin of perception, where you can either enter dreaming or fall off into the blackness of sleep. The idea here is to stay conscious as you fall into the blackness. You then allow your intent to bring images out of the blackness, and then establish a bridge into the images, and then let yourself flow into the images and into the dream.

Having a purpose for dreaming helps lubricate this transition. For instance, a few times I've mentioned using dreaming in order to write. This may be a suitable purpose for you as well. Or perhaps you'd just like to randomly explore. Whatever resonates strongly within you, use it to mount dreaming energies. Don't be bashful. Figure out what you want, what is part of your path, and then go for it.

Quite often you'll experience a surge of energy just when you're on the brink of lucid dreaming. This is your cohesion shifting, and this shift in energy may translate itself through the physical body as intense, raw emotion. This may make you very uncomfortable, or it may simply surprise you. Either way, you'll probably work hard to restabilize your normal cohesion and end the experience. For most people, letting go is the difficult part of stage one, or of any stage for that matter.

Level Two: Dreaming Travel

Okay, now you're inside a dream. What the heck do you do? Learn to travel, advises don Juan. For this, he offers an exercise that will deliberately change your dream. That is, you isolate a feature of your dream, and then use it to form a new dream, in the same way that television shows spin off a character from one show to make a new show (*Dreaming*, 44).

Don Juan maintains that the inorganic world is inhabited by intelligent, sentient beings and dreaming is a two-way bridge to that world. They're just not carbon-based intelligence as are humans and other organic life-forms of *this* world. Finding scouts from this other world serves several purposes. For one, you let them escort you into new dimensions. In the same manner that your parents helped teach you to walk, this is how you may also learn to travel in dreaming. As well, this is a huge test for weaknesses. If you pass this test, don Juan says you then head to the next level (*Dreaming*, 108, 111). If you *don't* pass, perhaps you'll become a petty tyrant—full of yourself and your grand accomplishments and never really learning how to handle your energy body.

The ability to control dreaming also gives you hands-on demonstrations of creativity. Since dreams are not subject to the influences of normal time and space that affect physical landscapes, you can significantly speed up, or slow down, any scenario. Paying attention to what unfolds offers lessons that you can bring back and apply to your daily, physical world. The general idea of level two, however, is to gain further command of cohesions. By shifting dreams, and by traveling within them, you increase your skills of energy management.

Level Three: The Dreaming Body

At this stage, the energy body is ready to act, says don Juan. Dreaming also begins to merge with your physical world (*Dreaming*, 142).

The effect on perception is that you produce the dreaming body. Again, I really don't think anything leaves the physical body, rather, as cohesion shifts, the movement of energy is translated by consciousness as movement of a second, nonphysical body. This second body then feels like it leaves the physical body. But the perception of second-body movement just echoes the movement of the focal point to another position, an "other-than-physical-body experience." If you re-identify yourself as an energy body, rather than a physical body, there is no "going out." There are just different kinds of physical and non-physical perceptions, all of which are within you.

A distinct advantage of having dreaming body experiences is that they help to break the fixations of the physical world. The energy body becomes more supple and more manageable. All in all, because you're working with the entire energy body, you get a better picture of what it means to be human.

Level Four: Dreaming-Body Travel

Just like you learned to travel within a dream in level two, now you get to travel using the dreaming body. During level three, your dreaming body typically ends up anywhere and everywhere, depending on how your cohesion shifts. At level four, you learn more locomotion skills. You learn to pinpoint your DBE travels. As a result, you can explore other dimensions, or take trips to your favorite places in this world. Bilocation begins with this level.

Level Five: The Double

All of your dreaming generates personal power. So by the time you reach this level, your energy body is such a powerhouse that some people notice your second body and think it's your physical body. This is what don Juan meant when he told Castaneda that sometimes the person he talked with was not his friend don Genaro but rather don Genaro's double (*Tales*, 48). And I think this is how don Juan interacted with me most, if not all, of the time.

Level Six: Teleportation

Remember that don Juan said level three is when dreaming and physical realities begin to merge? Well, at this stage evidently you can further connect your first and second energy fields and then apply your intent to shift your entire awareness to precise locations in your physical world. Relating your travels to the physical world not only binds your first and second fields together, it gives you a consistent reference, a home port from which to travel further.

One ability stemming from these travels is teleportation, which is what don Genaro did when he beamed himself to a mountaintop in the blink of an eye. It is a matter of mind, then, not of distance. Don Juan makes the case that don Genaro can do this type of thing when he is dreaming. As a result, he says don Genaro can do "more than if he were awake" (*Fire*, 237). The double is not bound by physical constraints. However, if the physical body is also energy, then isn't it possible to apply everything found through dreaming to it? Isn't it possible to teleport the physical body just as don Genaro teleports his double?

Evidence exists that this is so. For instance, Castaneda reports that he and the Little Sisters (female apprentices to don Juan) entered dreaming and disappeared from the physical world. Having difficulty returning, they were brought back to full awareness by the Genaros (male apprentices to don Juan) who were dumping buckets of water on them. This helped reconstitute their ghost-like images back into physical matter (*Second Ring*, 307).

Now, we can talk about dreaming until the cows come home. But it won't get us anywhere. It is *by* dreaming that we gain actual experiences with cohesion. This, in turn, enables the body to store and bring about these abilities.

Levitation, for example, is an aspect of level six; it suspends the physical law of gravity. Rather than beam off to a mountaintop, you float in the air, and not just with your dreaming body either. It's a real mind bender, a real cohesion shaper.

Level Seven: The Fire from Within

You have heard people say we only use a small percentage of our brain? Well, in like manner, we only use a small percentage of our energy bodies. To go completely past the Eagle (the Source), you must first become one with it. To merge with energy that intense must be why the old-timers used to experience the "spontaneous combustion" cohesion. Keep in mind that this might be a risk for you as well, since by tracking freedom you're activating your entire energy body. And you must do this to become one with the Eagle.

Don Juan says that, by activating the entire energy body, it's possible to stabilize focal point positions that are not of this world. Doing so, however, increases the risk of getting trapped in those worlds. He says that in order to avoid this pitfall, new-cycle Toltecs learned not to permanently stabilize any focal point position except that of heightened awareness. Experiencing other worlds was only a technique that was developed in order to learn about cohesion. This knowledge enables an alignment with the Eagle that brings all of the energy within you to life. This act of *will* produces freedom (*Fire*, 294–95).

The concept of burning with the Fire from Within describes the physical body transcending, resurrecting, as it were, this physical world. Looking at this from a Toltec point of view, don Juan wouldn't have been able to burn with the Fire had he not gained absolute control over his energy body. His control was so great that his entire physical body became only one of many manageable cohesions. Accordingly, this prior level is exercise for entering the third energy field.

Level Eight: Freedom Travel

The idea here is that once you're in the third field, maybe there's an exercise to better handle it. And maybe that exercise is learning to return to

Earth. You would then have a reference point to explore the immensity of the third field. You could launch, explore, return, assimilate your findings, and take off again. This would make the third field concrete, usable.

Based on my experience with don Juan, I think he did this. I also think that the ability to master the bridge between the human domain and the third field is what separates Toltecs, even the very best of the new cycle, from seers.

Level Nine: Beyond the Light

Just as a Toltec gets his fill of this world, and gleefully bounds into the third field, perhaps the seer gets his fill of the third field, and wants to move on. Therefore, just to keep the door open, I submit that there is a ninth level, a level that builds on the sense of freedom, and delivers awareness to . . .

DREAMING GATES

Dreaming levels correspond to gates, areas associated with the physical body, not unlike the chakras. One model of the gates, presented by Castaneda's teammate Taisha Abelar, places them at the soles of feet, the top portion of the calves and inner knee, the tailbone and the sex organs, the kidney region, between the shoulder blades, at the base of the skull, and the crown of the head.[1]

The gates are not simply the context as outlined in the prior section;

*Dreaming Gate
Locations*

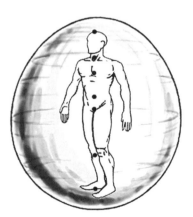

they represent a means of accessing and using dreaming levels as they offer a progression of ability in the same manner that movement up the chakras represents the evolution of perception. As such, there is way to approach them and a way to enter them. To help you into your dreaming body, here is an outline of the first three levels:

Level One
Approach: fall asleep while remaining awake
Entry: maintain constant images of a dream
Obstacle: randomness and novelty of dreams

Level Two
Approach: recognize the validity of another world
Entry: fully enter the dream and manage content
Obstacle: maintaining your wits and sobriety to control this lucidity

Level Three
Approach: feeling of movement, perception-shattering transition
Entry: classic DBE
Obstacle: indulgence, lack of purpose

DREAMING GATES AND CHAKRAS

You may have noticed that several of the gate positions are traditional chakra positions as well. In fact, it is not difficult to generate a model of dreaming that uses chakra locations rather than gate locations. If you think of chakras as dimensions of awareness, regarding them as equivalent to dreaming gates and levels is easy. A nice piece of research for someone would be to map the differences and commonalities and, in so doing, provide a map of the universal features, those that apply to the entire species. Some good work is waiting to be done.

The following list relates chakras to gates. What I find of interest is that there is a correspondence of the *energy* of each—even though the arrangement may be somewhat different, similar aspects of capability are presented in each, thereby indicating that, overall, the perceptions are universal to humans.

Chakra One

Raw energy. Primal awareness. Becoming aware of this power pack is like becoming aware that other dimensions exist, such as keeping yourself awake while entering dreaming.

Chakra Two

When you perceive two dimensions, you have the beginnings of a relationship. You can sense things around you. Dreaming level two deals with travel, and you can't travel without relation. If you didn't have another point of awareness, how could you travel to another location?

This emotional center that is chakra two is often related to the adrenal glands. When you get charged up, or endangered, adrenaline kicks in to save the day. Given the emotional surges that occur during the onset of dreaming, perhaps the onset of dreaming and this second chakra are connected in this way as well.

Chakra Three

Your physical body is perceived as three-dimensional (3-D), and with it you perceive the world as 3-D. Dreaming level three develops the dreaming body, which is typically perceived as a 3-D body. That is, due to our daily habits, the dreaming body often resembles the physical body. It might also assume the shape of an animal, or a sphere of energy, all of which are 3-D.

In essence, however, the dreaming body is a point of awareness. It initially emanates from the first chakra, from initial awareness. The sense of separate dimensions results from the interplay of different energies. That is, while all energies are essentially of one source energy, different states of energy produce relationships within ourselves as well as with the source.

As an aside, have you ever considered that our solar system has a yellow sun, just like the third chakra is yellow? And that Earth is the third planet from the sun? And that, just like the effect of chakra three, we can't seem to get out of our thoughts long enough to be aware of anything but ourselves?

Have you ever thought that we're now opening up to worlds beyond ours (such as extraterrestrial worlds) as the ozone layer is being depleted? Do you think that the reduction of this protective energy of the ozone is allowing energies from outside of our little home to enter our world and saturate our awareness? Is this making us awaken to them?

All of this is food for some very interesting thought!

Chakra Four

The heart chakra is where you begin to step outside of your 3-D self, and gain the perception of being connected with your environment. Remember, you always were connected to it; now you *perceive* it.

In terms of dreaming, at level four you begin to express dreaming in your physical world, in the environment of your physical body. Your expertise in dreaming-body travel begins to hook together your dreaming world and your physical world.

Chakra Five

The fifth chakra embodies communication: a form of relating with another consciousness. Resulting from your 3-D energies, you can talk about yourself. Add the fourth dimension and you can talk with others about your environment. This means you are gaining perspective and control of your environment. It also means you can talk incessantly about new forms of yourself, making it another entrance into the woolly world of self-reflection.

At this stage, the dreaming body acts. It is the time of the double. This means your dreaming body is developing movement. Therefore, you are gaining more perspective and control. As a result, you can move about in the physical world, and communicate with others by using the double. Perhaps this is why this energy is called the "double"—you get double the fun, double the trouble!

Chakra Six

This is the capstone of the second set of three-dimensional energies. Chakras one through three form the physical body, whereas chakras four through six form the complete double. Teleportation, then, means you have refined your ability to move the double in the physical world. Two sets of energies have hooked together to enable a most remarkable "double" relationship with the world.

Chakra Seven

This chakra is on the crown of the head, the last chakra within the normal human area, which means it resides on and within the physical body.

Burning with the Fire from Within means you have gained control of these energies, and you're stepping into other worlds. However, to illustrate a very important point, let's separate the Fire from Within from what I call the Fire of Freedom. You may burn with the Fire from Within and remain within the human condition as Toltecs define it; that is, remain within the energy body.

You may shift your cohesion so greatly that you evaporate from this world, but remain within the second field. This is what happened to the old-cycle Toltecs. Burning with the Fire of Freedom is a special version of the Fire from Within. It is shifting completely and unerringly into the third energy field, to a domain of energy outside of the human energy body.

Chakra Eight

Located just above the head, this chakra is removed from the ordinary human world, but remains within the energy body. Control of this energy means you can step in and out of the ordinary world. By shifting cohesion completely to it, you'd burn with the Fire from Within. You could then return by another significant shift. Again, however, just because you can do this doesn't mean you've learned the Fire of Freedom.

Chakra Nine

This is the white light for some, God for others, All that Is for still others, and the source of all Country Western songs to be sure, which means it contains all vibrations in the human world (be they musical or otherwise!). This chakra is the bridge between the human world—ordinary and nonordinary—and whatever lies beyond. For Toltecs, whatever lies beyond is the third field. Therefore, getting a handle on this energy is your stepping-stone to freedom.

Moving down the anatomies of the energy body and the physical body, I think the gates found at the knees and feet are chakras of a different model. I also hold that there are two other chakras. Just as there are chakras in the top end of the energy body, there is one midway between the soles of the feet and the bottom of the energy body and one beyond the bottom of the energy body. I currently think that the one at the bottom of the energy body deals with Earth-dimension physicality, while the one at the base of the spine deals with personal physicality. The next one up from the bottom of the energy body pertains to elemental dimensions as relating to Earth in a converse manner, and the chakra just above the head relates to extraterrestrials.

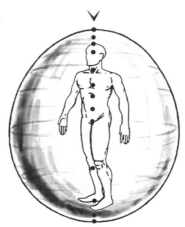

Expanded Chakra Model. It makes sense that an energetic circuit would travel through the entire energy body, top to bottom. As well, given our energetic connection with the environment, the role of the charkas pertains not only to the individual but to the whole environment as well, including planetary and otherworldly considerations.

Difficulties arise when you can't shift your energies. If you have a fixed-in-place cohesion, you can't entertain views that are not a part of that energy. There is no openness, no avenue for new information to register. At the same time, your energy should be stable. If it's not, you can't relate to new material. So be open, flexible, and yet very stable. The result is a transcendent life.

6

Dreams of Transcendence

Those Left Behind

I lay in my bed,
I see mist appear in my mind.
I feel my body go into my dreams,
I see my fellow friends floating in a bubble.
By magical wind, it blows along,
To find the energy to the gateway.
With my senses,
I help guide them through their adventure.

The Toltec Way outlines definite stages of growth. Each stage of transformation is a new cohesion, a new focal point position, and offers a new relationship with the world. The length of time it takes to bring a stage to life depends on the individual. It might take one person fifteen years to become a ranger, another only three years. If you're truly on the path, such distinctions don't carry much weight. If you're putting your all into the work, that sense of balance is enough to carry you forward. To some degree, the notion that "the journey matters more than the destination" is true. On the other hand, Toltecs are geared toward achieving success and so part of the journey *is* the result. And success is a great thing to experience.

Each stage represents experiencing a dream that transcends the dream of the prior stage. Each stage also reflects an ability to grow more into the moment. The more you plug in, the more you're aware of yourself and the world. The more sense you have, the more you can *be* in the moment.

At each stage you must claim your knowledge. You need to have experience, to develop skills to acquire more experience, and to have the wherewithal to make sense of your experience. Having good context for experience, then, is often as vital as *having* the experience. And you need to claim knowledge in such a way that you remain open to even more experience. To claim knowledge, therefore, it must become a matter of body knowledge, knowledge found throughout your entire being.

Your meaning in life, your values, and your interpretations, change at each stage. If they don't, you haven't done much to transform yourself. Keep in mind that changing your cohesion changes the world. To take a crack at freedom, the idea is to shed all meaning, values, and interpretations that stem from worldviews. Your cohesion has to be pretty clean to do this.

To get to a point where you can experience the world without the ballast of a worldview is a piece of work, to say the least. When you stabilize a new cohesion, a new stage, you'll feel natural in that energy. But remember that all secondary realities feel like home. They feel natural . . . until they exhaust you from complacency. Building an energy field relating to primary reality reflects a magnificent, awe-inspiring dream. It is a stage beyond stages. Don't settle for less.

The following is a general outline of the stages along a Toltec path to freedom. The *evolution* involves the dynamics of the specific stage. The *obstacle* is what don Juan refers to as a *natural enemy* (*Teachings*, 93).

THE APPRENTICE

Evolution: Simply put, at this stage you learn how to work your butt off. Expect to drill yourself on a variety of seemingly nonsensical exercises.

Don't expect to make any gains. Expect to be exposed to some wild ideas about the world. Don't expect to understand anything. But remember: From the perspective of a natural energy field, at each stage we're all beginners. The Zen mind is the beginner's mind: open, clear, yielding, strong.[1]

Obstacle: Fear. Fear is the inability to shift cohesion. This means that behavior is rigid and thinking is fundamentalist. Initially, this lack of suppleness is translated by the physical body as fear. Later, it is felt as a lack of momentum. In fighting fear, you gain new experiences because you act in unfamiliar ways. The more experiences you have, the more you bring your energy body to life. This results in having more energy and, therefore, more momentum.

Don Juan says the way to fight fear is simple: each and every time you find yourself at a crossroads, and you determine that the only thing keeping you from proceeding in a certain direction is fear, then you should head in that direction even if your fear seems insurmountable. To turn back is to be defeated. And don Juan says a defeated person may turn into a bully or just remain scared until his dying day (*Teachings*, 95).

THE RANGER

Evolution: My term *ranger* is what don Juan calls the *warrior*. Much to the chagrin of some, I changed the term to ranger to indicate a highly professional level of the warrior ethos. In part, this is a token of esteem for the U.S. Army Rangers; they are a cut above in training, skill, and character. The Toltec ethic, though, stems from not only waging war but the from the recognition that it's even more of a skill to stay out of war and to effectively wage peace. And so, in part, the change of term is a tip of the hat to the children's character, Ranger Rick, who diligently works with the animals of the wild. (Look, Toltecs are allowed to have fun with all of this stuff! In fact, don Juan considers doing so to be a matter of survival in the wilds of the second field.)

At this stage, it's important to keep doing what you've been doing: practice and refine your basic tracking skills. But you've also elevated your level of skill. Like getting a new belt in martial arts training, you're getting better. Just don't look for an outward symbol. You're not going to get sergeant's stripes, a new color of belt, or a sorority pin. By now, however, you do have a handle on your path. And you can apply your knowledge. You can deliberately (albeit modestly) shift your cohesion into different tracking and dreaming states. In a nutshell, you know what you want from life, and how to get it (*Teachings*, 96).

You've also committed to this path. It's part of your natural evolution, a piece of who you are all the way to your core. By developing this awareness, you've learned to wait. Having learned patience, nonattachment, responsibility, and the power of making decisions in the light of your death, you've become a ranger (*Separate*, 184). This is the core discipline of the Toltec path in much the same way that being a ranger is a core discipline of the more advanced commando-level training in the armed forces.

Obstacle: Clarity. "Lost within a vision" is a good way to characterize the negative effect of clarity. Oddly enough, becoming clear is an obstacle as well as a step forward. While you've enhanced your perception and thus gained a clearer view of the world, the work you've done on your energy body leads you to conclude that you've figured it all out. After all, from your apprenticeship you learned how to build your life, which means you built a foundation of strong cohesion, which means you can *see* clearly. But from the perspective of further evolution, you learned just enough to think you know more. Some patterns you now perceive will unfold just as you *see* them, others won't. Sometimes you're just getting ahead of yourself. Other times, you're too slow to act. This is frustrating, especially since you've paid a pretty hefty price to get here, and now have to start anew. But here's why it's important to continue practicing your basic skills: No matter what stage you're at, and at least until you can securely leave it all behind, the basics are what provide a solid orientation.

Clarity means that you have gained momentum. As a result, you're changing the direction of your life. It doesn't mean you know how to handle your new relationship with the world. This is why don Juan advises treating clarity as though it might be a mistake, and to defy clarity as you defied fear. Exercise patience. Make your decisions carefully (*Teachings*, 97).

One suggestion is to continue working with fear. By now you know that fear is inertia, a reluctance to change direction. Or you might consider it a lack of suppleness within the energy body that keeps your cohesion fixed. When you have a sensation resembling fear, track it. Find out its origin. Maybe you need a refresher in bouncing over the fear obstacle. Maybe you're learning the tensions associated with cohesion. In any case, you're working with the properties of energy rather than with the ordinary considerations of what fear once meant. Keep building momentum, which is the same thing as saying keep building your personal power. Fighting fear does this. So keep up the good fight.

To be defeated by clarity (or by any obstacle) means you've given up. You've hit the wall of a new level and have accepted the status quo. The wind has gone from your sails. Your tires are flat. If you don't overcome clarity, you'll stay on the surface of knowledge, or perhaps you'll become a clown as you go about telling others how much you know (*Teachings*, 96).

Let's take a practical business situation to look at the effects of clarity. Say you've been struggling tooth and nail to make your business go. You've built a reputation for service, quality, and dedication. Then, after years of toil, you hit pay dirt. You've got a product that everyone is asking for! Revenues soar. You've shifted to a new level. You've crossed the first obstacle to business success.

Like many businesses in this situation, you take your money and invest it in everything you've always wanted: more employees, better equipment, software upgrades. Your vision is finally coming to pass. You're *clear*. But wait—you've overextended yourself! You've missed a beat during the expansion and are no longer delivering your products in the timely manner your customers have grown accustomed to, which had earned you their respect (to say nothing of their money).

As a result, you're losing your business abilities; you're no longer managing your resources efficiently and with prudence. You've fumbled away the connection between your visionary goals and business practicalities. Your customers are now grumbling, almost begrudging your success. Having worked for many companies, I've seen this dynamic on more than one occasion.

The remedy is to go back to the basics, which is what enabled you to deliver quality and service in the first place. Return to your prior stage of growth to extract its wisdom. Relearn frugality. Remember not to recklessly overextend your grasp while pushing yourself beyond your limits. It's an interesting dance, knowing when to move and when to wait. This, in essence, is the dance of clarity. From this dance, you learn balance. You learn how to handle momentum, the movement of energy; the movement of your personal energy through these things we call time and space.

Clarity also has an effect on physical perception. That is, you begin to view the world as two-dimensional. A feeling of depth becomes the third dimension; it becomes just a sense of the world. Yet images are sharper, clearer, and colors are more vivid. The more you work with your clarity, the more you begin to figure out how the bubble of perception works. You *see* internal and external worlds merge, so that they do not have the same meaning as they once did. Each reflects the other. You gain a knowledge of intent that allows you to grasp how creating your life truly occurs; that is, by controlling your internal cohesion, you shape your external world. And by hooking onto the energy in your external world, you shape your internal cohesion. Having this awareness means you're just about ready to step into the world of the Toltec.

THE TOLTEC

Evolution: As a ranger, you've learned to wait for your *will*. Don Juan says that all people are connected with the world through *will*, through the luminous fibers centered in the abdomen (*Separate*, 33). For most people, however, *will* is dormant. The hallmark of the Toltec stage, therefore, is the activation of *will*. Throughout your journey to freedom you have in some way witnessed its expression and felt its power. Now it's alive and well. As a result, you have command over your cohesion. In doing so, you have completed building a nonordinary conditional energy field. You are a full-blown practitioner of Toltec knowledge.

During this journey of growing *will*, don Juan says a person performs impossible tasks, or impossible things just happen. He also says that the person may experience growing pains; yep, real pain, including convulsions (now there's something to look forward to!). Indeed, he says the more pain a person experiences, the stronger his or her *will* becomes. Don Juan continues, saying that when the convulsions end, the person can connect with and touch anything "with a feeling that comes out of his body" from a spot near the navel. This feeling, he says, is *will* (*Separate*, 185, 33).

A useful exercise for learning more about *will* is to observe whether you're perceiving the world with your reason or your body. When you're using reason, the world is distant, seemingly objective, and is upheld by your thoughts *about* the world. When you use your body, you feel connected, you sense your relationship and you have a knowing, beyond thoughts, that you're part of the world. This is body knowledge.

Obstacle: Power. Having command over your cohesion means you can determine the events in your life. It's all in the play of the bubble, a matter of focusing those mirrors to reflect whatever you want. But proceed in a narcissistic manner and you're doomed.

Relating this to the prior business example, having power means you can dominate. You can determine how other companies do business through the way you operate. A large distributor, for instance, can determine how a small production company must schedule shipments, file paperwork, and manage other resources. In some measure, for good or ill, the distributor is calling the shots.

On a personal level, power means you can literally create your own reality, and do so masterfully. Having control of your *will* means you have control of your cohesion. As you change your cohesion, you change your external world. You can have anything you want merely by aligning yourself with that energy. But if you give in to power, don Juan says you'll never learn to manage your resources. You'll never claim the fullness of your birthright and never learn to *be*—you'll stay lost in a sea of desire (*Teaching*, 97).

The way to manage power is the same as with the other obstacles: *don't* use it. With fear you learned to generate momentum, to move energy. With clarity you learned to temper and restrain your energy. With power you learn how to manage your complete energy body.

However, don Juan advises that there does come a time when you have all of your resources in balance. It is then, and only then, that you know when and how to use power. Such wisdom is gained only after a lifetime struggle, a lifetime of questing for freedom. At this stage you exit conditional energy fields and enter the domain of a natural field. You've become a person of knowledge (*Teachings*, 98).

THE PERSON OF KNOWLEDGE

Evolution: Don Juan says that while a Toltec may have a very strong *will*, it is possible that the person does not *see*. He indicates that only a person of knowledge perceives the world with his or her senses, *will*, and *seeing*. (*Separate*, 181). *Seeing*, remember, is the force of perception that splits energy away from ordinary and nonordinary conditions. It is a direct connection with the world, unencumbered by reason. Therefore, it removes you from the necessity of using metaphysical structures to bolster your quest. You're becoming free.

Up until now you've been caught in secondary realities. Your world has been fraught with projection; a world built from self-reflection. But at this stage you have the knowledge to break free, and rest within the embrace of all creation. Like a drop of water in the ocean, your energy body is fully connected with the Eagle's emanations. Hence, there's little projection. The mirrors of the bubble of perception have become so thoroughly transparent that "inner" and "outer" cease to exist. From having tempered your first energy field, your sense of order neatly meshes with the expansive energies of the second field. You're on cruise control, living life simply to be living it. You are now *being*. And you have fully integrated the discipline forged from the long haul to maintain this unparalleled state of awareness.

Obstacle: Old Age. The energy you've peaked for a lifetime begins to wear thin. Put another way, the energy you've built is getter harder to keep on track. You're old now, and you're getting tired.

Push this energy away! If you lose yourself in your tiredness, your energy will warp and reduce you to feebleness. Live your fate through, says don Juan, and you'll experience a rare delicacy. In what sounds like a pure mystical experience, he says the energies of clarity, power, and knowledge combine to produce an exquisite state of awareness that makes the entire journey worthwhile (*Teachings*, 99).

Remember: A viable system is not exclusive. It uses what works. It also has the means to transcend itself. Your advancement to being a person of knowledge is such an event, where the system becomes obsolete in service to continued growth. This is what the new cycle is all about.

THE SEER

Evolution: Don Juan says that *seeing* is the final accomplishment of a person of knowledge (*Journey*, 233). One must *see* to become a person of knowledge, and *seeing* continues the process. It seems as though it takes that much training not to get lost in *seeing*. Evidently, the old cycle of Toltec seers, who were considered masters in handling the energy body, became very fixated and obsessive about their *seeing*. So much so that they lost their nonattachment, dove back into fear, and became piously reverent, a terrible concoction for a Toltec (*Fire*, 18).

It is also my sense (and my rendering of Toltec teachings) that by the time don Juan had trained Castaneda, he burned away his energetic connection with Castaneda as he burned with the Fire from Within. Then, by the time he returned to take others under his wing, he had become a full seer, a consummate practitioner at managing energy. He was able to step in and out of dimensions, including to and from the third energy field, at *will*. I can only speculate about what passion and mysteries he must experience. Perhaps his energy ripples through creation, continuously expanding beyond worlds which are themselves at the very edge of imagination. Beyond this inkling, I have not a clue.

What I *see* now was quite beyond my imagination twenty years ago, and to make a couple more leaps of perception and place myself in his steps stops imagination dead in its tracks. Almost.

THE FIRE OF FREEDOM

Don Juan maintains that the process of growth along a Toltec path is threefold: to free existing energy, to use that energy to develop the entire energy body, and then to use that foundation to explore other worlds (*Dreaming*, 185–86). One such maneuver is the Fire of Freedom.

Again, this is a version of what Castaneda calls the Fire from Within. It consists of stimulating and bringing to life the entire energy body. At a certain point, the physical body evaporates from the physical world and completely enters another energy field. The old cycle of Toltecs fired off their energy bodies into the second field, possibly getting trapped for eternity (*Fire*, 230–44). Keep in mind that the first and second energy fields comprise the Toltec definition of what it means to be human. And this definition is pretty far-reaching. Shapeshifting into plants and animals, for instance, was evidently all part of a day's work for old-cycle Toltecs (*Dreaming*, 78). As a result, they were keeping themselves pinned within specific areas of the energy body. As grand as their accomplishments were, they remained locked within a certain domain.

The new cycle of Toltecs, of which I consider don Juan to be a shining example, gives the quest a different spin, that of pure freedom. This means evolving beyond the entire human condition into the third energy field; a radical transformation, a true evolution. This version of the Fire from Within is what I call the Fire of Freedom.

The idea is to become the essence of all that is human, retain this knowledge, then jump out of the human domain (*Dreaming*, 73). In her book *Being-in-Dreaming*, Florinda Donner, a teammate of Castaneda's, points out that a person needs a well-developed reason to make this leap, as it helps avoid excesses.[2] Rather than lose oneself in shapeshifting, for example, the logic of the path dictates that staying on track for even greater accomplishments is a higher priority. Shapeshifting may facilitate exploring the energy body, but is not the be-all and end-all.

Eligio, another of don Juan's apprentices, burned with the Fire because he knew how to let go (*Second Ring*, 46). He entirely accepted his fate. He blended with the world. He stopped the world. And so he was able to leave it. As a result, he gained the freedom to be human or to be whatever form of consciousness he experiences in other energy fields. However, discernments should be made as to whether these feats are of the Fire from Within or the Fire of Freedom.

The dynamic is that the focal point is pushed outward, bending uniformity into another position (*Dreaming*, 12). This permits some type of awareness of the third attention. This strikes me as a peek-a-boo arrangement of getting glimpses into something far greater than the human condition, be it ordinary or nonordinary. At the same time, especially when measured against a backdrop where one doesn't even recognize the influence of the energy body, the ability to perform such a feat, of having that much command over one's resources, is quite a marvel.

Don Juan maintains that at death awareness enters the third attention, and that by unifying the first and second fields death may be avoided (*Gift*, 249; *Second Ring*, 281). Evidently, during the throes of death, personal awareness expands through the entire energy body and beyond. Whether the Fire Within or Fire of Freedom, evidently the physical body—eyes, ears, nose, toes—leaves the physical world and consciousness is retained in another world. Relating this to Tibetan mysticism, one question that arises is: Does this maneuver break the wheel of rebirth, if there actually is such a thing? Just because consciousness may go somewhere in the cosmos, it doesn't necessarily follow that reincarnation occurs. The belief that it does could be the result of misinterpretations and projections of the death and dying process. It is possible that perhaps the various bardo states as outlined in the *The Tibetan Book of the Dead* are phases of experience or dimensions of the second energy field as one proceeds into death, and personal awareness expands throughout the energy body.[3]

If this is the case, the process of expanding through the second field might provide insight and experiences associated with the Tibetan map of death and dying. If reincarnation occurs, then perhaps one reincarnates because one does not break completely free of the second field, whereas fully entering the third field breaks the energetic chains that bind. If so, this process might illuminate key differences between the Fire Within and the Fire of Freedom.

TOUCHSTONES OF TRANSCENDENCE

Since dreaming accelerates experience, context is needed to help navigate the terrain. The following concerns provide just that; they are touchstones of transcendence that hopefully provide positive context for personal evolution.

Ethics

Ethics are governing principles of behavior: values, morals, and rules. Don Juan says that ultimately what anyone does is not important. Behavior is important because we think it is, because we have learned to regard one value over another (*Separate*, 107). He, however, has cleaned his bubble of perception in order to impeccably approach pure potential, something that is beyond the imagination of most of us. He lived at his core. To get there, he used the ranger ethic. He recognized the need for guidelines to channel energy, at least until a person is attuned to the rhythms of Spirit and can completely let go of any discipline.

Toltecs, says don Juan, are like anybody else pursuing a vocation. They can be good or bad. In fact, since they've learned to move their focal points, they can easily injure others. But don Juan, being a modern Toltec, says we must move past ordinary considerations, we must be governed by morality and beauty. Evidently Toltecs of the old cycle were so caught up in greed and the manipulation of others, they didn't even *see* invading armies coming their way. Finding an ethic based on personal freedom rather than on the accumulation of power was the challenge for the initial batch of new-cycle Toltecs. Part of this ethic is the practice of impeccability, which automatically gives others their freedom as well. Indeed, don Juan says that a person of knowledge would never, under any circumstances, harm another person (*Silence*, 102; *Tales*, 64).

When values clash, so do people. Wars have started over very simple things: the color of a person's skin, the shape of their eyes. These days, the topic of abortion often produces a heated environment. "Right to Life" activists have even killed "Right to Choose" adherents. And there's mud-slinging, arm waving, and epithet-calling galore when you put someone who thinks physician-assisted suicide is ethical in the same room with someone who doesn't. Perhaps we're in the midst of our own old cycle, as we can't even *see* ourselves acting completely contrary to our own beliefs. I'm not taking a position; I'm pointing out facts that illustrate incongruity and, therefore, a lack of balance.

Power

Power gives you the ability to actively mold your world. This is why it is also one of the obstacles. You may even want to be compassionate, to change things for the better, but power will see to it that you end up becoming a dictator. Its effects on behavior are very sneaky.

Ranger training as presented throughout this book is intended to guide you through this Herculean trial. To work through it, you need to connect with more than earthly powers. You need to fully connect with Spirit and let it guide your steps.

In essence, just remember not to *will* an outcome or even test the possibility of being able to do so. And don't exploit others. Work with the exercises, stick with the basics, and build your path. From this, any change that needs to come will come of its own accord. By not using power, you'll develop an exquisite balance. And, as don Juan says, there'll come a time when you have all of your resources and abilities in check, and you'll know when and how to use them. By then, you'll have become a person of knowledge (*Teachings*, 98). Having transcended all social bases, you'll be at your core.

Love

Just about anyone can give you a version of what love means. For some, it means you leave others alone so they may explore their own lives. For others, it means you step in to help out as often as is necessary, even if you're not asked to do so. And when it comes to intimate relationships, the needle tends to go off the meter; there is so much extra baggage involved! You can say you love your girlfriend, for example, but is this your hormones speaking up? Is it some kind of codependency that makes you feel a certain way? Do you need help paying the rent, and so you feel more open, tolerant, and loving?

Did you know that, in its native Greek language, the New Testament of the Holy Bible had different words, which meant different kinds of love? *Agape*, for instance, indicates a love that's more spiritual and expansive than romantic love. There were some dozen different words for different variations of love. In the King James version, these different words were all reduced to one word, one spelling: *love*. As you might imagine, some of the clarity, flavor, and sophistication was lost.

In addition, in most metaphysical environments people talk about "unconditional love." I still don't know what this means because everyone who has told me to love unconditionally places some kind of restriction on others. To actually have no restrictions, no conditions, is an amazing thing and requires intense, ongoing effort.

Perhaps love is awareness itself, or perhaps the feeling of ongoing expansion. After all, when we fall in love, we usually become more aware, and feel as though we're stretching out. Don Juan says that seers *see* love as pink, peach, or amber. Even then, only one of these is of the human domain (*Fire*, 163–64). But heck, only three colors out of the whole batch are love? This information doesn't support a view in which everything is love.

It seems like there's a lot of confusion over this thing called love. One thing that has always made sense to me, though, was expressed by don Juan just before his student, Carlos Castaneda, leaped into another world, burning with the Fire from Within. Don Juan spoke eloquently of how his love for the Earth had released his sadness, healed him, and eventually taught him freedom (*Tales*, 285).

Patience

In essence, patience speaks to balance and balance speaks to judiciousness, which is why this pertains to ethics. Patience is a silent force that forms cohesions. It is the posture of waiting, and waiting in such a way that you don't waste energy. Don Juan had a little singsong waiting drill: "A ranger knows that he is waiting, and what he is waiting for. And while she waits, she laughs and enjoys herself." In addition, since the ranger has a full life as a result of deliberately building their path, the ranger wants nothing. Indeed, don Juan says that not wanting anything is a ranger's finest attainment (*Tales*, 242).

This doesn't mean you can't like something, or you can't gather more knowledge. It means keeping your awareness clear and unfettered. It means you don't waste time and energy trying to be something, or have something. Each time you intend to be something, like a teacher, writer, scientist (oh, heavens, some kind of authority!), it removes you from the energy taking you to complete potential. By defining yourself, you've realized something out of potential, but not potential itself. You've become the pioneer who ended the quest and settled down before he wanted to, settled in a land he didn't truly love.

Patience is measured with the body, and is therefore a step toward managing body knowledge. Your body feels simultaneously relaxed and attentive, consistent yet fluid. And while you deliberately intend a particular result (like activating your *will*), you're nonattached to the outcome. From this posture, your cohesion can shift into alignment with a new set of emanations, lighting up your core and loosening the bonds of all inventories. Patience, then, helps create your life. As your life is now concerned with developing the energy body, your impeccability generates more personal power. As a result, awareness of dreaming, *seeing*, and the other cornerstones comes of its own accord. In time, you won't recognize you.

Impeccability

You can have tremendous psychic abilities, perform dreaming beyond belief, and still not be a ranger. Being a ranger is a matter of *beingness*, a way of relating to the world, a matter of character, a matter of integrity. And yet, there is no definite way to relate to the world, or to determine what character is. It is a matter of always measuring yourself through your eyes alone. In the midst of myriad different values, beliefs, realities, you're the only one who can assess your impeccability. There's a line in the British film *Cold Comfort Farm*, where someone says you have "standards inside yourself." This is what I mean. These standards produce the cohesion of impeccability.

Ranger perspectives and skills were created by new-cycle Toltecs to help you develop character, which is strength of heart and mind. It is also a lack of self-reflection. According to don Juan, getting to this point calls for "frugality, thoughtfulness, simplicity, innocence. . . ." He adds that while this may sound monastic, it's not. It's just the "best use of our energy level" (*Silence*, 248).

Impeccability is forged and tempered at each stage of evolution. Impeccability for a ranger is different than for a person of knowledge. Thus you must stay open, let go of your current thoughts and feelings, and aim for greater realizations. By the time you get to be a person of knowledge, you're no longer reflecting on the world; you're living in it, *being* with it. Being able to rest completely within your core, means you've become a seer, which means you've totally blended your energy body with creation at large, while keeping it very much intact.

I can write about being a person of knowledge as I have a sense of it, and I think I have a fair handle on the notion of impeccability. But I know I haven't evolved my cohesion, the actually energy of the matter, to the level of a person of knowledge. I haven't fully integrated the multi-dimensional experience known as "human" throughout my energy body. So part of impeccability is honest self-appraisal. This means it is also the ability to listen. The more you do, the more you naturally ease your way into other areas of your energy body, the ones you've never listened to, and thus never observed, before.

Emotional stability, calmness, and nonattachment are all signs and effects of having character, says don Juan (*Fire*, 178). These traits may also be considered to be aspects of emotional intelligence. Indeed, having emotional intelligence may be considered to be having character.⁴ The foundation for intelligence, then, is knowledge of the energy body. The more you've integrated a vast number of experiences, the more you've consciously stretched through the energy body. Therefore, you get riled up less because you're affected by less. You've experienced, worked through, integrated, then moved on to the next lesson, the next batch of karmic energies. This means you're getting that much closer to your core, to that cool spot surrounded by flame. And your backbone for doing this, says don Juan, is humbleness and efficiency (*Tales*, 280).

Being

We've discussed *being* before, but we will elaborate on it a bit more here. *Being* is arriving at and maintaining a connection with the core of your energy body. This might not be an objective, or a defined part of the energy body; core may be more like the essence of a person. This awareness is available to anyone, not just to Toltecs. Most consciousness-enhancing doctrines provide a way to access it. That's what they are good for. Remember, the mystical experience is a common element of spiritual traditions around the world. It embraces awareness outside of normal ways of perceiving the world. This transcendent experience may also tap the third attention, so we have a way to talk about it and compare notes. But like any novel experience, unless you have context for it—conceptual awareness that it exists—it will only be a fleetingly odd memory. Herein lies another benefit of a social base.

Awareness of core and the third attention returns our memory to primary reality, a reality where all the pieces of our lives connect, where there is an inner knowing of the world, ourselves, and our relation to the world. Without awareness of the third attention, we remain focused in a secondary reality where we can't reach beyond ourselves. As we have discussed before, focusing on the third attention therefore helps generate a continual mystical relation to the world known as *being*, as portrayed in Ram Dass's book *Be Here Now*.⁵

I don't think our awareness—however minimal—ever left the third attention. The energy body sails in this sea of consciousness. We've just become sluggish or preoccupied with other details. Plus, the third attention is so vast it is difficult to sense. The sights and sounds of the first and second attentions captivate us so that we lose sense of the more delicate and refined perceptions of the third attention. The various properties of the first, second, and third attentions are blended into one unit—our awareness. As we attend to relationships, jobs, problems and worries, joys, maybe even DBEs, we become so fascinated with focusing on the phenomena of our secondary reality that we forget our entire capacities, including an awareness of primary reality.

While *being*, we experience our lives from the vantage point of a flow of events, the circumstances of our lives. By actively cultivating a path that holds meaning, we help ensure these circumstances connect more to the core of our nature rather than reflect superficial needs and desires. The more we have experiences that connect with deep levels of our being, the greater the likelihood of our *being*.

The foundation for these perspectives of *being* results from inner discipline, such as that gained by adherence to perception-stimulating exercises (which are addressed in the following chapters). For example, clarity about your goals engenders a nonattached objectivity, preventing you from distorting how you feel, what you want, or what an experience is. Nonattachment, in turn, helps keep you clear. Clarity and nonattachment result in an attitude where you let yourself and your experiences be what they are, without a distortion or misinterpretation stemming from misdirected personal desires. This attitude increases clarity, which facilitates nonattachment, which develops clarity.

Minimizing self-reflection, in turn, allows you to get beyond yourself, or what you think of as yourself. You relinquish notions of yourself in order to experience more of yourself. As you cease trying to feel important, you lessen self-imposed constraints that keep you from tapping new aspects of yourself. As you stay out of your own way, you let Spirit flow through you more. When you don't block the flow, the flow maintains itself.

Potential is the sliver of new life between worlds, and it is the full force of all creation. It contains everything, while being nothing other than itself. Yet it is infinite. It is a state of energy from which all realizations arise, be they intellectual, emotional, or physical. The core of your energy body is part and parcel of this magical, mysterious force. Your core connects directly, intimately with potential, and all of your cohesions are realizations generated by it. The trick is to burn off the encumbering cohesions within the energy body, and fully bring your core to the foreground of awareness. Doing so awakens you completely. Again, I refer to this intensity of experience as *being*.

Being is necessary to arrive at freedom. Again, it characterizes the person of knowledge, which means it sets the stage for an evolution beyond the human condition. But being human is an essential ingredient to enact this evolution. You have a body, and it's a human one to boot. Therefore, being a ranger is about peaking the human experience.

Now the whole gig of being human, according to don Juan, is that we are luminous creatures. As such, our natural function is that of being aware, of perceiving. Indeed, don Juan takes this to a grand height when he says that "we are not objects; we have no solidity. We are boundless." Accordingly, he says that experiencing the world as material is a play of mind to make our passage on Earth convenient. He adds that it is when we get lost in reason that we develop difficulties (*Tales*, 100). It's like getting lost in a forest where every tree is of reason. By recognizing the value of the tree and then stepping away to view the entire forest, reason is relegated to its natural function.

Since we are boundless, the world must be as well. But we try to contain it through all of our thinking about it. All theories, all world-views, all conditional energy fields, all philosophies, all religions, are based in reason. They are formulations about the world; they are not the world itself. The world itself is perceived with the entire body through the epicenter of *will*, which then gives reason lots of stuff to play with. Being able to remain levelheaded while in a free-flow universe is done through *will*; more appropriately, through having a well-developed *will*. This requires the right and left sides of the energy body to strike harmony.

Until the first and second fields have blended and the entire energy body is awakened, we are in a self-reflective state. This is antithetical to *being*, and being totally alive. *Being* is arriving at your God-given earthly nature, as well as transcending conditions that bind. The particular path that unfolds from there is what will *be* (and perhaps what already is).

7

Dreaming Awake

Dream Ranger

I can dream with my eyes open,
and I'll tell you a story about a dream I dreamed:
a fox howling above the mountain,
crying for love and sorrow,
gliding through the sky,
calling, calling to me.
I try to catch him with my delicate hands,
but off he goes,
off he goes,
away, away.

Simply put, dreaming awake is taking what you learn from dreaming and applying it to your standing up, waking life. As Robert Monroe was fond of saying, you are more than your physical body and senses.[1] And, as wonderful as these senses might be, there is a heck of a lot more waiting to be explored and used. Dreaming awake is your launch pad for creating a magical, mystery tour of your life.

CREATING YOUR WORLD

Creating, or manifesting, is the process of determining what you experience. In general, this relates more to achieving something rather than simply witnessing that something has happened. Thus, it is an active application of dreaming.

For instance, if you tap the eighth chakra you enter the energy associated with perceiving ETs. If you deliberately seek that energy, you might manifest or experience them. However, you can also look at this as part of the species' evolution as we all expand from the seventh to the eighth chakra. As our awareness unfolds, our physical bodies will evolve with our perception. Our heads will grow to accommodate a larger brain, and the eighth chakra will then be at the top of the head, the new crown chakra. Humans will then be ETs. As this represents a more passive approach, one of becoming rather than of manifesting, creating also pertains to becoming aware.

Having said that, if you lock yourself into viewing creating a certain way then you limit your options. Whether you have the attitude that you actively create your experiences or passively allow your life to unfold, attitude is key to actual experience. That is to say, your attitude helps determine your experiences.

In the same manner, your identity—your own sense of yourself—can lock you up or release you to life. By letting go of having a sharply defined identity, you have taken a step to arriving at the fullest sense of yourself. For instance, do you identify yourself as being a physical body, or an energetic body that happens to carry within it a physical body? The difference is truly worlds apart.

From letting go, you receive. By incorporating an attitude of non-attachment, you can deliberately seek specific experiences while remaining unattached to the results. This helps you let go of your thoughts about cohesion in order to find what is really there, something beyond your thoughts. In so doing, you discover yet another cohesion. By taking charge of your life in this manner, you can allow your experiences to unfold at a natural pace, rather than forcing your desires. This deliberateness is *tracking*, and it has abundant application to dreaming.

TRACKING AND DREAMING

Tracking and dreaming are two major aspects of Toltec philosophy. (The term *tracking* is commonly called "stalking" in the Toltec tradition, however, due to the ominous connotations associated with the term *stalking*, I've changed it to *tracking*.) Tracking and dreaming relate to types of energy as well as to types of people. Tracking is energy of stability, of definition, of pattern, of controlled growth, and of the skills relating to these. Trackers tend to be practical, easygoing, and relate well with people. Although this has raised the ire of some Toltec devotees, I also think it is more descriptive of the process of aligning internal and external energies in order to perceive and to shift perception, a procedure discussed in this book.

Dreaming is energy of expansion, of natural wildness, of swift transformation, of raw power, and of the behaviors relating to these. Dreamers tend to feel like they're never at home anywhere in the physical world, strain the resources of those with whom they come into contact, bounce freely from one energy to another, and act like they're not grounded in what's going on about them (quite often, they're not). In essence, dreaming shifts the focal point and tracking fixates it into position (*Dreaming*, 69).

Toltecs groom both of these energies. You can, for instance, tap dreaming to boost your level of tracking. I frequently enter dreaming to establish the logic or pattern of my books. I just place myself in the energy of what I'm writing about, and then let the dreaming energies go to work and reveal what's on the agenda. I either *see* what is to be written, or come out of dreaming with a sense of several new paragraphs.

In turn, you can make greater headway in dreaming by becoming a better tracker. Proceeding to a new dreaming level requires that you have a degree of control over the previous level. The tracking skills of being grounded and centered, remaining inaccessible, and having stability of purpose, all provide a constancy that carries over into dreaming. Dreaming pulls you into your energy body, tracking pushes you into it; dreaming explodes you into it, tracking ushers you into it.

Each supports the other, and in a leapfrog manner, they expand your growth.

In addition, tracking relates to the first energy field and dreaming to the second field. By consolidating these energies, you bolster the entire energy body. By intending to reach freedom, you stand a chance of lighting up the entire energy body, experiencing all that is human, and then evolving beyond the human condition to pure awareness.

TRACKERS AND DREAMERS

Trackers and dreamers have different experiences of energy. Each personality connects with the world in different ways, and deploys or uses energy in different ways. As Emilito (a member of don Juan's team) says, whether in dreaming or in waking, trackers plan and then carry out their plans. Dreamers, on the other hand, jump into any reality without regard for plans.[2] So that you may better acquaint yourself with these energies, the following tidbits compare and contrast them. Watch for both of these expressions in your behavior.

Trackers build cohesions step by step.	Dreamers enter new cohesions in one swoop.
Trackers purposefully consolidate energy.	Dreamers keep awareness open to radical transformation.
Trackers develop flexibility and fluency among different worlds.	Dreamers are often black-and-white, totally in a perspective or totally out of it. Literally.
Trackers tend to be lighthearted.	Dreamers often become morose and obsessed, seemingly lost within the energies of their world.
Trackers find knowledge through shifting social identities.	Dreamers find knowledge through shifting the various dreams of reality.
Trackers find meaning in stability, then hook dreaming into the physical and build from there.	Dreamers take their awareness, fixate on it, then project that onto others.

Trackers have a difficult time accessing the full robustness of dreaming.	Dreamers have a difficult time relating to what they consider limitations of the physical world, and the requirements of building something over time.
Trackers isolate components of a problem, then apply strategic pressure to open doors.	Dreamers sense options, then open doors.
Trackers need training in dreaming to stretch into their energy body.	Dreamers need training in tracking to get down to earth.
If trackers don't commit to dreaming, they get lost in the nuances of their wondrous accomplishments.	If dreamers don't commit to tracking, they get lost in the currents of their own dreams.

If it seems that I am slightly kinder to trackers in this portrayal, it is because you're relating these features to normal social considerations, to what has meaning in the ordinary world of people. A dreamer wouldn't give a fig for all this chatter about what a dreamer is like, and a tracker would assess it under his or her own terms. At the same time, I may have given a slight edge to trackers because I have found that tracking is essential. Without it, time and time again, I have seen people squander their potential for realization as they lose themselves in the mysteries of dreaming states that have no purpose other than to instill a fake sense of accomplishment. Having a clear head and heart is required for this journey. Tracking and dreaming are professional skills. They require ongoing development. Getting lost in a dream occurs more frequently than we realize.

Tracking is a relatively recent Toltec innovation. It arose from the old-cycle Toltec need to change from their greedy and manipulative ways to a philosophy of freedom and transcendence. Tracking, as taught by don Juan, offers the balance and the stability to pursue the greater quest of personal evolution (*Fire*, 166–73).

You need a firm foundation to enter the unknown, whether you're exploring the outer reaches of the first field or journeying into the second field. In short, you need stability of mind and purpose. While tracking promotes fluidity, stamina, resourcefulness, and resilience, the gist of the whole matter is obtaining sobriety. This is another way of saying that you're aware of and capable of managing your energy body.

Managing your energy body, then, is the equivalent of managing awareness, meaning that you can manage what you're aware of, whether it is your diet or an entrance into other dimensions. Like any skill, there are levels of proficiency, of ability. In this light, here are a few dynamics at work and play within your energy body.

Chakras

As presented in chapter 2, chakra energies correspond to specific perceptions. For instance, the first, or red, vibrational energy is, of course, physical matter. The second, or orange energy, is of the emotions. Since each relates to a specific function, each is independent. Hence, each is its own domain. At the same time, since all chakra energies swirl within the energy body all the time, each influences the others as well as the whole of the network. So if you're always on the lookout for sex, your first and second chakras control your behavior. If you're studying at a university, your third chakra receives lots of attention. In other words, the energy given the most play entrains the others toward it, thereby influencing your overall behavior. Hence, while the chakras may be in a straight line up the spine, they don't necessary play themselves out in a linear manner. It's then up to your intent to corral your energies, aim them, and watch the results.

Biocognitive Interface

During a series of sessions while I was under the influence of Hemi-Sync in the Monroe Institute's lab, I contacted an energy that identified itself as extraterrestrial, from the Pleiades star system. Now, whether or not I actually talked with an ET might be a book in itself. But if you take it at face value, the experience offers some interesting possibilities.

One of these is the *biocognitive interface* model of creating, a concept given to me by the ETs and a concept mentioned earlier in this book. It means that the more you think about something, the more emotionally comfortable you'll become with the idea (such as the existence of ETs). Then, the more emotionally comfortable you become, the greater likelihood that the idea will manifest in your physical world. In other words, by thinking about ETs, you become more emotionally comfortable with the notion of their existence. The more emotionally stable you become, the greater the likelihood of having contact with them. As a result, the energy works from mental to emotional to physical, the third chakra down to the first, if you will.

Of course, your thinking is influenced by how your heart connects with the world, or how much psychic activity you have, or what your primary spiritual discipline is. In other words, the way you feel about something determines how or what you think about. This is especially true if you are emotionally charged about a topic, as strong biases influence your thinking as well as your physical behavior. Plus, if you're naturally psychic, you have even more to feel and think about. So, again, all of these energies play off all the others, each taking a lead role at some time or other.

And you needn't have a get-together with something as bizarre as ETs to see this dynamic at play. If you're starting a career in business, for example, you might read business books and magazines, perhaps take a few courses. You talk with business people and learn of success and failure. All the while, you're becoming more intellectually aware and so more emotionally in tune with the world of business. You may also just dive in and land jobs to provide this training. The long and the short of it is that the more mentally and emotionally comfortable you are with your business, the greater your chances of success. You have to do your homework to realize your vision. It's common sense.

As you gather a range of experiences and integrate them, you form a base for further experience. From one cohesion, you build another, then another. From this process, you grow in leaps and bounds. This is the biocognitive interface at work. To make it work efficiently, be careful to gather a wide range of experiences and integrate them carefully. The dreaming/tracking combo offers such breadth and depth. Using the chakra model is also quite helpful because you have several energies to relate to any given experience. Simultaneously managing several facets of the energy body serves to make what you've integrated lasting.

Let's look at the biocognitive interface from a different angle. As all of this talk about chakra energies plays itself out in mainstream society, more will be said and written about them. As a result, more people will recognize experiences associated with chakras. The more people acquaint themselves with chakras, the more chakras will be studied, leading to a greater understanding and a more detailed logic. Then, just as any subject grows in depth and breadth, this knowledge will become part and parcel of society's daily world. The cohesion of the social consensus will then change.

The essence of the biocognitive interface is that it helps you connect with your body, and therefore with the energy of what you're creating. Dreaming provides a huge amount of experience; tracking delivers you to your goal.

Cohesion

As we know, cohesion is the pattern of energy within your energy body. This pattern reflects how your personal energy is aligned with emanations outside of your energy body, be they having a cup of coffee or talking with ETs. The bottom line is that alignment translates into perception and experience. Therefore, if you change your pattern of energy, you change what you perceive. A very minor change is walking down the street. A greater change is having a DBE. A huge change is the Fire of Freedom.

By deciding what you want, then applying yourself to that goal, you shift cohesion. Your level of skill is the hinge of time. If you lack raw determination, the biocognitive interface offers a structured approach, which is what systems are for. The more you learn, the more your mind will relax, and the more capable you'll feel.

If you're starting a business, don't flail away. Approach it with determination, apply what you've learned, abide by ethics you consider worthwhile, remain attentive to your intuition, and place your work in the context of your spiritual growth. Everything considered, you're working with a variety of energies toward a common goal. You then begin to realize that experience. If all channels are tuned, you should realize success. If something is out of whack, you'll discover the problem. If so, retune that energy and proceed again. There are no guarantees. There are, however, potentials waiting to be realized. Remember that in large measure your cohesion is built by, and simultaneously reflects, your worldview. From this energetic pattern come your options. From your options comes your behavior. By changing your options, you change your worldview, your cohesion, your behavior, and the world that you realize.

Decisions

For reasons just given, your decisions are governed by your cohesion. You make decisions according to your cohesion and you make new decisions in an effort to shift cohesion. Also, referring back to body knowledge, we find that a recurrent lesson from don Juan is that the body knows what is what, then it decides how, when, and where to act. Therefore, grooming body knowledge is equivalent to becoming aware of your cohesion (*Journey*, 292; *Tales*, 158). You then let your body do the work.

To say this another way, your cohesion makes up your mind for you. To act consistently after having established a decision is acting from power as you deliberately work to stabilize a new cohesion. This is what produces the changes in your outer world.

When you create a decision, you've probably experienced enough to know you don't want your old behavior to rule. But when you begin to act, all sorts of memories, influences, and longings rear up as the old cohesion begins to snap back into place. This is simply momentum and inertia. You'll find that bursts of energy from old cohesions, reflecting old habits that you wish to leave behind, surface to throw you off the mark.

Sticking with your decisions saves the day, and sometimes it may take years to fully form and use a new cohesion. But the constant focus of energy that comes from holding fast to a decision eventually supplies enough energy to offset the old patterns. An unchangeable decision, says don Juan, generates *unbending intent* (*Silence*, 241). And unbending intent is a condition of personal power. So make your decisions carefully, and then don't turn back . . . unless you make a new decision.

Expectation

Your expectations aim energy, a kind of loosey-goosey intent. As you think and feel in certain ways your cohesion shifts to follow along those lines of energy. Like almost anything else, there's a high side and a low side.

The high side is that your expectations help you create your goals. If you expect to have a positive experience, you increase the odds that something favorable will occur. If this doesn't happen, just remain nonattached to the outcome. Live, let live, and learn. The low side of expectations is that you might get in the way of greater creations. For instance, if your goal is to teleport your physical body but you expect it to happen in a certain manner, then that expectation might prevent anything from happening at all.

Of course, sensing the potential of something, or being clear in your thoughts about it, may not be sufficient to realize it. You may need to take a few steps first. You may need to grow into it. Handled properly (and only you can determine what's proper), your expectations can assist your growth. In and of themselves, expectation is not unbending intent.

Intent

Intent is a mysterious force, silently weaving its way through your life. It's a neutral force that moves to your beckoning, thus it's a good thing to have your priorities in order. Otherwise, you intend the least little thing. Or perhaps you'll have a multitude of conflicting intentions, which then produces a lifetime of conflict. Whatever you set your mind to is pretty much what you'll get, including all the stray desires along for the ride.

Don Juan once related intent to manipulating your feelings in order to change your relationship with something. And it's feelings handled with deliberation, with conviction, and with focus, that produce intent

(*Silence*, 230). Therefore, you can use feeling to gather sensations and use them as channel markers. From this you can determine your cohesion and alignments of energy, which are the substances of creating. The result is that intent is focused, directed energy, which is in balance. If you focus too much, you squish energy away from you. If you focus too little, you lose your connection with it. In either case, you diminish the inherent power of intent. Naturally, this reduces your ability to create. Moreover, when you establish intent, get out of the way of your thoughts. Nurture intent by balancing the focus of it with body knowledge, then let the results come of their own accord.

Herein lies another value of working with a system. It helps you reduce haphazardness. It gives you interlocking tips on how to behave, such as letting go, remaining nonattached, tracking, etc. This structure, combined with definite goals to measure your growth, provides support to enable you to learn better. You need to understand how your bubble of mirrors is created by your thoughts and how this binds you to a world of self-reflection, how energy fields affect perception, and how to manage these influences. A good system provides all of this and more.

Purpose

One of don Juan's female apprentices, la Gorda, says that the key for a ranger who desires to be an impeccable tracker, is purpose. Her purpose was to enter another world (*Second Ring*, 223–24).

Purpose is a combination of focusing toward, and flowing with, energies associated with a goal. It is an expression of your innermost wishes and thereby connects you intimately with the world. As with focus, if you shut down the flow of energy, you lose sense of your quest. If you open the nozzle too far, you squander your resources.

It is also interesting to note that Edgar Cayce recommended astral projection only to some. For these people, he thought it to be a faster way to reach Christ consciousness. Before embarking on the journey, though, he advised that one should first know why he or she is taking up the quest. More on this and other advice from Cayce is presented in chapter 11.

Visualization

For our purposes, visualization may be considered a form of dreaming. When used as a visualization exercise, dreaming speeds up learning as you work directly with cohesion. That is, dreaming lets you witness what you place into motion faster than you can in the physical world. So you can test and measure your steps more easily. You can run a program by visualizing different scenarios—feeling if they make sense, making adjustments, running the program again—and then letting your body adjust to that energy. In other words, imagine different scenarios and watch the results unfold. Your body knowledge then helps you reconstruct the program in your outer world, and thereby create it.

By using visualization and feeling together you can also get a handle on intent. "Intent is beckoned with the eyes," says don Juan (*Silence*, 144). For instance, use your imagination to connect with the first chakra. To help, use red as a focus. Then feel that energy. Now imagine orange. Feel it. Work your way up through the chakras, then back again. As you do, feel the movement of energy with your entire body. You're now learning to manage cohesion.

In psychological experiments, athletes who used visualization improved their abilities at rates higher than those who merely physically practiced their sport. They used their imagination to refine their "athlete" cohesion, which translated into better performance. Some studies included the use of hypnosis and found the subjects learned how to relax and concentrate better.[3]

Furthermore, you reinforce your image of yourself throughout the day by what kinds of images you create. Notice how you think, feel, and visualize yourself at various times of the day. These imaging sessions occur in a split second. But over time they build a self-profile within your energy body. This, in turn, aligns you with that image of yourself, which then manifests that result. And this applies to your health, your finances, how you drive, and how you talk; in short, to all facets of your life.

Waiting

As a discipline, waiting is also force. It automatically provides focus, removes obstacles within your cohesion, establishes an energy line to the goal, and thereby aligns perception with the emanation of your goal. It allows all the shifts in cohesion to fall into place in order to stabilize it. As it does, you've created what you were waiting for. Thus, you don't have to search for something; you can let it come to you. By shifting cohesion, you produce the intended results.

Will

As discussed earlier, *will* is the active force of shifting cohesion. It gives you command over your cohesion. As a result, it gives you command over your complete energy body. For example, whereas the heart chakra is the balance point of the physical body (it is the fourth among seven), *will* is the balance point of the energy body as a whole. As a result, by shifting your cohesion, you can manifest your heart's delight. However, doing so may turn the tide of freedom against you.

It seems that *will* has plenty of interesting and nontoxic uses. When don Juan's friend don Genaro climbed a dangerous waterfall, he used his *will*. In doing so, he gave Castaneda a lesson in how to control *will* and the abilities it rendered. When don Juan prevented Castaneda's car from starting, he used his *will* on the car's "key joint," by preventing the spark plugs from igniting. In a grander maneuver, don Juan says that Toltecs tune their *wills* by playing with death, by stretching out into the unknown, and then letting their *wills* reassemble their bodies (*Separate*, 132, 239, 240). It seems as though Toltecs still live in the wild, wild, West!

In general, by intending yourself to develop your *will*, you gradually bring it to life. So throughout the day, bring yourself back to this point of reference. Learn to isolate the differences between perceiving the world through reason and through *will*. You may do so simply by establishing an intent, then paying attention. Are you reflecting on the world through thought, or are you actually in touch with it? Doing so continually grooms your body knowledge. This, in turn, awakens *will*.

Tips

A few odds and ends, and reminders:

1. Manifest from the moment, from the here and now. If you want your world to manifest in the future, keep it there and away from you.
2. Be aware of opposite effects. If you try to keep your lover from slipping away from you, you'll cling. That will most likely drive the person away. And if the person was leaving anyway, let go gracefully.
3. Don't leave something to chance. Do everything you can to fulfill your purpose.
4. Focus toward, but don't fixate on, your goal.
5. Remember that optimism is a sign of emotional intelligence, and an indication of those who achieve success. It is the lubricant that helps energies shift, thus making it easier to build a "success" cohesion.
6. Each decision adds to, or subtracts from, your cohesion and your quest.
7. Don't have cross purposes. Align your primary and secondary programs to work in support of each other.
8. Tension in your body often reflects work you're doing to create a new cohesion, and to manifest a new life. The realignment to new emanations is work, and so your body feels it. It's body knowledge at work.

Creating is bringing something into awareness, and having it remain stable and usable. This occurs from the interaction between form and potential. Form is of cohesion, a type of energy field. As we've discussed, potential is abstract energy; that is, energy which has possibilities for realization but isn't here yet. Pure potential is completely abstract, the infinite creation which contains everything. How these two energies play together determines what is realized.

Remember that whatever is realized directly reflects your cohesion, or what pattern of energy you've stabilized. It also governs how you continue to connect with potential, which governs what you'll manifest next. So you have the energy body meeting greater emanations. This meeting produces a dance between potential and realization: the disco of creating.

If you're not hooking up with potential, you're just circling within the cohesion you already have. This may keep you amused, but you're not going to grow too much. Plus, when you squarely face your potential, you're placing your life squarely on the line.

Dreaming awake is, for most, a highly unusual state of consciousness. As such, it might be easy to get lost, in more ways than one. So let's examine a few aspects of guidance, of how to navigate away from rocky shorelines and toward positive destinations.

In some way, shape, or form all guidance hinges on body knowledge. As such, all require paying attention to what the body senses, and to how you relate to any given event; in other words: listening. Since we're first addressing inner guidance, let's place listening in terms of the energy body's innate modes of perception, the cornerstones: dreaming, feeling, and *seeing*.

MODES OF PERCEPTION FOR INNER GUIDANCE

Dreaming

Some people say that you must have the same dream a number of times for it to be considered revelatory or meaningful. From personal experience, dreams that repeat themselves usually mean something is at work, and the message within the dream is begging for attention. At the same time, while a one-time only, very vivid dream might be the result of too much pizza; such a dream might carry enough weight by itself to be considered as holding a portent, as signaling bona fide guidance.

The way to figure out which is which is to educate your intuition. Sense what a dream tells you. Does your body tell you that your interpretation feels right? Recapitulate the dream to discover its meaning.

Did you eat too much, or does it carry a prophetic note? This helps you figure out your feelings that much more easily.

You may also set up dreaming to find specific guidance. Carry a question into dreaming, for example, and let your dream play itself out. Pay attention to the images, and to how you feel. Don't censor your dream. Give yourself plenty of room to experience whatever, and I mean *whatever*, unfolds in the dream. Anything can happen in a dream, and usually does; after all, you're in dreamland! But typically, a dream settles down once the energies behind it discharge. So if a dream is violent, it may turn peaceful if you don't repress the images. Let it work itself out and discover where it will take you.

You may also apply this as an exercise of stretching out your *will*, a playing-with-death exercise. To do so, enter the blackness of level-one dreaming, then let your awareness disperse, ooze, or flow far into the dream. Then let your energies be at rest. Next, observe your energies returning, consolidating within your physical body. This reorganization occurs when your *will* is ready to let it occur.

Feeling

Realizations stemming from emotional outbursts are fleeting, says don Juan (*Fire*, 278–79). This means that when you click on insights that are packed with emotion, they tend to be of very limited value and don't withstand the test of time. Hence the need for educating emotions, feelings, and intuition. In this way, we cultivate feeling as a viable method of guidance.

Intuition, an aspect of feeling, is a full-bodied, multi-dimensional form of guidance. It's full-bodied in that it requires body knowledge. It relies on being fully aware of how you're feeling. And for that, you need your body. It's multi-dimensional in that at some level, conscious or not, you're aware of different dimensions, and are connected with various modes of perception.

Feeling gathers many influences, and then delivers insight. Feeling may even be thought of as having tentacles extending throughout regions of consciousness, such as the regions dealt with in chaos theory.[4]

As a result, you're aware of irregular, or unknown, patterns in the universe, as well as regular, or ordinary, patterns within your known world. This means you can be intuitively aware of something without a rational foundation to explain why this is so. As you can imagine, managing such complex behavior requires rigorous education and self-discipline.

Applying feeling to work in your life requires listening to gentle nudges and ever-so-soft feelings. If you don't, all heck may break loose. Not that it will, but one little thing not in place may produce very large ramifications. In other words, if you overlook even a tiny form of guidance you may experience catastrophic results. For example, a Toltec-minded friend of mine told me an interesting story. It seems as though she was having her silver-mercury dental fillings replaced with quartz-based composite fillings. Her purpose was to remove the toxic substances from her mouth. Just before entering the dentist's office, she felt a twinge to have only one large filling replaced that day. Eager to get the procedure finished, though, she had several fillings replaced during the one visit. However, one replacement filling was not shaped exactly like the previous one. This threw her entire bite off, requiring numerous additional trips to the dentist in order to restore a proper alignment of her teeth. While the dentist did own up to making a mistake, my friend assumed complete responsibility, realizing that if she had been more patient, and listened to her guidance, the difficulty would not have occurred. With only one filling to concern himself, the dentist would have remembered the exact size of the filling to be replaced.

As a result, contrary to the popular method of filing a malpractice lawsuit, she used her guidance to help the dentist restore her bite. Before she continued with him, however, she set up an omen to see if she should stay with him. She did so by asking Spirit for guidance, intending that she'd receive an answer, and then waiting for a reply. Receiving a favorable indication, they set about the task of restoration. (By the way, she said that her body felt better as soon as the mercury was removed.)

I'm sure you can recognize something similar that has happened to you. How many times have you felt like behaving one way, only to behave according to your habits, or according to your personal thoughts or wishes? Then, later on, it dawns on you that you should have acted on how you originally felt.

Seeing

Seeing is like peering through something, through outer manifestations into deeper, root energies. This makes it a marvelous technique for guidance. Like any skill, it requires training to develop. Don Juan says that at first *seeing* carries many distortions, making it difficult to figure out and use. Later, it becomes a direct link with intent, a direct way of knowing (*Tales*, 154). Keep in mind that its visual nature may be misleading. *Seeing* hinges on connecting, or merging, the entire body with what is being *seen*. Even though it may include using one's eyesight, it's not something that's done just with the eyes.

In general, guidance reveals itself in many ways. *Seeing* is no different. You might experience a bundle of energy, which leaves you with a knowing. You might have a vision, or simply perceive a mental image. Or a response to your request for guidance might come as a voice, a silent voice. In each case, it's a matter of establishing an intent for guidance, then getting out of your own way in order to perceive an answer. Using *seeing* for guidance is very much like obtaining guidance while dreaming. But, since *seeing* tends to be a more direct method, you become instantly aware, rather than having to decode or interpret a dream.

As you develop *seeing*, you learn to discriminate among images, body sensations, and voices, learning what to trust what you can bank your life on. To begin, start with questions that aren't very complicated. Should you eat a hot dog? Should you take a day off from work? While these are simple enough, keep in mind that however you act carries weight. The smallest decision in your life is capable of creating the greatest effect. So be responsible. Pay attention. Experiment.

THE GUIDANCE OF SPIRIT

Perhaps the most difficult part of receiving guidance from these modes of perception is cutting yourself loose from *all* of your concerns in order to be aware of the promptings of Spirit. Spirit speaks in many languages, and comes in many forms. You might feel a soft, inner voice, or have a traffic sign, an omen, placed directly in front of you. When you give yourself permission to be guided by Spirit, you're tapping higher orders of awareness. Therefore, a request from Spirit for seemingly nonsensical behavior usually turns out to be quite brilliant after the dust settles. Spirit has a full sense of the entire playing field, not just the position *you're* playing.

One of the ways that Spirit manifests is through omens. Omens, or signs, have been around a long, long time. Julian Jaynes, for example, explores many varieties of omens in his book, *The Origin of Consciousness in the Breakdown of the Bicameral Mind.*[5] From comet trails to cloud formations to eclipses, and from facial characteristics to dreams to hallucinations, omens have always been part and parcel of the human condition. And there is no doubt they are a key element of a Toltec lifestyle.

Indeed, until you get a good handle on intuition and *seeing*, omens serve as an excellent bridge to understanding the communications of Spirit. Additionally, until you establish a firm direction in your life, intuition and *seeing* also help guide you through the random influences that push and pull at you when you first enter formlessness.

In a manner, omens are like the signposts found in dreaming. By serving as external reference points, they help take you out of your normal habits. Indeed, they help elevate perception into heightened awareness, or dreaming while awake. That is, they help transform your ordinary feel of the world into the perception that daily life is a type of dream.

Omens also help you figure out internal guidance, because intuition is a key to deciphering them. When you witness an omen, for example, don't tell yourself what just occurred. Ask yourself what it means instead, and wait for an intuitive reply. Make sure you don't bend an interpretation to suit your personal desires. As you build up your omen vocabulary, you'll recognize some omens immediately. Others will be filed for future reference. You'll have to wait and watch how your life unfolds, then match the omen on file with whatever occurs. You may start building this language by determining your positive and negative colors, your "yes" and "no" omens.

For example, during a trip to London, my companion and I were walking about town as I explained omens to her. Since she was curious, I asked Spirit to show us what her positive color would be for the day. I told her she could change it later, but for practical purposes we needed references for that afternoon. As I asked Spirit this question, a red automobile pulled up to the curb and stopped in front of us. Okay, red it was! I then asked for her negative color. A white taxi turned from another street in front of us. Now, part of this was that these events were out of the ordinary. We had not seen any red cars stop in front of us, nor had I seen too many white cabs that day. They stood out, which is part of what omens are all about.

So there we were, cruising about town having a great time reading omens. Then we decided to eat. She was not familiar with the area we were in, so she wanted to turn left and head back to where she knew the turf. I said "Let's use omens, instead." After all, that was the curriculum for the day. As soon as she agreed, a red car passed us, and turned right, heading in the opposite direction. Even though this was not the direction she had wanted to go, we turned around and followed it. After we walked three blocks, a woman dressed in black stopped, bent over, and adjusted her shoe. To me, black means death, which means the event gets an exclamation point. Black is neither good or bad; it just means: pay greater attention. Then we noticed a white car parked just past the woman. We stopped. Immediately to our right was a pub. I asked if this is where we should eat, and a man wearing a red shirt walked inside. We followed.

I had been hungry for a traditional English meal of roast and vegetables. It turned out that this was the pub's evening special. My friend had fish and chips, which she raved about, saying the pub was a true find and she had to return.

Other times, when meaning is not so readily apparent, ask Spirit what the omen means. You'll then receive inner guidance, or perhaps another omen will pop up in front of you. You can decipher omens from virtually anything. An omen might be the same for several people, or it might mean several different things. It's up to you to figure out your agreements with Spirit in order to create your very own omen dictionary.

This may sound nuts to some, I know, but Spirit communicates with all of us all the time. Think of the wonder of that!

Here are two more examples just to give you an idea of how fun all of this is. The first occurred years ago, when Halley's Comet was passing by. Even with the entire media hullabaloo, I had not been paying too much attention to this cosmic wonder. But the morning it passed closest to Earth, I found the rear window of my automobile had been shot with a pellet gun. A small hole was surrounded by shattered glass that formed what looked like a comet and its tail. I asked what this meant and the silent answer was, "Pay attention." I had been too caught up in my own thoughts, in my own drama of living, and was totally oblivious to stretching further into life.

Another way to tap awareness beyond the ordinary is the mystical experience, which is found in all major religions and is typically characterized as one of the more refined levels of consciousness. I think it is also a prelude to *being*.

For our purposes, the term *mystical* should not be equated with the term *occult*. Occult typically concerns the experience, use, and application of psychic forces, forces that remain hidden to the perspectives of ordinary reality. An occult view may fence in seemingly supernatural events, often without requiring us to expand our vision past the event at hand. As valuable as occult phenomena may be, they do not necessarily point the way to freedom.

Mystical experience relates the fullest possible experience and understanding of ourselves as part of a greater, perhaps Divine, order. It dismantles fences in favor of extensive and continual growth. It requires us to break barriers because it can't be contained. For example, as I walked along the water's edge near my apartment in Virginia Beach on a warm, summer day, I stopped to pick up and throw away a beer can lying on the sand. Without malice or scorn, I thought that if every person who visited this beach threw away one piece of litter, the beach would stay clean. Continuing my stroll, I noticed a gull's feather on the sand. Because of my last name, I identified with the feather, thinking that I was also it. I thought about the birds flying over the ocean and, since I was the feather on the sand, I also belonged with each of them. I then reflected that birds exist over the entire world and that I was a part of each of them.

With that thought, my thinking collapsed and what felt like a quiet fire started within me. I perceived myself as a complete and intricate part of the world. I then recognized the intellectual steps I had just gone through in order to arrive at that perception. Yet it was as if the recognition was also experiencing me. From individual humans on the beach to an individual feather to unity with all feathered creatures, I went from a neutral and natural relation with humankind, to the uniqueness within me, to a connection with all parts of the globe. From that point, the fire grew as I understood that I was connected at the deepest level of my being to the entire universe. Exquisite energy coursed through my physical body and my mind soared with my brethren creatures past the ordinary world, past the heavens, and into the heart of creation. Consumed by intoxicating bliss, I nevertheless felt relieved when these feelings passed.

Just as a certain pattern of stars indicates a constellation, a specific pattern of individual perceptions indicates a mystical experience. In *The Varieties of Religious Experience*, William James outlines four components of a religious experience. It is ineffable (the inability to transfer a full sense of one experience to another), noetic (it instills awareness beyond the limits of the intellect), transient (short-lived), and passive (it comes of its own, has its way, then leaves).[6]

Although a mystical experience may be transient and passive, I think engaging a good metaphysical system loads the dice in favor of your having one. They are also bound to occur if you aim for *being*, which is an effect of reaching the stage of being a person of knowledge. This is a stage where one lives in dreaming awake, and I can tell you for certain that when you're in dreaming awake you may have out-of-this-world adventures while your feet are firmly planted in this one.

All of the experiences described above are wonderful dreaming awake experiences, but perhaps the most refined one is *being*. On several occasions, I have been fortunate to slip into this form of heightened awareness. On three of these occasions I remained in this state for at least ten days. This awareness was characterized by feelings of calm, self-assurance, deep relaxation, and alertness.

I felt immersed in a natural order, and felt a natural pace, which caused me to walk slower than normal. It seemed as though I was in a mild current, a flow of electricity that directed my life. Rather than continually checking my watch, I intuitively knew when to leave my apartment to meet someone, or to be someplace on time. I fulfilled all of my needs and obligations as I shopped for groceries and attended college classes. I also had more enjoyment as I visited inlets and rivers during the early morning, and watched the sun set in the evening. I entered deep meditative states more often and required less sleep. Actually, it would be more accurate to say I felt as though I was meditating twenty-four hours a day, with some experiences reflecting deeper meditative states than others.

Abiding by the thoughts and actions that then became "me," I gradually learned more about who this "me" actually is, rather than distorting this information by habits associated with maintaining an identity that I felt comfortable with. In Toltec terms, I accepted the quiet directives from Spirit and allowed that force to guide my every action. As a result of these experiences, it was obvious that entering and maintaining this state of consciousness provided a more intelligent way of living. I felt more peaceful, had more energy, and experienced more life as I felt more alive.

It seems as though undergoing a mystical experience promotes a natural sense of internal timing. It also turns out that timing may be quite important in more ways than one. I say this because don Juan maintains that his version of inorganic beings are slower and consequently live longer, whereas the natural speed of humans exhausts their energy more quickly. As a result, the consciousness of inorganic beings is evidently deeper and calmer. (*Dreaming*, 45). Also in this mix don Juan is saying that the inorganic world is separated from our world due to a barrier of energy existing at a different speed (*Dreaming*, 47). Speed, vibrations of energy, and timing are part and parcel of the same dynamic. What might we discover if we take just this one facet (the slower-paced consciousness of inorganic beings) and use it to examine the following: emanations; Earth in relation to other dimensions; energy bodies among species; and the effect that timing has on human health?

This natural timing associated with *being* is also reflected in having a sense of flowing from moment to moment with the world. This experience has been well studied by Mihaly Csikszentmihalyi, who wrote the best-selling book *Flow: The Psychology of Optimal Experience.*[7] To simulate this feeling, try the following exercise. (It's also a good one to help set up DBEs.)

☀ The Waterfall Meditation

. . . Imagine, visualize, feel, or otherwise perceive yourself as a river. Identify with the river as you feel rocks on the riverbed, the churning of the water over boulders, the wet earth along the riverbank. Perceive yourself flowing as the river.

. . . The river now flows over a cliff and turns into a waterfall. Droplets of water separate from the river. Change your identity to one of the droplets. Feel it drop downward at the same speed as the waterfall.

. . . The waterfall and the droplet enter a lagoon. Shift your identity to the calm pool of water. Languish in its gentleness, in its depth.

. . . You feel another force as a current pulls you away from the lagoon. You enter another river and re-identify with it as it flows downstream and empties into the ocean. Shift your identity to the ocean. Perceive the myriad of life forms within you. Expand your awareness outward in all directions.

. . . Now you feel another force acting on you. You feel pulled upward and your identify again shifts, this time to vapor, as the heat from the sun evaporates water from the ocean.

. . . As you rise, you feel yourself becoming denser. You then identify with a cloud. You feel wind currents gently move you over the ocean and over land.

. . . Feel yourself becoming even more dense. You then begin to rain and your identity shifts to become drops of water. You fall downward into a river.

. . . As you merge with the river your identity again shifts to the river, which completes the cycle.

. . . Proceed through the cycle again, as many times as you wish.

Our next chapter will bring you a very wonderful dreaming awake experience that I had and am eager to share with you.

8

The Dream of Vixen Tor

Vixen Tor

Silent at night foxes come leaping
across the hilltops, sniffing their prey
away, away.
Whispers of the moon cry,
shining brightly,
reflecting on the faeries' pond
in the lavender field.
Stars come and go,
passing their lives in five seconds.

The Dream of Vixen Tor" is a true story, an honest-to-goodness dreaming awake adventure. It occurred during the fall of 1999 while I was presenting a workshop in the magical moors of southern England. We were housed at Grimstone Manor, owned and managed by a community of people seeking to live a more spiritual life and do so on their own terms. The manor is located very near Dartmoor, in the county of Devon. Except for the placement of the story in time, all of the events are depicted exactly as they happened, rather, exactly as I experienced

146

them. Yet even the time period of the story was inspired by my *seeing* and feeling the energy of a large rock, which I perceived as the spirit of King Arthur. The feeling became what it was, and is what it is. The shape of this dream occurred no differently than that by which any other dream of reality takes form. To my reckoning, this makes it a true story. For what is real, anyway?

THE ADVENTURE

After the passing of King Arthur, the lessons of the crown slipped uneasily into disarray. Arthur's subjects had lost their sense of nation and self, and floundered amidst feelings of having no direction to travel. Even with the prosperity of his legacy, it was a time of great confusion and despair.

It was Arthur's last request to the Knights of the Round Table (the most able of men, who had gathered simply to share one of the greatest adventures ever known) that before dispersing to the four winds, they train a special breed of men and women, beginning a longstanding lineage of trackers and travelers known as rangers.

It was to the rangers that the task of restoring the crown, of restoring the relationship of the people to the spirit of all things good and whole, and to the spirit that contained all worlds, fell. Merlin, adviser to King Arthur and one of the greatest wizards ever born, was even thought to have participated in this training, as the quest for freedom was firmly fixed within his heart as well.

This, then, is the story of one of those rangers trained by the bold dreams of King Arthur's knights and, yes, of Merlin, himself. It also begins the story of a gentle waif seeking her way through the night into womanhood, and that of a coachman seeking to claim the knowledge of her heart.

This is about the nature of dreams brought from night to day, of courage and wit, and of lands long lost. Among rangers it has become a new myth about the quest to reclaim sacred journeys, within and without. Forged within the dream of Britain, this, ladies and gentlemen, my fellow travelers, is a true story. Like any dream, it is a way to learn of the seen and unseen forces of this world. For we carry with us many kinds of dreams: those of ourselves, our families, our native lands, our quests, as well as the dreams of others, and those of other worlds.

The Traveler

He walks to the sun like a ghost.
He lies like a new blanket on my bed.
My face shines like a penny.
The birds gaze at me.
Why do they stare at me?
My cloak, I wrap it around me
like a blanket.
Sweet sleep . . .

Upon learning from the coachman that Vixen Tor was but a short distance away, the ranger knew he had to visit. Formed by the earth itself, tors were often thought to harbor strong magic, Vixen Tor being no exception. Indeed, the legends of the Vixen were strong, the tales were many. In his efforts to restore the crown, the ranger had traveled to many lands, visiting many races of people, always trying to inform and intrigue, and to cajole stories, myths, and legends into reality. And here was a legend waiting to be lived, again.

So he hired the coachman, asking only that she deliver him directly, but without undue haste, to the Vixen's keep. Although a female coachman was more than a mere curiosity, she seemed capable. It was for this reason and this reason alone, that he was willing to risk the journey with her.

A waif, small in size and large in heart, asked to join them. Neither the ranger nor the coachman refused. There was no sense of dread surrounding the simple request. Still, the ranger did not like the feelings brought about by the other half-dozen or so who wished to travel with them. Too many people would make things a bit too clumsy.

Their journey crossed the moors, magical fern-laden lands speckled with grazing sheep. Gently sloping, rolling hills eased their tension and eased their minds as to what might lie before them. As in any good dream, the air was laden with an elixir for the senses, with an awareness that circled about, ready to connect with the feelings of any creature that simply took care to notice.

Directing the carriage this way and that, the coachman evaded the followers seeking the ranger's company, for they knew bits and pieces of his quest, and sought in some way to reclaim the crown themselves. But the ranger was keen on his scouting mission, and the coachman, sensing this, adeptly backtracked over the roads she traveled and so dispelled the image of their line of travel.

The main road then veered away into the night, the fog and rain reclaiming it as its own. This left them on a narrow, seldom-used trail . . . all to the ranger's liking.

Wolf Rock
Carved faces in a rock,
Glittering pieces that shine like diamonds.
I stand beside the stream,
watching my reflection in the flowing water.
Travelers come and rest with me,
My sound is like an echo in the wind,
covering the land like a wavy blanket.

This sliver of a trail cut abruptly to the right, leaving the small band of travelers at the beginning of the path into the Vixen's most private domain. They eased out of their carriage, stretched, looked around, and then continued their journey on foot.

Surprisingly, a large stone on the left shone with a visage and the energy of King Arthur. The ranger then knew that all of this land, including that of the Vixen, was of the crown, an auspicious omen, a message from the crown itself. He trusted this connection with the most high, a domain above human concerns, above the trials of earthly travel. He also knew he must remain couched in respect, for their journey was about to enter the unknown, into lands that lived only in ancient tales told over ample mugs of mead. He was at once anxious, intrigued, humbled, and keenly aware.

In the distance he saw a line of tall trees showing their strength through the rain, through the last light of day. The coachman, who had traveled this region once before, told the ranger that no, those were not trees. They were, in fact, the line of Vixen Tor. "A clever disguise," mused the ranger, his full instincts now on alert. His appreciation of the Vixen rose within his heart not unlike the illusion rising before him through the haze.

As if to signal this reality, the path quickly became jagged and rugged; stones littered the path, to keep the timid away.

Few words were spoken, for they walked quietly, almost tenderly, as they were filled with awe, wonder, excitement, and more than a hint of fear. On the verge of reaching her keep, marked by a craggy stone wall nearly two meters high, a blackbird darted from a nearby tree. It flew in a straight line to the Vixen, her messenger performing its task well. The ranger knew that they had lost any element of stealth and surprise.

As the three stepped closer to the Vixen's domain, the Vixen changed. Out of the fog and shadows rose tall, jagged rocks that contained a wicked, mighty energy. She was a temptress, a conjuror, a mother of sorceresses openly displaying her power.

Part of worlds never to be touched by humans, she was not evil, although that feeling was thick in the air; she was only herself, with her own ways in this and other worlds. And she would never reveal her true self but to those she chose, and to those she gave just a hint of respect. Part of this bargain, however, was being fully subjected to her ways.

The Vixen

Old rooted trees,
have been here at the beginning of time.
seasons come and go like the gift of future.
I feel the sun like bristles and whiskers.
The moon is like a crystal ball,
shining on my sacred land.

Few lived to tell their stories of meeting the Vixen. Her legacy of myths was cluttered with stories of broken limbs and hearts, pitiful reflections of those who had sought to tame her. As if to accent this point, a goat with a broken foreleg hobbled away from the three, not making a sound, an omen reflecting this land, to be sure.

The ranger knew King Arthur had respected Vixen Tor, even had considered her an important part of the crown. Legend had it that after his passing, she banished herself to the center of the moors, cloaking herself in longing for the one who understood, avoiding the passing of mere mortals, and keeping them at bay by entangling them in her magic.

The ranger parted with the others to track out a sure path, his mind unrelenting, as he was set on learning the lesson of the Vixen's dream. The coachman, knowing of a ranger's training, gave way to his instinct. The waif, ever fearful of the unknown, steadfastly inched her way forward while remaining a good distance behind her companions.

Stepping mindfully on rocks to pass over a small river, the ranger then passed through the Vixen's open, weathered, wooden gate. The outer edge of the gate rested on the ground, the other end barely was hinged to a wooden post. He allowed his steps to be guided by flashes of light from the dirt and rocks, a simple trick Merlin had passed on to him.

Immediately upon stepping through the gate, a black beast appeared. The ranger stood silently, attentively watching and assessing this guardian. The beast's broad head turned to the ranger, its ears flickering while trying to apprise itself of the presence. Its rain-soaked, furry body remained abreast of the path, firmly blocking the ranger's advance.

The Guardian

He shapeshifts into a crow;
I feel the breeze on my face.
Two seconds pass, now he's an oak tree.
He is very threatening to me.
I feel a big spiral around my body,
spinning, spinning,
I'm surrounded by him,
he's everywhere.

The ranger stood motionless. Heeding a quiet, deep, inner voice, he knew he should use his feelings to ask the beast to move on. He was here to learn of Vixen Tor and her place within freedom's dream. Their energies mingled, duly assessing one another. He was neither predator nor prey. But he was unsure of the beast's intentions; he neither gave way nor tried to advance. The dream before them spun anew, coming to life from the dreams of each: a dance of unseen forces shaping their worlds.

The beast then shifted, slowly giving ground to the ranger. Although respectful, the ranger grew wary, ever cautious of the distorted feelings about him.

As though out of thin air, the coachman appeared next to him, then just as quickly disappeared as she sought a trail with better footing on the far side of the hill. The waif remained behind them, near the gate, filled with fearful wonder. Even so, she was able to keep her attention on the ranger and coachman, eager to participate in some small way in this adventure.

The ranger felt that the coachman could fend for herself. Looking a bit nervous, she was up to her ears in something, which was probably hers alone to figure out. With the waif remaining behind, he felt more at ease to continue his quest.

The Witch

From her brew, mist appears,
moonlight reflecting on her dark cloak.
Spells glitter in her mind,
candles lit by her soul.
Her hands are webbed,
her eyes are crystal blue.
Her face shines like ruby marble,
her footsteps mold in the ground.
She disappears in the misty air.

Directly in his path was a huge rock that created an overhang, a dry spot amidst the slushy, mushy turf of the hill. A strong sensation throughout his body informed him that he had to pass under it. By not passing under he would lose his edge, and his instincts would then fail him. He also knew that the magic of this land could make it fall squarely on top of him. As he stepped firmly under the massive rock, the tension mounted and the air became thick with converging energies. Just as quickly, the strain eased as he passed fully under, and he felt a noticeable weight removed from his shoulders. Although it was part of a ranger's training to proceed without reservation in the face of fear, he would only later realize that he had passed the Vixen's first test of courage.

Another beastly guardian then appeared before him. It blocked the easy trail to the Vixen's heart on his left, leaving a steep climb up rocks and moss open to his right. He moved in that direction to begin his climb. The rain had made the rocks slippery and the moss pulled out from the earth with much too much ease, making the ranger's footing unsure and his climb treacherous.

With little effort he slipped into his training from Merlin, again using dream images to guide his steps. A flash of light here; a gesture from the rocks there. Over the years this had become a matter of simple navigation for the ranger. He was not truly a wizard, for wizards journeyed in ways he could not yet; but, yes, he had learned some magic from the great wizard of King Arthur's court. Even in the dead of night this bit of dream-tracking, as he liked to call it, always guided his steps surely and steadfastly. From tests of time, he had grown to trust it completely.

Suddenly his footing gave way, and to his horror he nearly plunged to the rocks below, a sure fall to his death. As he slipped, his world turned to slow motion; he saw a root jutting out from the wet ground. In one deft motion, he grabbed it and so managed to save himself. Then just as quickly, his instincts told him the Vixen was turning his own dream against him. She was controlling his magic, his destiny. Hers was the greater power in this other-world, and he had better acknowledge this. At the same time, he remained attentive to his task, letting all the energies between them move about gracefully and lightly on the surface of his awareness while allowing his attention to continue engaging and tracking the Vixen's energies. Doing so, he became at once part wizard, part knight: the true mark of a ranger.

Falling back on his early training with the Knights of the Round Table, he withdrew himself a little further from the magic, shifting himself to rely solely on his physical senses. He now grabbed on to tufts of grass and moss, testing his hold not once, but twice and three times, before he pulled himself further up the steep, jagged slope. He gradually lifted himself over the rim, onto the plateau of the tor. He had passed the Vixen's first test of wits, and her second test of courage.

The Ranger

He has the strength of a tiger;
he can hear your fear,
see your footprints before you have made them.
You can see him galloping on his horse,
and watch him doing his sword practice in the woods.
Then he walks with power to the castle tower.

Now over the ridge, the ranger entered the heart of her home. He was suddenly engulfed by a flash of fear. A goblin appeared before him, looming toward him out of the twilight. It must have sensed the ranger was ready to fight, for it quickly dissolved back into the rock from whence it had emerged. Its markings remained on the rock's surface. Mirth flickered on the ranger's lips.

He circled about some small boulders and found a cave. He stepped into it and found that it was warm, dry, peaceful . . . too peaceful. It did not feel like a part of the surroundings. He could not even feel the onslaught of rain. He queried his heart. Then he knew! It was a trap! Offering a respite for complacent travelers, the cave would ease them to their doom, into deep sleep or perhaps into the bellies of the beasts who wandered about the tor. Seemingly in one step, he moved quickly back into the cold, a single act of will and determination. He had passed the Vixen's second test of wits.

Looking up, he saw her face brooding over him. Perhaps chiseled into the rock by the forces of nature, or perhaps by her own making, she loomed above him. At first, she looked somewhat like an elegant eagle, yet she had two beaks, two tongues. Repelled by the sight, he knew he could never trust her. In the same breath, he now knew her. She carried a treachery unmatched. But as taught by both knight and wizard, he continued to apply no judgment as his was a mission of learning, and for this he must remain objective and not laden with ordinary human concerns.

As he walked in the direction of a gentler path, which he thought would lead him away from her home, he glanced over his shoulder. He wished to once again glimpse her strange, savage beauty. He found himself holding two opposite thoughts, two opposite images in his mind: "Wicked beauty." Her face turned toward him. "What magic is this?" he wondered, his heart jumping an extra beat.

Sensing another person, he turned abruptly and found himself straight in the path of the coachman. She was a bit dazed, as though her world had turned upside down and was spinning out of control. Feeling as though he had gained what he had sought, the ranger suggested they leave. She agreed. He took care not to close off his awareness of the Vixen. It would still remain a tricky departure.

Spirit
He runs like lightning,
flames come from his hooves.
He races with the wind,
with his mane traveling behind him.
He appears from the mist,
with astonishing force.
Then he fades away,
only leaving his legend.

Walking side by side, they began their departure. Taking only two steps, to the left the ranger noticed a crevice of sorts, a small hollow joining two larger formations of rock. It was sweet, enticing, delicate, yielding, and yet full of the Vixen's terrible energy. He knew it was her essence, carrying a power that turns girls into women and drives men mad. If a woman isn't careful, the power imprisons her, leaving her full of empty power as she loses sense of the higher power of the crown, leaving her to live only within the Vixen's dream. If a man never learns to grow beyond this seduction, he remains forever estranged from his own heart, subject to the whims and dreams of others. It is a power greater than most mortals can ever bear to witness.

It was then that the ranger decided he would never return. He thought he had learned what he needed to learn, so he began turning his attention to which lands he would soon scout so he might finish his quest. Noticing that he was a bit full of himself, he returned his attention to the moment and aimed himself away from the tor.

Still, he wanted one more look. Turning toward the Vixen, he found that she had turned her head once again and her double beak smiled at him, mocking his lack of understanding.

His ranger's mood returned suddenly, ferociously! He would not allow himself to have a weak relationship with any part of the crown. He would never bow to, or be bowed by, any creature, of this or any other world. Nor would he allow another to bow to him. This manner would be the only way he could learn, and then tell others of his missions so that they might catch the mood of what freedom brings.

He then vowed to return, but knew that to do so, to live so that he could return, he must maintain his alertness to the steps that lay before them. Later, in deep reflection, he would work this journey over and over until it was threadbare, reducing his perceptions of it until they were sharp and objective. He would then assess whether his turnabout of decisions arose from his ranger's training, or from an inflated sense of self; the difference between the two often being a matter of life or death in a ranger's world.

Now matching stride with the coachman, he glanced at her and saw that she had been transformed. She told him that through her adventure, she had learned from her heart that she was an apprentice sorceress; the Vixen had touched her so deeply and so thoroughly. The ranger wondered at what magic was stirring within her.

"I am very much of her," said the coachman to the ranger. "Yet will

I have to be like her? She makes you feel free without giving you true freedom."

> Coachman
> *Guided by the moonlight,*
> *trickling stream in sudden sight.*
> *Waters beneath the night,*
> *an owl leaves a willow tree.*
> *Its haunting cry follows me,*
> *traveling into jet black.*
> *Not knowing my plight.*

The ranger acknowledged the Vixen side of the coachman. But he also knew the goodness in her heart; their separate dreams had mixed long enough for him to *see* fully through her.

"The Vixen is a dream within us all," he replied, "but the greater magic of the crown will always guide your steps."

Accepting the ranger's prophecy, the coachman relaxed and felt herself come more to life with each passing step.

Noticing that she had quickly become ready for the next instruction, the ranger added, "Find the core of spirit within and you will have taken a step to restore the crown of the land. The crown, you see, is also a dream within us all. We have simply let other dreams command our attention, so the crown has become something barely noticeable by most." Feeling the truth of his words, the coachman sighed heavily.

They departed the top of the tor, amazed, bewildered, and thankful for their lessons. A keen vigor surged through their veins.

On the bottom of the slope, they reunited with the waif and all began the walk out of the Vixen's land. The coachman, having completely accepted her fate, was continuing to come to life in a new way. The waif was busy placing one foot in front of the other. The ranger began to feel transported beyond this adventure into dreams yet waiting.

As they walked, the ranger gently coaxed the waif as a father would his daughter. He didn't hasten her, because she might fall into the water, or crash into the soggy turf. He simply sent her strong feelings of clarity and surefootedness, leaving her to figure out her path. Testing, moving, and retreating through the invisible maze, the waif crisscrossed the stream that flowed just outside the wooden gate.

The Coachman and the Waif

Swish, swoosh with the whip;
gallop, gallop the horses go.
Hurry, hurry chuckles waif,
gallop, gallop faster!
You can come on;
come on!
Now we'll be late for our sleeping dream at night.
I'm getting tired of this ride.
Come, come now,
I'm flying away.

As the waif found the path away from the tor, the ranger and coachman stepped up their pace, yet continued to walk carefully so as not to make a mess of the land. They stopped now and then so the waif could catch up. While they waited, the two compared notes on how to find a sure path away from the tor. As soon as the waif came into view, they were off again.

Although she was deeply troubled by the Vixen, the waif stayed alert, and while never fully advancing, never once retreated. Indeed, it was she who pointed out poison mushrooms growing along their path, a reminder to the coachman and the ranger of the nature of this land. *The waif has mettle*, he thought to himself, a character deep within that waited to grow stronger with the passing days, something that would allow her to one day engage her own adventures.

Stopping, and then turning back toward the tor, they found the Vixen had again cloaked herself. Simple, raw power emanated from the land, through the rocks, into the heavens. Yet she was a bit gentler now, with no trace of treachery. A golden toad hopped across the path in front of them and disappeared into the fern.

Vixana, the Sorceress
At dawn she appears to be an owl,
you see her wings catch the sunlight.
The dew glistens like her tears,
The frost goes into spirals,
dancing dandelion seeds.
Twilight showers like glitter,
faery dust scatters her beautiful body.
Her black hair looks like sea at night,
she whispers to the universe.

At the end of the trail that marked the outer edges of the Vixen's territory, they found a rock set deep within the earth and dead in the center of the path. It was in the shape of a heart. The ranger turned back his gaze once more, for he could not completely comprehend the meaning; it came as such a jolt. But by now the Vixen had slipped quietly and completely into the night, no trace of her remaining.

The ranger banished from his thoughts all considerations about what might belong to the crown and what might not, now knowing that what might be seen as evil may not really be. It just was, and it had its place. It was the power of dreams, to be used for good or ill.

Still not caring to share the story of her transformation with the others, the coachman had awakened to her heart. Once jittery with doubt, her stride was now sure. Never again to fear what strangers might say about her, she set upon her own journey of learning and discovery, soon to embark on her own path to restore the crown.

She had learned that the Vixen entices people to arrange their dreams for themselves, and not to strengthen their connection with pure freedom. *Perhaps people needed to know this lesson to hold their own in this world*, she thought. But she also knew that it was vital to learn the proper use of this energy, this manner of dream. In days yet to come, it would be the greater learning of this lesson that would guide her steps deeper into sorcery and, through that journey, deeper into freedom.

The waif, filled with the others' daring, walked stronger, in fact, a bit stronger than she should. But all the while she kept trying, trying to find her place in this strange world.

> Waif
>
> *A pretty young girl in a four-acre wood,*
> *I imagine I'm in a warm, cozy blanket*
> *with a lively fire opposite me,*
> *going higher and higher.*
> *I'm magic;*
> *I can make lovely Sunday dinners for my stomach.*
> *My shelter is a tree;*
> *an oak tree is my special home.*
> *I'm to become the woman inside me,*
> *but I can feel the different ages within me.*
> *I have no friends at all,*
> *and no one knows me.*
> *I run like the wind*
> *in a cold dusky day;*
> *I float in the sky like an eagle,*
> *but land in sudden silence;*
> *then I fall asleep in my tree.*

Each had gained from the moment, and each had lost a part of the past. They did not yet fully know, yet each did sense, that they had moved closer to the crown. And each understood well that forevermore the dream of Vixen Tor would remain alive within their hearts and minds.

COMMENTARY

My adventure at Vixen Tor was an effect of having explored Toltec arts and crafts for some thirty years. It was also influenced by the participants of the workshop I was conducting at that time. Connecting with them in different ways took me into the realm of the abstract. In other words, I had become removed from a concrete, fixed way of perceiving the world. My internal energy then became freer and more fluid, and thereby more capable of interacting with external, or environmental, energy in a different way.

I was also in a bit of turmoil due to being physically separated from someone I cared deeply about, and the only way I could connect was through shifting my relation with the world and entering dreaming awake. The workshop participants, in turn, kept me working to remain at that level in order to present the workshop, which dealt with heightened awareness.

In addition, my arrival at Vixen Tor seemed a bit orchestrated by a force beyond human contrivance. The prior year I had made plans to visit the tor, which is a natural rock formation on top of a hill. Everyone in the workshop wanted to experience Vixen Tor, as it was deemed to be the female-energy counterpart of the male-energy tor we hiked to every afternoon. As it was somewhat of a distance away, we all piled into automobiles for the sojourn. But the automobile I was in became separated from the rest of the convoy. My group ended up heading in a different direction and we found ourselves at St. Michael's Church, also on top of a hill. It was there that we felt the "Dragon's Breath," the energy of the wind that travels through the rock walls of the church. The Dragon's Breath is so noticeable that it is part of the everyday legend of St. Michael's. The church itself is remarkable in that, while it has no heating, it stays warm inside, even when a cold, wet wind blows outside. At any rate, the trip to Vixen Tor never materialized . . . that year.

Upon my arrival the following year, the manor we had traditionally used to hold annual workshops seemed a bit odd to me. Maybe it was simply that I felt off-center. Trying to settle down, I walked around its large front yard. Looking off to my left, a row of bushes and small trees suddenly seemed to become the queen and her court. One tree even looked like an illustration on the back of an English pound coin. Then the outlying trees assumed the emotional manner of wizards and knights. They simply felt that way, and seemed to present themselves to the world as such. After all, I was now in Albion, the very land of King Arthur and his trusted adviser, Merlin.

I let all of these impressions be, neither trying to uphold the fantasy nor trying to develop it into something more. It turned out, however, that this magic of the land set the tone for the workshop.

In short order, the theme of the workshop spontaneously emerged as "restoring the crown," which carries an obvious connotation of English royalty as well as the crown chakra. For the workshop, it took on the meaning of regaining one's center of awareness, one's immediate connection with God. You might also think of this as cultivating Christ consciousness, stimulating the entire kundalini tract, or getting in touch with the core of your being, whichever perspective works for you.

The notion of restoring the crown took full root during an outing to Plymouth, where our troupe took on individual disguises for the afternoon. A computer programmer became a full-fledged beggar, for instance, or a mild-mannered accountant became a rogue. The point of this exercise was to discover the relativity of how we see ourselves in daily life. While walking about the very city from whence the Pilgrims had departed to their New World, I came upon a large, green lawn that had an obelisk in plain view. On top of the ten-foot cement structure, a crown had been chiseled. In a flash of intuition, the obelisk represented the core of awareness and the crown represented elevating this awareness to its highest state. Dreaming awake, a principal exercise of the workshop, was then viewed as an avenue of personal awakening in order to "restore the crown."

During the workshop, a window of time unexpectedly opened to allow us to pile into automobiles and drive to the Vixen. Amid fog and rain, several cars left the manor. Only one arrived at the path leading to Vixen Tor: the coach that carried the ranger, the coachman, and the waif. Just as I had been separated from the group earlier when I ended up at St. Michael's Church, now the group had become separated from us. And so it was that we three were left alone with our adventure, to join up with the rest of the participants at the end of the trail that both began and ended "The Dream of Vixen Tor," for they arrived later but never embarked to the tor.

You might say that this is all imagination. Well, yes, I agree with you.

At the same time, our daily world is upheld by imagination: a dream by another name. It's all a matter of us agreeing on which of our imaginings are real. And we have also worked very hard to squelch the capacities of imagination so that we may feel comfortable within the cloak of consensual social agreements. Toltecs think that most humans have opiated their imagination, and, as a result, have dulled their sense of allowing reality to continually unfold and become refreshed at each turn; indeed, to remain a mystery.

As with my experiences on the manor's front lawn, with my coparticipants, and with Vixen Tor, the key to allowing reality to unfold is managing how the internal energies of yourself meet the external energies of the world. Allowing yourself to let go of a fixed, concrete world enables your internal energies to move about more freely. In so doing, you connect with the world in a different way; in so doing, you allow the perception of new worlds. What kind of dream you live is an adventure uniquely yours. This is the craft of imagination, and the art of exploring perception.

Skillfully practiced, dreaming awake loosens the reins of perception and lets imagination bear its fruit. If more people made this agreement to live more completely in freedom, it would also be possible to retain the positive effects of objectivity. That is, we can all share the quest of restoring the crown, and allow transformation, in whichever way it manifests, to arrive. This can be a new agreement of reality, a new objectivity, and so a new *objective*.

Like the courageous and adventurous explorers before us, and those who are among us now, I invite you to go with your dreams, wherever they occur, and allow them to reveal their stories, so they may give you the time of your life. It is also with this awareness of how things are, how maybe they aren't, and how maybe they could be, that I invite you to enter, and to live, the journey of the ranger's spirit.

As we know, tracking dreams is the skill of entering and stabilizing your dream life. In other words, you wake up inside your dreams. This applies to whether they are of the night or of the day, and whether you are asleep or wide awake. As dream research often indicates, our dreams are reflections of ourselves. The people, symbols, or events within a dream carry meaning; it's only a matter of being able to interpret what is occurring. In this light, tracking your dreams is learning to track the hidden knowledge within yourself.

For instance, while all three of our story's travelers are individuals, I'm sure you can recognize that, at some level, the three travelers are one; and you can probably see these different aspects within yourself as they represent different stages of growth, evolution, and maturity.

The waif is the uncertain child, yearning to know more, desiring to be free, not yet fully capable of action. The coachman is the somewhat more mature person who, after searching for a release from the mundane, finds his or her heart and, in so doing, finds his or her path in life. The ranger is the actualized person, or at least the person who has matured sufficiently to be able to walk a path leading to actualization.

In addition, we can most likely see ourselves and others in the Vixen, her messenger, King Arthur's spirit, and in the other elements of the story. As a result, we can recognize ourselves within and throughout the *entire* story. This notion of oneness, of being part of everything, is a central component of many of the world's spiritual traditions. Indeed, a core component of heightened awareness is being able to perceive yourself as one with your world. Dreaming, especially dreaming awake, is an exercise to begin this quest, as is *seeing*, or gaining an immediate *knowing* about your circumstances. Keep in mind this immediacy of knowing is direct, and therefore transcends reason as a means of understanding our world. Reason works from subject-object relations, from a separation among things.

Many people have told me that after a second reading of "The Dream of Vixen Tor," they spontaneously entered a heightened, dreamlike sense of the world. So why not give it a try? It'll only cost you the time of your life.

9

Preliminaries for Dreaming

Dream Door

When I close my eyes at nightfall,
my dreams become magical.
An eagle flying beside me,
and faeries I can see.
Moonbeams reflecting on a river,
glittering brightly like stars.
A waterfall like a running jaguar
traveling toward me.
A butterfly comes and flutters beside me,
bringing a message of a new rainbow.

Exercises and techniques such as minimizing self-reflection and nonattachment have been referenced throughout this book. In this chapter, we come to better grips with the ranger discipline in order to begin managing the energy body. In other words, these are all perspectives and skills to temper the energy body, and therefore to directly engage and experience dreaming. So here we go.

Accept Your Fate

Accepting your fate is a common theme throughout don Juan's teachings. You meet your life (and death) head-on, living the challenges that are set in your path. In a nutshell, what manifests in front of you is an effect of your cohesion. Therefore, accepting your fate allows you to work with and through these reflections in order to build a stronger energy body.

The more you control your energy body's resources, the more control you have in a variety of ways. Don Juan's close friend don Genaro, for example, could teleport his awareness over great physical distances; he had that much control. As don Juan explained to Castaneda, don Genaro was a person of knowledge and therefore had the ability to control himself without controlling anything else. He saw people and events, decided his course of action, and then accepted his fate (*Tales*, 63–64).

It is by accepting your fate that you remain open. This allows cohesion to shift, and so forms new dreaming abilities and worlds.

Accessibility and Inaccessibility

Accessibility to the world is when you're not centered in the here and now, and you float around, subject to stray influences. Accessibility to Spirit is when you're in some way connected with the ultimate creative force and are allowing that force to govern you, to hold sway over your decisions. Accessibility to all other energies is what requires counterbalancing, as they limit your expansion through the energy body. You have to learn by trial and error, and by trial and success, when to be accessible, and when not. According to don Juan, this is a quintessential lesson for becoming a hunter, whether you're hunting food or knowledge (*Journey*, 83–95).

Inaccessibility to the world of people is one of the most difficult lessons around. It does not mean to exclude energies, to block awareness, or to become a hermit. You need to be aware of what's going on all around you. But you also need to remain connected primarily to Spirit as potential, rather than to the features of Spirit, such as people, Earth, and other dimensions. When you're accessible you lose energy. It drains right out of you.

You are inaccessible when your cohesion is stable, integrated, and energy flows to and with Spirit. You can then better connect with other energies as you can measure and assess them more objectively. And then you may play out the rhythm of your life. Following your path with heart helps you avoid entanglements with the energy lines of others. Also, don't contend with the dream of daily life. Know your role in it, perform it well, then let it all go.

Inaccessibility also paves the way to enter other dimensions. The fewer energy connections you have with this world, the more energy you have to head elsewhere. Dreaming, for instance, is a controlled shift into the second field. Such a shift opens the doors to other worlds, some of which are inhabited by creatures of one kind or another. Remaining inaccessible helps you explore these worlds, as well as return to this one more readily.

The combination of accessibility and inaccessibility acts like a power generator at a dam. You manage your resources to give yourself energy reserves, and you let energy flow in a controlled manner to produce even more energy. Again, the trick is knowing when to open the gates or keep them closed. The flow of *being* is the effect of this balance. Other exercises in this chapter support this dynamic duo of energy management.

Here are a few tips, which will help you develop this stance:

1. Use death as an advisor. In the face of death, why waste your last moments with worry?
2. Listen to your inner thoughts and feelings.
3. Accept yourself.
4. Don't force yourself on the world. Try not to force your views on others.
5. Sense the difference between the directions of others and yourself.
6. Assess situations as they are, not as you want them to be.
7. Speak freely yet thoughtfully.
8. Aim to align yourself with Spirit, not with the thoughts and desires of others.
9. Direct your life toward strong, purposeful goals. Work to achieve them without bending them, yourself, or others out of shape.

10. Take only what you need and leave the rest. Use the world; don't abuse it.

Alignment

A main tenet of the Toltec worldview is that alignments of energy produce perception. When the energies of an emanation intersect energies within the energy body, cohesion is produced and perception occurs. The location of the focal point is an indication of what manner of alignment has occurred (*Dreaming*, 7). In very general terms, if it's on the right side of the energy body, you're attentive to the physical world. If it's on the left side, you're dreaming. Therefore, to have stable perception, your cohesion must be stable. Otherwise, you'll experience myriad meaningless shapes and sensations. For instance, ordinary dreams tend to come and go, and be very unmanageable. This means the dreaming cohesion is not stable, the focal point jitters about, and you flit from dream to dream and scene to scene.

Attention

Attending to something enables you to perceive. As you attend to your growth, your attention to the details influencing it automatically quickens the process. The more you pay attention, the more you become aware. The following steps are general guidelines to get the most out of the exercises in this chapter:

1. Pay attention as you practice these exercises. Notice the effects of the techniques. You may not perceive any differences at first, so practice.
2. Test, retest, and measure the exercises. If you find a way that works better for you, implement it.
3. Exceed your limits periodically. Stretch your awareness.
4. Adjust and adapt yourself to your goals. Rearrange your life to provide support and direction to those endeavors.
5. Pay further attention to where you have been, where you want to go, and most of all, where you are now.

Balance

By developing the path that reflects the deepest aspects of yourself, you will find balance and harmony. You will then find it's no longer a matter of striving for balance, but of maintaining it. Since you have the experience of obtaining it, this doesn't present a problem.

Preventive maintenance enables you to handle daily problems more easily and often eliminates disturbances before they occur. Happiness, too, is no longer an uncertain by-product of behavior that may or may not deliver results. Now you'll know what it takes to be happy. One maintenance technique is the Chakra Tune-Up found on page 38; it will help balance energy between and among your chakras.

Controlled Folly

What you say about the world is not all that important. How you behave is. One of the things don Juan gained from following a Toltec path was to *see*, and *see* very well. From the grandeur of this perspective, he learned that nothing mattered. Yet he choose to act as though everything mattered to him. In his words, this is controlled folly. And he indicates that if another person learns to *see*, then to that person everything might matter. This is also controlled folly (*Separate*, 106).

By don Juan's reckoning, he has gone beyond all ordinary relationships with people and the world. When Castaneda challenged him to explain this lack of normal meaning in his life, don Juan said, "I go on living, though, because I have my *will*. Because I have tempered my *will* throughout my life until it's neat and wholesome and now it doesn't matter to me that nothing matters. My *will* controls the folly of my life" [italics mine] (*Separate*, 101).

This abstract relation to life is the hallmark of controlled folly. It is a blend of nonattachment, inaccessibility, accessibility to Spirit, observation, fluidity, and more. In short, it is the consolidation of all tracking skills. Controlled folly can give you your life and help you move smoothly through anything you experience.

Death as an Advisor

Ultimate terror, to me, would be a person on his deathbed realizing he had never lived his life.

Relating to death as an advisor makes life personal. You drop pretense to get to the core of what matters to you. When faced with death, other concerns pale in comparison. Meaning wells up from the heart and you clearly understand how you want to live. The humility this inspires tempers and molds character. For me, its greatest value is as an agent for focusing on what matters.

It's not necessarily so that when we physically die, we die forever with no experience in the hereafter. That is another question and problem altogether. Using death as a focusing agent provides a functional way to center and to align energy within yourself in order to maximize your life.

A strong focus on death permits a strong focus on life. If you push away the knowledge that you will physically die, you push away one of the most significant events in your life. This results in blindly refusing to take hold of your life. Adapted from don Juan's teachings, here is a simple way to use death as an advisor (*Journey*, 46–57).

1. Simply ask your death how you should behave.
2. Simulate the feeling that this is your last act on Earth.
3. Implement nonattachment so you don't become morbidly obsessed with the technique.
4. Allow energy to flow out from your heart, offering you direction. Reflecting the deeper parts of yourself, what guidance does your heart give you? Remember you are using your death as focus to receive guidance. Rather than seeking advice from "How do I gain material wealth?" or "Why is the world against me?" and using such attitudes for focus, you pinpoint what has significant meaning for you.
5. Act accordingly.

Dissonance

Dissonance is used to shift cohesion. In other words, by placing yourself in between opposing tensions, you set the stage to move the focal point. Therefore, you deliberately place yourself in the midst of turmoil. Perhaps the best example of this is having a *petty tyrant*, a mandatory Toltec lesson. Further along in this chapter, you'll read about petty tyrants—the quintessential way to place added stress in your life!

Another example of dissonance is the tension resulting from experiencing the Toltec world. Your thoughts may tell you that humans can't suddenly appear from another dimension. So when this occurs, experiences, thoughts, and beliefs clash. This happened to me every time don Juan showed up, as he popped in clear out of the blue. He always threw me off balance, then left. Months later, just as I had regained my emotional balance, don Juan would appear out of nowhere again, say or do a few things, then leave me to regain my balance again! His doing so became a significant point of reference for me. Over time, I learned not to think as much and just try to fully engage whatever experience I was having at the time.

When people experience tension, a common response is to lash out. The tension within the energy body often produces violent behavior. This may be especially true for dreamers, as they have a hard time with physical-world stability. Dissonance becomes home territory for trackers, though, as they know it helps them manage their energies better.

Drugs

Mind-altering substances, often known as hallucinogens or psychotropics, sometimes play a role in allowing a person to obtain glimpses of nonordinary reality. In addition, just as a medical doctor might prescribe penicillin for an infection, a Toltec might use a mind-altering agent to become aware of, and then correct, an imbalance.

In *The Teachings of Don Juan* and *A Separate Reality*, Castaneda reports his use of several mind-altering substances, including peyote, jimson weed, and certain mushrooms. Don Juan usually required Castaneda to perform a ritual prior to ingestion. The ritual helped Castaneda focus his energies; as well, it let him know this was not a recreational activity. In the introduction of *Journey to Ixtlan*, Castaneda tells us that don Juan administered the drugs only because Castaneda was too slow to catch on to other techniques that helped to accomplish the same goal.

A principal difference between perceiving nonordinary states with drugs or with meditative techniques is that meditation is nontoxic. Drugs alter perception by forcing cohesion to change and the focal point to move. However, drugs distort or bend perception, often causing a permanent imbalance. Although a particular experience while under a drug's influence may be perfectly valid, a side effect is an inner distortion that prevents a clear assessment of how to use and move the focal point. Overall perception is not as clear as it could be, since an artificial agent stimulates it.

The benefit of using drugs is perceiving that there is more to us than what we previously thought. Hallucinations are usually thought of as perceptions of something that don't exist, except in the imagination of the perceiver. Don Juan holds that hallucinations are glimpses of non-ordinary reality by using modes of perception that are dormant. Drugs stimulate and bring to life these faculties. Once recognized, the different modes of perception may be further explored and developed without using drugs.

We must also remember that except for isolated instances—such as medical research and certain religious rituals—these substances are illegal. Given that much drug use is abuse (witness the detrimental effects of cocaine addiction on the fabric of society), it doesn't seem likely that legislatures will legalize drugs anytime soon. But as a society, we do not have a complete knowledge of these agents. We haven't learned that we can use such drugs to help restore mental, emotional, and spiritual balance. For instance, with proper education, peyote could be used to heal in the same manner that penicillin is used to heal. Just as we wouldn't think of using penicillin unless we had an infection in the body, so we wouldn't think of using peyote unless we had an infection of the mind.

I am not advocating the use of drugs. Getting the focal point to move without them is by far the better route. But in some circumstances, I think drugs are used because people recognize at some level of their awareness that something productive occurs. Because there is no context to adequately make use of and learn from the experience, the emphasis gets shifted to the thrill, the energy boost, the high. Use becomes abuse.

Gazing

Gazing is an energy-body posture that enables you to tap the second field. It is also a direct avenue to *seeing*. It involves letting go. It requires fluidity. In one motion, you must simultaneously relax and remain very attentive. You then gaze at, and relax into, the energy field you're studying.

Put another way, gazing lets you merge your first and second fields, thereby making a direct connection with energy. As you align your energy body with energies at large, you begin to *see*. You might say gazing helps the energy body become more supple. As such, it helps you explore and strengthen your awareness with a field of energy totally distinct from the field of physical energy you're most familiar with. For this reason, don't gaze while driving or operating machinery, as you might remove yourself too far from the ordinary. You can, however, gaze while talking with people. As you gaze at their energy bodies, for instance, let your speech arise easily and naturally.

You can gaze at nearly anything. Don Juan's apprentices, for example, gazed at trees, clouds, shadows, rain, and other forms of nature (*Second Ring*, 285–87). You can also gaze at music, traffic, art, and the air itself. Gazing at a specific thing acts as an aid to hold your attention so that you can eventually learn to gaze at anything, anywhere.

To begin:

1. Relax, try to be nonattached.
2. Establish your intent to gaze.
3. Don't focus on the world as you normally might. Don't, for example, pick out an object and then look at it. Let your eyes go soft, unfocused.
4. Feel your body merge with the world.
5. If you *see* a haze of light, or swirling dots of energy swirls, as they're often called, let them be. Don't focus on them or you'll

go back into physical-world focus. The light is the second field breaking into your awareness. Later, when you have gained more experience, you can focus on the light and it won't disappear. But until you train your eyes and your body, your normal habits of perception will take you back to your ordinary world.

6. The more you practice, the more you'll *see* different things, like the spirit of King Arthur emanating from a rock! Or the aura of a tree. Or the energy body of another person. Or . . .

Internal Dialogue

Your internal, verbal dialogue binds you to the world. It consists of a constant stream of thoughts that upholds your view of reality. By interrupting this flow, you will allow new ideas and perceptions to surface. Eventually, you will *stop the world*, an experience where reality as you know it, vanishes (*Journey*, 291–302).

When you stop the world, you bring to bear a very unusual focus of time. In the *Star Trek: Next Generation* episode "Journey's End," for example, young Wesley Crusher stops the world with the help of the Traveler (a very Toltec kind of guy). In so doing, a battle among the Cardasians, Federation troops, and native villagers stops in mid-motion. The Traveler and Crusher freeze-frame the world, and pull themselves out of the social base of time, the time everyone else is focused in. Then they just step out of the picture, literally, enter a new experience, and let everyone else go about their business of fighting. It's all in the wrist of focus.

You don't have to be part of a *Star Trek* script to do this. While I watched a Little League baseball game in which a young friend of mine played, for example, a Navy fighter jet from a local base flew directly over the field. Even though it seemed a nuisance, I looked up and calmly watched it, trying not to condemn the ferocious scream of its engines. I placidly accepted the event, letting all thoughts about it slip away. Then it stopped in midair, as though it were a toy model suspended from the ceiling of a child's bedroom. As I reflected on the situation while the jet hung silently in the air, I noticed that the ball game stopped as well, the players motionless in midstride. After what seemed like five to ten seconds, the world engaged again, the jet thundered by, and the game resumed. Once you experience something like this, it's easier to assimilate alternate views concerning our perceptual abilities. You might say it's proof positive that holding onto ordinary reality limits us.

Don Juan also says this of perfect dreaming—one must stop their internal dialogue (*Dreaming*, 93). Dreaming at this level is a professional shift of viewing and interacting with the world. You must literally step out of one reference to enact another.

To begin quieting your internal dialogue and exploring nonordinary perception:

1. Pay attention to your thoughts. Allow them free reign. Don't censor or judge any of them.
2. Gaze with unfocused eyes at an object (such as a vase or rock) or blank wall. If you gaze at an object, gently cross your eyes until you can see two identical images of the vase. Place your attention in between the images. If you use a wall, exercise your peripheral vision, allowing yourself to see as much of the wall as possible.
3. Continue to let your thoughts flow without censorship. Regardless of the thought, acknowledge its presence and then let it go.
4. Casually bring all of your mental attention to one subject. Then let that topic slip away while maintaining focused attention on the wall or vase.

Or try this technique that I've slightly modified from don Juan's instructions to Castaneda (*Journey*, 38).

1. Take a little walk with your hands in an unusual position that does not attract attention. This will direct your attention away from your head to your hands. If you hold your hands too awkwardly, you might have to contend with other people wondering what you're up to.
2. Direct your vision slightly above the horizon. If you are in a hilly or mountainous environment, look 10–20 feet in front of you.

3. Unfocus your eyes, allowing your peripheral vision to absorb as much as possible.
4. Listen to and smell the environment. You are trying to get out of your head and into your body.
5. Walk at a normal pace, or slower than your normal pace.
6. In the beginning, for safety, you may want to walk where you know you will not have to contend with traffic.

With time and practice, you'll experience a floating or similar sensation that indicates you have stopped your internal, verbal dialogue.

Meditation

Meditation involves exploring your deepest recesses. It often acts as a solvent to help remove obstructions, a lubricant to enable you to explore new perceptions, and a guiding force to help you make sense of it all. A key point for any meditation is not to analyze what occurs during the meditation; allow any and all perceptions to come and go without censoring or editing them.

You will find meditation provides practical benefits of facilitating relaxation and enhancing problem-solving capabilities. This quiet listening facilitates exploring and realizing your entire being, including dreaming. In some way, all of these exercises are a form of meditation.

Nonattachment

Nonattachment is most often, I think, perceived as mental agility, or perhaps emotional distance. Thus, while a person may be viewed as being adept in coming up with just the right answer for a given situation, they may also seem aloof. But nonattachment is more than this, and has wide-ranging effects. Don Juan says he existed in quiet desperation and had only ordinary needs when he temporarily lost his nonattachment (*Silence*, 208).

Without nonattachment, it's difficult to place your life on the line. The terminal velocity of life will drain you. So let me propose that you never will really have a house, a car, a relationship of your own unless you can let it all go, release the desire to the four winds in order to see what remains. Or, when you find yourself in turmoil, nonattachment lets you assess the situation, and take appropriate steps. And if you do lose your control, it helps you reclaim your power more readily. Nonattachment, then, gives you maneuverability. You're not invested in a particular outcome so you're freer to act as you wish.

Focusing on your death, remaining inaccessible, and staying fluid all assist the development of nonattachment. But don't expand this into not caring, or not feeling your connection with the world. It is not an absence of passion. It is not severing your ties. Indeed, it is an enhanced relationship with the world. As Shunryu Suzuki writes in the classic book, *Zen Mind, Beginner's Mind*, nonattachment is something that can help you find the reality in each moment.[1]

Nonattachment, or *detachment* as many term it, is a necessary attitude when exploring dreaming. It offers a quiet zone or space between an external circumstance or event, and an internal reaction or assessment of the event. It is a neutral, yet personal, relation between the environment and oneself, offering the ability to perceive what is at hand more clearly. Here are suggestions that will help you develop this attitude:

1. Recognize that you are fully connected with the world and responsible for your actions. Nonattachment is an attitude, a relation to the world, so it doesn't disconnect you from the world.
2. Strive to remain calm and centered within yourself. Frequent meditations will assist you.
3. Participate in group activities without regard for how you are perceived by the group. This doesn't mean to act foolishly, but if you should behave contrary to the group's protocol, let any criticism slide away from you.
4. Instead of criticizing, mentally and emotionally accept—without comment or reaction—situations that usually spark you to react.
5. Cultivate a sense of self-observation. As though you were standing in back of yourself, watch yourself without judging or censoring your behavior. Try not to identify with any roles. Just

allow yourself to act normally. Over time, you will identify the behavior that you wish to modify or eliminate.

6. Be aware that you are developing nonattachment and patiently let that awareness provide the lessons. In other words, you will set into motion lessons around nonattachment simply by intending them. So once again, pay attention.

Nonpatterning

This is a central Toltec exercise and is part of every form of meditation I've experienced. Regardless of your involvements, it is also one of the most practical tools you can develop. Also known as *not-doing*, this technique requires that you accept events just as they happen. No inference is made regarding origin or outcome of the event (*Journey*, 219–39). This means that on a regular basis you don't organize, formulate, or structure a situation. As you mature with nonpatterning, when anything unusual occurs act *as if* you are unaware of it being unusual, while paying attention to details. This will prevent you from jumping to conclusions while allowing you to rapidly accumulate information.

Even when it is necessary to formulate or pattern something, you can still apply nonpatterning. For example, say you are working outside and hear a particular sound, a noise that, through experience, you identify as "squealing tires." By nonpatterning, you would not translate the sound into an interpretation of a squealing tire or the screech of a pterodactyl. During your travels, you might find yourself in an environment where tires don't exist and pterodactyls do, and if you translate a sound similar to squealing tires as such, you might ignore the features of that other land. It's possible that interpreting the sound as a tire will alert you to the danger of an out-of-control car, enabling you to get out of its way. However, you can still apply nonpatterning by affecting a nonchalant and unfettered acceptance of almost being run over. You disengage perception in order to engage it more clearly. By waiting to organize data, you enter wider horizons of reality. You do need to remain alert as to whether you're in dreaming or waking worlds.

Structuring a situation activates the cornerstones of thinking and reason. Nonpatterning activates feeling, *seeing*, dreaming, and *will*. Exercising feeling, you find a neutral balance between positive and negative feelings, as though you were suspended in between the north and south poles of a magnet. Resting in this neutral area enables you to focus and direct your attention wherever you want. Exercising *seeing*, you stop the world and direct your attention to fields of light. These fields might consist of auras, the luminous body, or other dimensions. Exercising dreaming, you break the routine of ordinary dreaming and develop it as an information-gathering tool. As you exercise feeling, *seeing*, and dreaming, you automatically exercise *will*.

For the most part, all of these exercises consist of nonpatterning. Here are a few more ways to help you grasp nonpatterning:

1. Unfocus your vision and gaze at the environment. Here, reversing a figure-ground relationship (such as between leaves and the shadows of the leaves) is particularly helpful.
2. Reverse the order of statements. "Dreaming-body experience helps develop perception" turned around is "Developing perception helps dreaming-body experience."
3. Do not label or conceptualize your actions or the actions of others. Don't refer to yourself as a physician, a mechanic, or a teacher, for example. Perform your actions well, but don't identify yourself with them. If someone asks what you do, respond that you collect information, that you live, that you walk the face of Earth. If this seems unrealistic, remember you strive to be unreal in that you seek to expand your notions of reality, not strap yourself further into them. In turn, offer the same consideration to others.
4. Throughout the day, accept without interpretation at least five events.

Path with Heart

Your path is not only what you give your life to, it's what brings you life. It's an energy line that connects you with your core. Thus, it's what connects you with *flow*. A path with heart is continually unfolding, ever changing. Yet it delivers a constancy that enables you to connect with potential, the crucial element of *being*. By remaining with potential, you stand a chance of elevating your life to its highest potential. Just remember to intend positive results. Otherwise, you become an expert at manifesting the unusual and the bizarre, but never really get anywhere.

Gazing places cohesion in neutral. It lets you open up to new patterns of energy, new cohesions. Intent, on the other hand, is the stabilizer. It's what connects and binds the energies that are aligning themselves. Intent, therefore, produces stability of purpose. A path with heart yields stability throughout one's life.

I am familiar with two methods to cultivate a path with heart. I implemented the first way after reading Castaneda's *A Separate Reality* (*Separate*, 261–62). I learned of the second method from Robert Monroe's *Far Journeys*.[2] Doing so provided the fundamental techniques enabling me to heal my internal distress and disease. Interestingly, Monroe told people that his "ABC" method helped him cure his ulcer by placing himself on a path more natural to him. Both methods offer a way to achieve patience.

Remember that waiting is a force in creating your life? Patience, the principal element of waiting, is obtained by forging your path with heart. When you have built your world from the stance of a ranger, you've acquired patience. Combined with purpose and losing self-importance, you've gained balance.

In general terms, if you have your path, you have yourself. As a result, you're not in the cohesion of "want" or "need," which means you're prosperous.

☼ Don Juan's Way to Develop a Path with Heart

1. Develop an acute sense of your death as a physical being. Or, turned around, how do you want to live your life?
2. In order to prevent this awareness from becoming debilitating, apply nonattachment to everything.
3. Deliberately select several things such as friends, work, and hobbies in which to involve yourself. The criteria for selection

is simple: Does the activity provide peace, joy, and strength?

4. Test and retest these selections to ensure their strength in your life.

5. These items should assist you in obtaining and maintaining balance in, and control of, your life.

6. Select items for the physical, emotional, mental, and spiritual sides of yourself.

7. Go ahead and dream, selecting items which give the deepest meaning to your life, so you may live a life worth living.

☀ Robert Monroe's ABC Method to Find and Complete Your Life's Work

1. Make an "A" list with all your worries, anxieties, and concerns about which you can do nothing.

2. Make a "B" list with all your worries, anxieties, and concerns about which you can do something, large or small, today.

3. Make a "C" list with all your needs, hopes, goals, and desires yet to be fulfilled.

4. Destroy the "A" list knowing that you're also dismissing it from your consciousness.

5. Take some kind of action, large or small, for each item on the "B" list. If you're addressing your problems, you're gaining control of them and not letting them control you.

6. Take some kind of action, large or small, for at least one item on the "C" list, knowing you're building momentum and direction.

7. Do this each day until you have no "A" list, no "B" list, and you are completely devoted to your "C" list. It doesn't matter what time of day you prepare your lists.

8. You then will serenely complete your human life purpose.

Petty Tyrants

A petty tyrant exerts pressure on your energy body from the outside, and perhaps by pushing your buttons from the inside as well. To meet and exceed this energy requires an internal shift, the internal shift being a shift in cohesion. This is why Toltecs can't get enough of these cosmic bullies. Petty tyrants ensure that you have plenty of practice in shifting and stabilizing cohesions. Get enough of their nonsense and the work required to taste freedom begins to make sense.

This doesn't mean you must be a passive dishrag. There comes a time when you have to stand up for yourself. But before this magic moment arrives, you should be able to parry most of your petty tyrant's maneuvers to control you. Therefore, each time you are thrown off the mark by a petty tyrant, recapitulate the event (see the next exercise on page 188) in order to track your self-reflection.

Then parlay your efforts into the management of your energy body. Use the external pressure to step aside from petty influences and aim for your core. Tons of pressure turns coal into diamonds. The more you discover yourself being unaffected by the onslaughts of others, the more you'll silently rejoice in your evolution.

You may also use petty tyrants to work your way through your chakras. For example, when petty tyrants push emotional buttons, don't suppress your energies but don't fly off the handle either. In order words, one of your goals is to not let the situation get the best of you. Otherwise, you place undue strain on your body. In this example, by not managing your emotions, you interfere with the flow of energy through your chakra system. You then distort your first chakra's energy, those related to your physical body. This leads to further distortions of your second chakra's energy, your emotions. Also, by interpreting the petty tyrant as a moron, you distort the third chakra, your intellect, by the way you think.

Continuing up the ladder, speaking calmly promotes the flow of energy to the fifth chakra. Stepping away from the turmoil of petty tyrants and into dreaming eases energy into the sixth chakra, and remaining true to your primary program lets energy fully enter the seventh chakra.

A positive relationship with your energy body stimulates a harmonious flow of energy throughout the entire chakra system, and thereby energizes the entire energy body. An even, well-regulated flow is an optimum state for you to produce results while generating the least amount of energy loss. *Being* is having attained expert-level status with this process.

Your struggle with petty tyrants is magnified if you seek retribution. If you do, you're letting the situation get the best of you. You're also becoming a petty tyrant yourself. Remember, the idea is to learn non-attachment, how to let go and remain unaffected, and so figure out how to remain focused in the heat of battle. To do this, you must behave from the reference of a larger view.

Petty tyrants plunge you into dissonance, which, again, is experienced as conflict between your thoughts about the way you think things ought to be versus the way the world really shapes up. You get to look at yourself and the world inside out. Petty tyrants help you hone your strengths and address your weaknesses. You become more secure, more stable, more in touch with what matters. For these reasons, they're great to have around.

Quite often, your petty tyrants are the people you work with. For instance, there is a peculiarity about some managers that cause them to inflict pain on their subordinates without ever addressing their own inadequacies. I don't know, I think this is some kind of law; it happens frequently enough to be one. Anyway, a good petty tyrant has authority over you in a situation that magnifies the energy, causing you to squirm. After all, your livelihood is probably on the line.

Don Juan says that the Toltecs of the old days came up with a scheme of petty tyrants. In descending order of ability to exasperate and cause misery, they classified petty tyrants as petty tyrants, as little petty tyrants, as small-fry petty tyrants, and as teensy-weensy petty tyrants (*Fire*, 30). You can see they had loads of fun with the matter. Joining the ruckus, I developed my own scheme. I came up with headers such as *one-way artists, people of experience, rebels,* and *spiders*.

One-way artists always call attention to themselves at the expense of others. They twist words and events to suit themselves. For instance, a one-way artist quickly says "I did that" when something good unfolds, says "We did it" when someone nearby has success, and says "You did it" when there's trouble. Double standards rule the day with them, and you rue their company. People of experience typically justify themselves by saying they have experience in the matter at hand, and therefore they are right. Just ask them. Naturally there are times when a person's experience shines. But as far as petty tyrants go, people of experience bend the world out of shape in order to rule.

Rebels torment others by playing a game of how wonderful they are because they think that they are bad in a good way by flying against the rules. Contrast this with *heyokas*, or sacred clowns. Heyokas are visionaries who work impeccably to disrupt social norms, and are a long-established part of Native American cultures. The difference between them is that rebels aim to confine others and heyokas work to liberate all.[3]

Spiders, as you might imagine, weave a delicate web to trap others. They ooze warmth and grace, and gently pull you into their domain. In each case of petty tyrant, their guiding light is to control, to confound, and to manipulate. They use all means to do so: peer pressure, anger, ridicule, paychecks, and maybe even guns.

To handle petty tyrants, enact all the tracking skills you can muster. Pay attention, let go, assess strengths and weaknesses, remain inaccessible, nonattached and nonreactive, stay fluid, lose self-reflection, control your folly . . . you get the picture. Rather than run screaming from the situation (which you'll want to do from time to time), use it as an obstacle course to build your personal power. Don't try to change or educate a petty tyrant. Use the occasion to deal with the world the way it is, not the way you wish it to be. Learn and adapt. There's too much waiting, too much wonderful mystery, too much power in the universe to think you can change a darn thing. If your petty tyrants want to change, let it come from *their* hearts, not your desire.

As you become embroiled with petty tyrants, use the pressure on your energy body as a catalyst to shift your focal point. That is, use the situation to temper your energy body. What do you want out of a job? Out of life? What can you live with, and what is a deal breaker? Where will you place your life on the line, and where will you gracefully exist? With whom do you want to associate, and what influences do you wish to avoid? What promotes strength and wisdom, and what entrains you to the dregs of pettiness? By encountering petty tyrants, you'll answer all of these questions, plus many more. You'll strengthen your cohesion, your *will*, your intent. So remain focused and balanced in order to enable a natural outcome to occur. When you learn what the petty tyrant represents within your cohesion, the situation evaporates, one way or another.

A key point: Don Juan says that petty tyrants are not only to help you lose self-reflection, they are to help you perform the "very sophisticated maneuver" of stepping out of this world (*Fire*, 42). When you peak your relation to potential, you're automatically inaccessible to worldly energies. A petty tyrant gives you training to peak potential by requiring that you intend your awareness away from the force at hand. After all, it's having an excessively regimented cohesion that turns a person into a petty tyrant. By working with this entire process of plugging into potential, you are delivered deeper into potential, and, therefore, closer to the Fire of Freedom.

Recapitulation

This is a marvelous way to spiff up your energies, reclaim your energy, and get yourself clear of obstructions. It discharges the energies of old habits, casts off the muck of that fight you just got into with your friend, and primes you to move deeper into the unknown. It's effective for all types of energy and works for anyone. Detailed exercises to perform it are also presented in Taisha Abelar's and Victor Sanchez's work.[4]

In most instances, this exercise uses the breath as a means to free your energy. First, inhale and bring the energy under scrutiny into full view. Then, exhale to release the binding force of it. You never lose the memory or the knowledge of the event. You just lose the fixating tension of it. One idea is that by recapitulating you discharge enough energy to be able to cruise past the tension of the Eagle as you enter the third energy field. If you don't offer up your energy, you get snared by the unrelenting force of the Eagle and your energy body is pulled apart, dissipating your awareness and squelching your perception (*Dreaming*, 149).

I have also found that the recapitulation may be used without using the breath. In dreaming, for example, you apply the intent of recapitulating and allow the energy release and rejuvenation to occur. As with most dreaming exercises, the procedure is accomplished faster than during the physical-body version. The key is intent. And the best way to learn this intent is to practice the complete method, step by step. After learning the basics, experiment to find innovative ways to speed up the process.

There are also two principal schools of thought regarding how the breath is employed. In one camp, you inhale as you sweep your head across your chest, or, from another perspective, through your energy body. Some say sweep your head right to left. Others say it doesn't matter as, again, intent is the key. In this case, it's the intent of pulling energy into your immediate awareness to process it, which is a sub-intent, if you will, of the overall exercise. Personally, I like to inhale starting from my right shoulder, as it has an effect of hooking me into a reference point of the first field. That is, as a tracking exercise I ground myself in my daily world and then expand from there. I then work my way into the more subtle areas of the second field, into the unknown areas of my life. Then I exhale from left to right.

To illustrate its effects, some time ago I woke from a dream in a cold sweat. During the dream, a friend of mine was stabbing me with a knife. While I recapitulated the dream, I remembered an incident several years prior. The person in the dream had emphasized a point in our real-life conversation by shaking a knife at me. Evidently, the incident had left an indelible impression in my energy body. I was only now discharging its energy through the recapitulation process. Through employing the breathwork the recapitulation, by definition, includes the process and breathwork.

Abelar indicates that you may use the formal method of making a list to enact this process of recapitulation to enact the recapitulation. This is where you list everyone you've come into contact with throughout your life. Then you recapitulate the entire list front to back, or vice versa.[5] Don Juan adds that a fluid style may be used (*Dreaming*, 150). For example, several people I know prefer a method of recapitulating whatever comes to their awareness as they enter the exercise. They also make sure to work through any of the day's turmoil to better clear their minds. Then, from time to time, they pre-select an event to work with. For instance, they might choose a photograph out of an old album, then recapitulate it. Regardless of your method, I do think it's important to maintain an intent to work through each and every piece of your life. Take time to come up with your own innovations, being careful to test them thoroughly to make sure they work.

From years of practice, for example, I've come up with my own "Gunslinger" method of recapitulation. This can be done virtually any-where, anytime. I aim my energies to peak the potential of the moment, to get the most out of the session, and then let whatever wants to sur-face, surface. That is, I try to plug myself fully into the moment. Then I wait for an energy that needs recapitulating to enter my awareness. It could be anything: a family dispute, a job-related problem, or even which movie I want to see. I then retrain my intent away from potential and plug fully into the energy to be recapitulated. Then, in one deft movement (which is akin to how my recapitulations occur in dreaming), I discharge that energy by letting it evaporate as though I had popped a balloon.

Whatever your method, make sure to enter—indeed fully live again—the experience you're working with. You need to discharge the fixation which that energy has on your energy body. This is what allows cohesion to shift. In fact, don Juan says that the recapitulation allows the focal point to move slowly, steadily, surely. He adds that most people can't tap dreaming because they're loaded down with heavy energy. This sludge keeps people from shifting out of their own stuff (*Dreaming*, 147–49).

In addition to the formal breathing exercise, periodically assess and reassess where you have been and where you're going. As you retrace your travels, you mold information into knowledge. For me, writ-ing this book provided me with this exercise, as it required me to list events and formulate models of what they meant or related to, thereby synthesizing years of experience. While writing it, it had its own direc-tions that often surprised me; it shaped me as much as I shaped it. This transported me beyond it. I collected, assessed, integrated, and then left each level of activity. I stood renewed and refreshed, waiting to explore another stage of growth and learning. A few tips to start your recapitulation:

1. Establish the intent that your recapitulation will enable you to study, integrate, and transcend the object or area of assessment.
2. State or restate your short-term and long-term goals associated with this exercise.
3. Look back over recent and long-term behavior to determine if your actions support reaching your goals.
4. Collect your thoughts and experiences by writing, talking, and/or thoroughly mulling them over.
5. Meditate, allowing this energy to saturate you.
6. Notice the results. This process contains the seeds of your next endeavors. By the end of the recapitulation, you will leave this study with a clear sense of your renewed direction.

Responsibility

Don Juan maintains that assuming responsibility for yourself means to behave as though you are continually placing your life on the line (*Journey*, 58–69). He thought that this stance, this attitude, created a clarity, which enabled a person to live life to the hilt. After all, you need gumption to consciously enter dreaming. Personal responsibility also requires that you stay at peace with yourself. This allows you to stay in touch with yourself and cultivate deliberate behavior, behavior that originates from within you as an expression of your deepest self. To further develop responsibility:

1. Fully assess a situation before you decide how you will act. Carefully weigh the pros and cons from a variety of perspectives. Be honest with yourself about yourself. You gain nothing by refusing to acknowledge how you feel.
2. Throughout the day, ask yourself, "If this were my last act on Earth, is this how I want to express myself?" After this assessment, don't be too serious or morbid.

3. After you make a decision, abide by it and the results. Don't second guess yourself or blame someone else. Spend your energy on the next problem, while using the knowledge gained from previous situations.

4. Dare to try new and innovative solutions. Build a wide base of experience from which to draw knowledge.

5. Understand and appreciate that you are building your life. Treat it with respect.

Routines

Your habits keep your cohesion stable. So in this regard, they are highly beneficial. Otherwise, your mind would be off and away all the time, which is generally the case anyway. Routines, however, also dull awareness. They keep you focused on the same things, day in and day out. This is why don Juan taught Castaneda to hunt for food by having him disarrange his habits. Castaneda had to let go, tune more into his body, and develop a new set of skills in order to be successful. It is this new set of skills that became a new set of habits. Don Juan then guided Castaneda into using his new skills to habitually hunt knowledge (*Journey*, 70–82).

There are physical, emotional, and mental habits, each influencing the others. Driving the same route to work is a physical habit, consistently getting angry when someone disagrees with you is an emotional habit, and always thinking that the world is material is a mental habit. Each of these habits reflects an energy pattern within the energy body; in other words, each habit originates from cohesion. Fluidity is what you're aiming for when you begin your habit-breaking endeavors.

Altering routines involves deliberately breaking habits (*Journey*, 96–104). As you break a habit, you open yourself to new behavior, new ways of looking at the world. New experience provides new knowledge. To help loosen perception, try these exercises:

1. Do something just for the heck of it. Move all the living room furniture to the middle of the room and leave it there a few days.

Rearrange it again based on feeling. Where does it feel like the sofa should go? Where does it feel like you should place the rocking chair? Don't worry about the way it looks. Let feeling guide you. Have some fun with it.

2. Place your left shoe on first for one week, and then place your right shoe on first for four days. Vary the exercise randomly.

3. Drive to work on different routes, at different times.

4. Every day for 20–30 minutes walk around your house or neighborhood guided only by feeling. Don't censor where you walk by "should's" and "shouldn'ts." If you have an impulse to bend over and pick up a candy wrapper, do so. If you feel good about knocking on a neighbor's door for no apparent reason, do so.

5. Pay attention to your activities. You may discover some comfortable habits may be superficial, serving no purpose. You may also realize how habits in behavior create habits in what you perceive. If you want to perceive more, give yourself more options.

6. One problem you may encounter is thinking you are altering routines when you are only creating larger ones. If you vary the route to work each and every day, you are creating the routine of varying the route to work. To correct this, again use feeling. You might drive different routes three days in a row, and then drive the same route twice.

Self-Reflection

This is the big enchilada, the major league show, the reason a person travels a Toltec path in the first place: to get rid of self-reflection. The less you reflect, the more you perceive of what is really in the world.

Don Juan says that self-reflection has two sides. One part consists of all that is good. It makes us stretch into the unknown and tackle challenges. The other side, and the side that we are dealing with here, consists of all that is putrid. It's what turns people into petty tyrants, and keeps perception imprisoned. And getting rid of the putrid stuff, says don Juan, is a masterful accomplishment (*Fire*, 28). While self-reflection has two sides, in essence it is a cohesion, a state of energy. Invariably, it reflects having a specific energy field, whether ordinary or nonordinary.

So let's isolate these two features. The first is emotional. This is where you measure yourself, reflect to yourself about whether you're good or bad, are proficient or not, or are worthy or unworthy. The second is mental. This is where you define and interpret yourself, others, and the world in general. Both of these must be brought under control to proceed at any stage, through any level. This is because losing self-reflection opens doors of perception, frees up energy, gives you personal power, and thereby strengthens your connection with Spirit.

The emotional side, or self-enhancement, is bolstering or diminishing one's sense of self. People tend to invest huge amounts of energy into whatever it takes to defend themselves against the onslaught of everything that seems to be outside their sense of a personal self. Just let someone say you aren't the way you think you are, and then watch your reaction. One hallmark of self-reflection, therefore, is getting irritated, or even angry, when someone sets forth an idea not in line with your thinking, or behaves contrary to what you feel is appropriate. One value of working with a metaphysical system is that when you erupt, you have a tool to guide you through the turmoil and back into balance. For instance, you can work to regain your nonattachment, intend to remain inaccessible, and aim to lose more self-reflection.

Another aspect of self-enhancement is self-righteousness, or indignation. This is when you pump up the volume of an emotional outburst to let everyone know that you are right, no doubt about it. Indignation usually erupts when another person's cohesion doesn't match yours, as they are having different thoughts or feelings. Sometimes this mismatch of energies produces anger, which, at times, may be an effective means of communication, as it gets across your point. But to use it as such, it must part of your tracking skills and not part of self-reflection. In other words, your anger must be under control, and not occur simply from reactiveness. You want to manage your resources; you don't want to enter the kingdom of the petty tyrant.

To me, one of the most intriguing aspects of Toltec studies is the mental side of self-reflection. The bottom line is that your interpretation or definition of anything, in any way, is a reflection from yourself to yourself within your energy body. This has a high and a low side. By defining something, you bring it into view. By saying there is a second energy field, for instance, you may begin to perceive it, and then explore it. The down side is that if you don't continually let go of your definitions, you won't remain open to the next new awareness. Shifting from an ordinary to a nonordinary field, for example, takes a heap of work. The grandeur of the newfound reality can keep us interested for a lifetime.

The more we become fluent with this other world, the more we stand to engage self-reflection. There's great power in this. There are many prison bars as well. It is so much fun interpreting the world in grand ways, then playing with our magnificent views, that we often forget to summon the courage to go even further. To overcome these distractions don Juan says that modern seers must create a very detailed description of their world, then laugh at it and throw it away (*Fire*, 256).

To lose self-reflection, here are a few exercises:

1. Don't judge or criticize others. You may gaze and *see* their energy bodies in order to assess their energy fields, but don't make yourself judge and jury. Any time your sensibilities are offended, look within yourself before you pin the tail on the other donkey. Remain vigilant for projection.

2. Don't define yourself. When you say "I am a writer" or "I am a mechanic," you structure your continuity within the margins that you've just defined. By buying into a definition of yourself, you lose yourself to that domain. Use your experiences to activate and balance your energy body, not to place yourself in a straightjacket.

3. When your self-reflection surfaces, track it. Find the seeds of it. *See* what reveals itself. Then recapitulate it. Or recapitulate it to find the seeds of it.

4. Engage nonpatterning often. Gaze frequently. Stop your internal (infernal) dialogue.

5. Study the effects of petty tyrants and projection. You'll soon see

your own pettiness, your own sludge that keeps you from connecting with Spirit.

6. Don't let the behavior of others offend you. Develop the attitude that people are part of nature and how anyone behaves is no different from the behavior of any other creature of nature.

7. Provide service to others. From clearing the table after dinner, to volunteering community service, to establishing a service-oriented business, these activities take you out of and away from yourself, providing useful experiences and insights about yourself and others.

Strategy

In *Warfighting*, a book on applying U.S. Marine strategies to the business world, General Gray, Commandant of the Marine Corps, says, "War is an extreme trial of moral and physical strength and stamina."[6] As you may know, don Juan often relates the Toltec world to warfare, hence, the use of terms such as "ruthless" and "warrior." Toltec strategy, however, is not adversarial as is military warfare. Modern Toltec endeavors are the struggles to find true peace within the heart and mind. The rigors of a Toltec path, however, do echo General Gray's sentiments. You need "moral and physical strength and stamina."

To make progress, especially the progress of tracking freedom, you must align yourself strategically with your entire life; that is, you must realize you're in it for the long haul. The goal, the quest, the war, is that of freedom. Elements of the long-term strategy include tracking and dreaming, and whatever else needs to be done to zip past the Eagle to get to the third field. Employing tactics such as erasing personal history, gazing, and losing self-reflection, make up the daily battles to claim your being. The only way to lose the war, says don Juan, is to quit. Joining the ranks of petty tyrants, for example, is a dead giveaway that you've lost. However, if you become a petty tyrant and then regain your senses, the good fight is still on. In essence, when you lose the strategy of being with Spirit, you've lost the struggle for your own heart (*Fire*, 42–43).

Don Juan also gives examples of grand maneuvers of strategy—

behavior that is more far-reaching than individual exercises or tactics; these are called *attributes of warriorship*. Each of these maneuvers brings you closer to your core. Therefore, rather than create five-year plans (as you might normally design in a strategy), Toltecs strategize to maximize the moment at hand. These grand elements of strategy include control, discipline, patience, timing, *will*, and interactions with petty tyrants (*Fire*, 39–42).

The gist of it is that control allows you to easily shift out of anger and regain your composure. Discipline enables you to recognize the strengths and weaknesses of someone, a petty tyrant for example, even when you're being pummeled by their energy. Patience lets you restrain yourself and wait for what is rightfully yours. Timing reflects an exquisite intuitive sense of when to act and when not to. And *will* is a defining element of your evolution to freedom, because you have earned greater control of your energy body; and the petty tyrant is the means to ensure that you always have plenty of practice with strategy and tactics.

These exercises enable the perception of a different worldview, be they Toltec or something else. Furthermore, they provide the foundation to enter those worlds. This applies to the world of business, science, or dreaming. In these terms, I think you'll find that they have universal application.

10

Transition into Dreaming

Gathering of Rangers

Off we go to another dimension,
in a world that doesn't make any sense.
A landscape without any feelings,
time lasting for infinity.
Have we all been here before,
or is it just a distant dream?

Regardless of the journeys we undertake, we face prerequisites to help ensure success. If we're going camping, we take a blanket or sleeping bag, a change of clothes, a knife, and perhaps a tent and food. Before a long drive, we check the radiator and brake fluid, hoses and belts, tires, and anything else that crosses our minds. Traveling the paths of dreaming is no different. We acquaint ourselves with tools and techniques that pry our energies loose, and offer support and balance if we stray into never-never lands that may cause us to lose touch with our normal sense of reality.

Practicing the techniques in this chapter can stimulate awareness of the chakras and the eight cornerstones of perception, thereby empowering us to use more of our capacities. These exercises enable the focal point to move, taking perception out of the routine and ordinary and placing it into the sublime and magical. As this occurs, we grease perception so that it moves fluently in and out of different landscapes. We can explore dimensions of time and space, visit other forms of life, and travel to the most sacred of places within ourselves. Theories and views about reality establish a guiding force for perception. Exercises and techniques provide a way to experience that force and its effects, as well as allowing us to continue to expand our views.

Experience sustains knowledge and vice versa. It is the substance from which we derive our temporary and lasting truths. We tend to perceive and to experience the views we have been taught. While viewpoints stimulate the quest for knowledge, experience provides knowledge that may transcend viewpoints. A sufficient amount of out-of-the-ordinary experiences often overturn the way we look at the world, which in turn opens doors to more nonordinary experiences. In this leapfrog fashion, we evolve.

Techniques also enable us to remain alert and balanced when we leave our assumptions about reality at the door and cross into experiences for which we have no previous reference. We may then assimilate the experiences without fear or concern. This enables us to maximize experience as we incorporate it into our daily lives. Suppose, for example, you have been taught that there are absolutely no extraterrestrials. What happens when you witness such a phenomenon? How can you use the experience without arbitrarily dismissing it? Techniques that provide for the exploration of consciousness create the needed perspectives to accept that something out of the ordinary has occurred, while not jumping to conclusions.

The following perspectives will therefore help you establish a strong base to begin, renew, or further your travels in consciousness, with particular attention being paid to DBEs. You will also find exercises to experiment with, techniques to perceive and control nonphysical energies, and methods to balance your daily life—a major emphasis when working with the first energy field. Some of these exercises may be found in almost any system of consciousness development. The names may be different and the steps modified, but their consistent appearance is one mark of their effectiveness. In my conversations with don Juan, his peers, and their apprentices, I referred to many of these techniques. They invariably understood the concepts and often used the same terminology, which underscored the value of Castaneda's work.

I've found that the more we experience identifiable changes, the more the shifts begin to have quality. Inconsistencies dissipate. We can then return with greater and greater ease to specific locations in our consciousness. Just as we learned to play in the yard without trampling the flowerbed, we learn to return to locations within consciousness, such as accessing past lives, or traveling in dreaming. Then, as we experience more and more shifts that relate to each other, we begin to build a new framework.

Whatever the specific exercise, your relation to technique forms a bond that can lift you into the sky or keep you in a cave away from the light. You are always encouraged to combine, innovate, or create new exercises. Don't get lost in techniques; use them for support. When used within a context such as the Toltec Way, they can make your steps surer and stronger.

TOOLS FOR MORE PREPARATION

Attitude

One of the tools that makes or breaks us is attitude. As you travel deeper or further within dreaming, your attitude can lift you over barriers or keep you ramming your head into them. Changes in attitudes result in changes in your relation to the world. Developing your own signature of behavior can be fun. Here's one way to proceed:

1. Strive to remain aware of how your attitudes affect your behavior and how they result in different outcomes.
2. Tell yourself you want to learn more about your attitudes. Make it a commitment within yourself.
3. Feel the energy of this commitment centered deep within your chest. Push the energy out and away from you, letting it seep into the world. Release all of the energy associated with this pursuit. Allow yourself to have new experiences as the energy of your request returns.

4. Pay attention to how your attitudes reflect your relation to the world. Notice how people respond to your moods, the tone of your voice, and your physical mannerisms. Don't worry about changing anything yet. You're still on a fact-finding mission. Accumulate as much information as you can.

5. Study attitudes by watching other people and movies. A well-scripted character behaves consistently and provides an excellent subject. You might enjoy the flippant attitude of a policeman, or the humorous slant on life a college co-ed uses to help her through difficulties.

6. Play with unusual attitudes. For instance, if you're under unusual stress, imagine that you are already dead, that there is nothing more that can harm you, and that you have a gift of living out your life even though dead. Pause, relax, and reassess how you want to behave. For another example, see yourself as part of a motion picture production. Whatever occurs—from a traffic accident, to a fight with your lover, to winning the lottery—imagine that it is part of the script. Whatever happens, happens because that's the way the producer and director want it to happen. Responsibly assess your feelings and proceed, feeling that you are a full participant in the film. Attitudes that push you out of your normal behavior provide more perspectives with which to look at and understand them.

7. Take some time (weeks, months, years) to study and assess your attitudes. Determine how you want to positively and purposefully express yourself. Develop your own tailored set of attitudes that assist you in your endeavors.

Body Knowledge

Many of the ills of today are from not paying attention to the world and to ourselves. We have lost ourselves in a symbolic world that has no direct connection to what's really going on.

Mental reflections cannot account for everything in the world. But since our physical bodies connect with the world, we simply need to connect with our bodies. By doing so we tap an order that transcends the intellect. Often social consensus has us disavow our knowledge, our sensing of what's afoot. Yet this natural intelligence supersedes conceptualization.

Listen to your body. If you have an ache, for example, feel it. Let the energy from it fully enter your awareness. This allows you to discover why you ache. If you're nearsighted, ask yourself why you won't look into the distance . . . clearly. Don't get me wrong, I'm not prescribing a cure-all. However, I am very much saying that listening to your body provides more knowledge than most people can imagine.

Will activates when you have sufficiently stimulated your cohesion, and have integrated that energy into your daily world. The only way I know how to do this is to own up to your body knowledge. Through it, you *know* that the first and second energy fields are not separate. They are distinct categories of energy, but they are also interwoven. In the final analysis they are one and the same. Making the distinction between them, however, serves to call your attention to different worlds and ways of perceiving. Cultivating the distinctions helps you evolve. Leaving the distinctions behind helps you evolve further.

All of the exercises and perspectives in this chapter facilitate the learning of body knowledge. Being in your body, feeling *flow*, is by far the best exercise for dreaming.

Clarity

Perhaps you became involved with nonordinary realities because your goal is specifically to develop DBEs. Or, perhaps you were attracted to that path for no apparent reason, and now that your steps are more certain, you consider DBE a next step. Whatever sparked your interest, it helps to refine your thinking about, and your motivations for, DBE. Ask yourself why you want to experience a DBE, what your fears are concerning it, and how you would like to use it. Fully accepting yourself and your circumstances engenders clarity.

But clarity may also inhibit you. Sometimes you may arrive at such a sense of clarity that you think and feel you have solved everything. This kind of clarity is an obstacle to further growth. To offset this effect, patiently measure your endeavors. Proceed step by step and gain strength from these steps. Question, explore, and further examine your involvements.

Learning Tasks

One of the best ways to harness your intent, to be active in dreaming, and to keep pushing through levels of dreaming is with a learning task. Determine what you'd like to learn, something a little far-fetched from the ordinary. Then apply yourself to entering dreaming in order to accelerate your learning of that topic.

Observation

Pay attention to what happens, how you feel, what you think about when you enact these exercises, or as you go through your day. Watch your thoughts. Track your emotions. Listen to yourself, to others, to the world. Indeed, listening allows new alignments of energy to occur. It enables you to become aware of the world in different ways. It is a principal means of observation.

Through observation, of self and the world, you can become a dispassionate witness to life. Again, this doesn't mean to leave passion behind. Just be nonattached to it. By choreographing several nonpatterning skills, you may better study your energies, and what behaviors build or dissipate your personal power.

Self-observation is tracking yourself. It is not looking at yourself in the mirror and being ever so pleased, or displeased, with what you find. Rather, you must establish a point of awareness away from your physical body, and then observe your behavior, all of your behavior, from that outside vantage point. This promotes objectivity so that you may change your behavior as you see fit. Furthermore, by stepping outside of yourself, so to speak, you reduce projection.

Through observation of self and world you'll find your path with heart because you'll discover how your energy connects naturally with the world. This is a step toward having a natural energy field.

Personal Power

This is an essential ingredient for personal evolution. It pertains to how much usable energy you have. By developing personal power, you can do all sorts of things: give psychic readings, have DBEs, manipulate others, or bestow blessings on others. The idea, however, is to use your energy for your continued evolution. As such, personal power is best found by matching your energies with Spirit, not with lesser powers. Spirit opens all avenues to freedom if you simply open yourself completely to Spirit.

At the same time, personal power is there to use. You need it for intuitive guidance, which is the soft and silent voice of Spirit. You also need the energy of personal power in order to discover your path with heart. In all cases, whether you have just a wee bit or a huge chunk, don Juan says that a measure of impeccability is trusting yourself (*Journey*, 204).

Staying in touch with yourself enables you to discern the proper course of action. While you probably won't abandon society and seek to live a hermit's life, trusting personal power requires that you govern your behavior by measuring it through your eyes alone. This doesn't mean you avoid asking for advice; it means you assess all the information you can by using as many modes of perception as possible, then pave your own way. You may find that the more you discover yourself, the more you surrender to power and allow your behavior to flow from that awareness. Less and less will you look back, second guessing what might have been. You will be too busy building a better life as you walk into the future, while remaining in the present.

Projection

No, not astral projection. This type of projection occurs when you attribute to others what occurs within yourself.[1] If you angrily pronounce someone as being egotistical, it is because you, yourself, are egotistical. The more the behavior of another person bothers or upsets you, the more that characteristic is alive and well within you. Projection also occurs for good tidings. For instance, if you say another person is a kind and loving being, it is because you also have those qualities.

Our consensual social reality is projection on a massive scale. Projection also becomes a problem when you cease feeling responsible for yourself and try to judge the behavior of others. The more you allow others to be as they are, the more balance you develop within yourself. Nonpatterning and minimizing self-reflection are the means to get a handle on projection.

Relaxation

Okay, now you have to relax. So go ahead and tense up. And if you do, remain nonattached. Doing so helps you observe yourself. By observing yourself, you'll eventually notice you're no longer relaxed. Then you can let go, use your death to remind yourself what's really important to you, become inaccessible, and then once again relax. See how these exercises bolster each other?

If you're not relaxed, you'll expend energy wantonly. Your body will have a difficult time adjusting to new energies and new cohesions. So you won't apply your efforts correctly, which means it's going to take more time than you want to achieve something. But if you remain nonattached and relaxed, it may seem like your learning is taking longer, but it really isn't. You're just more aware of yourself learning.

To relax, let any pressures you feel settle throughout your body. Allow your cohesion to gradually shift to the focal point position known as "relaxation." Pay attention to yourself, observe yourself. Let go, step by step, down and throughout your body. Counting to ten as you let go of tension in different parts of your body is a popular meditation, but makes some people tense. In addition, accepting your fate and remaining accessible to Spirit help to establish priorities. These relationships are your energetic posture. With the correct posture you automatically relax into your life and then live it without recrimination and with joy and abandon.

Shields

Behavior forms from predilections, the preferences and personality traits that you express to the world. While you may had have a predilection to watching films, during childhood it may have been expressed as a penchant for watching animated movies. During adolescence, your pre-dilection may have been for teen-idol movies. As an adult, your prefer-ences may lean toward mysteries. Or you may have given up movies altogether. Predilections may change subtly within themselves or come and go completely.

Your conglomerate of traits provides an identity and reflects your path in life. One person may feel drawn to the medical profession. Once there, the path splits in many directions: internist, radiologist, or sur-geon, for example. Another person seeks the drama of police work, and again the path splits: homicide, vice, or forensics. Your predilections may offer you sustenance to fully enjoy your life as well as to get you through hard times, or if they are not the deepest expression of yourself, they may cause you to shrivel. You may sense of lack of meaning, a nag-ging depression of not having purpose.

Setting the stage for DBEs requires a complete assessment of pre-dilections, bringing to the fore those that sustain balance and harmony and offer the most personal meaning. Previous exercises provide a way to suspend how you relate to the world. This break in the action offers a way to reassess where you are and where you want to go.

Predilections also act as filters, a means of protection that prevent the immense amount of energy that surrounds us from flooding our aware-ness to the point of inaction, to where we are so overloaded with data and energy that we are unable to make sense out of anything. As filters, they affect the specifics of what we perceive. Out of all of the physical and non-physical energies surrounding us, these filters hone our awareness along certain paths, paths associated with, and reflecting, our predilections.

Power predilections express your innermost traits and characteris-tics. They provide a base of meaning from which to expand awareness by providing the strength to set yourself momentarily aside while you tap new resources, new perceptions. You have the strength to surrender yourself to Spirit since you have something worth returning to or living with. Since these paths reflect the deepest currents within, they provide profound personal meaning. Behavior becomes more consistent as you travel deeper within.

In addition, these predilections allow you to store personal power; their meaning offers strength of purpose and direction in life. What you give returns in abundant measure. This precisely focused energy enables emotional balance as you find yourself matched with the world. As you blend with the world, individual integrity and sense of purpose reflects itself in positive ways within society. For don Juan, the careful evaluation and selection of shields places one on a path with heart. Walking *your* path provides the best shields for dreaming you have.

Worry

This is being inaccessible, placed into action, as worry often manifests the very situation that someone was worried about. For example, an elderly woman expressed concern that she might not want to return from a DBE, an activity that had previously added quality to her life. She said that some of her friends once tried to wake her in the midst of a DBE. They had difficulty rousing her and, since they didn't know of the possibility of DBEs, they thought she might be dying and became very concerned. She woke just before an emergency call was placed. Since she was worried about troubling her friends again, she no longer tried to have DBEs. This attitude made her enjoy her life less. She then grew worried that maybe she wouldn't return from a DBE if one occurred spontaneously.

After hearing her story, I remarked that, since she didn't enjoy life as much, maybe that would prevent her from returning. Perhaps if she would not feel responsible for her friends and how they viewed her, she would renew her enjoyment of DBEs, which would then help her enjoy life, which would then make her want to return. When she saw the relationship between her attitudes and her experiences, she lightened up. Her tension eased and the light about her glowed stronger.

OTHER CONSIDERATIONS

1. If you sleep in the same bed with another person and are concerned that they may roll over and touch you and, in so doing,

interrupt your DBE, program yourself not to return from a DBE unless your physical body is in danger or discomfort. Before entering or during a DBE, tell yourself the conditions under which you will stay out or return. Focus on the specific circumstances you face (such as your partner rolling over).

2. If you unexpectedly find yourself in your dreaming body looking at your physical body, leave the area and do something—anything. This will break the habit that leads us to believe that we must be in the physical body to be able to perceive. Also, don't let surprise interfere and ruin your DBE. Remaining focused on your target destination (knowing why or where you want to go) is a way to overcome surprise and its tendency to refocus your attention back to your physical body.

3. Try not to feel so committed to the goal that you become uptight or inflexible.

4. You may experience depression. This often results from changing the way you view the world. Developing a powerful daily life and continuing your exercises takes you away from the blues.

5. Patience. Just as a child learns, you need sensation prior to recognition, and recognition prior to control. In other words, you might perceive fleeting features relating to separation before you begin recognizing and controlling your DBEs.

Transitions

During the transition from a DBE to wakefulness, meditation, sleep, or dreams, almost anything might occur. You may simply find yourself outside of your physical body with no sensation of having had any transition. Or you might feel as though you have entered a high-energy zone. This involves a usually short-lived sensation of being in the midst of tremendous energy. This is also a high-potential zone, a state of consciousness where anything can occur. Your slightest doubt, concern, fear, or wish might bubble to the surface. It may seem as though you have entered an enhanced, super-dream of amazing clarity where you confront whatever is on your mind.

My experience indicates the transition to a DBE from a meditative state enables more control, which makes sense since you will already be more awake and alert. Yet the high-energy zone might still buffet you about like an airplane in a storm and passing through this region might seem a little freaky. During one meditative transition, my awareness shifted from my bedroom (where my physical body rested) to my living room. Just as I thought I had a clear view, the scene fragmented and bits and pieces of the living room tore apart as though I were dismantling a jigsaw puzzle. This proved disconcerting, which drew my attention back to my physical body, thus ending the attempt.

During some transitions—especially those where I am meditating and trying to induce a DBE—I have sensed five levels. First, I feel tension. As I work through this customary surface tension and allow it to dissipate, I begin viewing mental imagery. Through nonpatterning, I allow this imagery to come and go, to be whatever it wants to be. Doing this takes me to a third level where I am enshrouded in blackness, which is also a very restful area. Shortly, I enter the fourth level of a new series of images. This time, through a relaxed effort, I maintain the images. I allow them to shift if necessary, but my emphasis is on gently holding them constant. As this level stabilizes, I am delivered into a DBE, the fifth level. I don't think it is necessary to experience all of these levels. You may have all five, or may bypass one or more. The idea is to acquaint you with as many DBE features as possible, not to create a rigid, inflexible model.

The transition also brings normal fears regarding DBEs to the fore. One of these is the fear of dying. While discussing DBEs, Robert Monroe said he thinks our physical survival instinct presents a barrier to get to the dreaming body. If we sense we are heading toward a DBE, we instinctively turn away from it, since separation from the physical body conjures images of dying. Monroe thinks that breaking this fear barrier is a major step toward achieving a DBE.

Getting past the fear doesn't mean you lose your survival instinct. It's been my experience that the dreaming body responds to the needs of the physical body and that if survival is in question, the DBE ends and physical perceptions are restored.

A closely related fear stems from the disorientation experienced during the transition. While thinking about DBE may clear up your sense of purpose about it, actually leaving your physical body may deliver the shock of finding yourself squarely in the midst of nonordinary reality. The support derived from your ordinary worldview may falter, leaving you groping for some way to ease this shock.

The issue, then, is whether you have committed yourself to your DBE explorations. Especially in the early stages of developing DBEs, you may feel your lack of control. You may sense that a force more powerful than yourself is influencing—even controlling—your perception. This *is* scary. You're now faced with the knowledge that forces beyond your comprehension can determine your fate. Thinking, reading about, and experimenting with a variety of DBE views and techniques offers well-rounded perspectives, which provide support and help ease this tension.

Not all people have these concerns. And even when a person has one or more, most of the time completing the transition and being fully in your dreaming body diminishes or erases them. Not panicking and holding your purpose in mind facilitates the transition. A full commitment to entering the dreaming body not only smoothes out the transition, but helps guide you to your preferred destination.

Barriers

In addition to fears associated with a separation, you may run headlong into other barriers. We build barriers during the course of our lives, and most of them result from the way we perceive and define the world. A common barrier is thinking that a DBE is impossible. Another is the limitations we place on ourselves because we think something is supposed to be a certain way. As we think, feel, and act in certain ways, we create borders for our thoughts, feelings, and actions, which then determine how we think, feel, and act.

If you practice medicine, for example, much of your thought, feeling, and activity have been established for you as you develop and refine your knowledge and skills. You open in one direction and close down other avenues as a matter of choice. You set priorities since you can't do everything. You manage your time and energy between work and play. Insufficient flexibility, or rigid thinking and behavior, hardens these borders into barriers.

The filtering effect of predilections allows us to selectively perceive meaningful information from the immense amount of data that continually impinges on our awareness. Predilections filter this data, allowing us to perceive what has meaning to us.

Fluidity

It is by matching personal energies with the Eagle's emanations, says don Juan, that we become "fluid, forever in motion, eternal" (*Fire*, 68). Thus, becoming fluid and flexible is building that type of connection with Spirit. Fluidity helps keep perception open, and lets cohesion shift. This doesn't mean we should be wishy-washy. Shields provide stability, balance, and strength and, in relation to flexibility, they let you shift easily while remaining steadfast.

Humans tend to have fixations, and these equate to pieces of cohesion that are locked in place. Fixations differ from watermarks in that watermarks are deliberately forged from strength and flexibility; fixations are more like barnacles. Fluidity gracefully pries away the barnacles and lets cohesion shift more easily.

Our urge to hang on to things is immense; it's a force in itself. But letting go is the only way to explore new horizons, and to tackle the unknown. Otherwise, you remain fixated by only that which you know. Or more accurately, what you think you know. By letting go, by becoming fluid, you discover your innate self, your God-created self, not the society-created self most people walk around in. To begin working with this notion, ask yourself: "When I let go, what remains?"

Compared to the quest of sparking an awareness of your core energy, it's easy to let all else go. There is no greater adventure.

Intent

Intent is focused energy; energy firmly fixed on something, or aimed in some direction. It carries a blueprint that forms our experiences. If we set our mind to something, we usually achieve that goal. The more we focus on a goal, the speedier the results. Often a specific intent wanes as we find an interest in something else. But we may have planted a seed. You often witness levels of intent as you get nearer to your goal and your experience and resolve deepens. Clarity replaces vagueness. Knowledge replaces ignorance. To learn more about intent try the following:

1. Establish an overall strategy. Where do you want to go in life? What do you want to experience and learn?
2. From this strategy, make your decisions carefully. Examine many features and relations around a situation before actually deciding on a course of action. Keep your decisions focused in line with your strategy.
3. If you make an on-the-spot decision, do not waiver from it. Trust yourself to have acted properly, and believe that your intent is acting on different levels in order to assist you in reaching your goals.
4. Pay attention to how you feel regarding your decisions and how you are trying to achieve them. Do the energies feel different? Do they have focus, direction? Can you direct the energies?
5. Be flexible. Allow unexpected events to direct you toward your goals.
6. Listen intuitively to your inner thoughts as they guide you.

Partial Projections

It's quite common to experience a partial projection where you *see* or feel a nonphysical arm or leg rise out of your physical body. This kind of projection might seem more dramatic if you sense most of your awareness residing outside of your physical body but you still feel partially connected with it.

Partial projections are more common during the early days of trying to have your first DBE. Later they may occur because you need to resolve something in your daily life, so you can't let go completely. They may also occur because you're learning something new. As you split your perception, for instance, you're also on your way to bilocation, which, as we discussed earlier, is a more advanced stage of DBE.

Separation

When you undergo separation, it will seem as though you took your physical senses with you, and they will most likely operate from a heightened perspective. Colors will appear deeper. Shapes will look clearer and sharper. Feelings will intensify. Sounds might seem magnified. It is possible to duplicate any of the five physical senses, although developing taste and smell may, in general, require more effort, while vision is usually the first to develop.

There will be times when your vision embraces a 360-degree panorama rather than a straight-ahead, stereoscopic vision. Traveling as a sphere of energy readily lends itself to maintaining this perspective. In the beginning, however, your vision might appear foggy. And you may not have any of your other physical senses. With time and practice, difficulties will clear.

Even though you perceive as though using physical senses, other physical requirements don't matter. During a DBE, you may stay underwater or in deep space for as long as you wish. You may also travel through physical objects such as walls and mountains.

Once you have completed the transition, you will have experienced a shift in your perception from your physical body to the dreaming body. You now have at your disposal different states of awareness. You might hover about your room, fly around Earth, or go to other planets or other dimensions.

If you don't like a particular situation, it is up to you to travel away from the environment, not try to change your external landscape. This is a key distinction between lucid dreaming and DBE, and it is accomplished by aligning thinking with feeling. Merging your thoughts and feelings creates the maneuvering intent. This provides the force or energy, which enables you to travel. You may travel to any destination in the blink of an eye, or poke around. Often, as soon as you think about a place, you'll find yourself there instantly. If you need to think during a DBE, and don't want your thinking to effect where you go, separate your feelings from your thoughts and you can contemplate whatever you wish for as long as you want.

You may also run into forces more powerful than you. Knowing that they exist and dealing with them in a manner similar to physical experience makes them nonthreatening. For example, people periodically drown in deserts in the southwest as they attempt to cross a wash (a dry river bed) in four-wheel drive vehicles. During flood season, washes may suddenly come to life as water thunders through them. Underestimating the force of the short-lived river may result in death, as the vehicle meets a stronger force and is swept away by it.

This analogy of DBE with physical experience stops short, however. If you encounter a situation where you feel overwhelmed, you always have the option to return to your physical body. Through internal, non-verbal dialogue you may also ask to understand the nature of the threatening force, where it originated, and why you are dealing with it. Then allow your experience to unfold without fear or concern. In such a circumstance, it might prove beneficial to adopt the attitude that you are watching or are participating in an educational movie.

By now, I'm sure you've gotten the notion of the variety of dreaming states. Generally speaking, experience follows from the seeds you sow. If you organize your life in a certain direction, related experiences follow. This applies to DBEs as well. Keep in mind, though, that offhand or unexpected events may also occur. Any new event might happen only once, or it could signal the beginning of a new area you'd like to explore.

Just as there are different countries, states, cities, and neighborhoods, there exist different landscapes in nonphysical dimensions. You might find yourself in a foreign country and have to learn the language of extraterrestrials. A visit to a neighboring state of consciousness might take you to a dream-time Silicon Valley, or you might find yourself in a nonphysical equivalent of a church where you meet guides and helpers who offer insight on how to grow spiritually.

The next exercise simulates shifts between states of consciousness.

It also incorporates an exercise on how to handle unexpected shifts.

1. Determine a destination and two intermediate stops along the way. The two pit stops and the final destination should be places you enjoy visiting.
2. Center your energy within your physical body.
3. Send that energy directly to the destination, bypassing the intermediate stops.
4. Return to your physical body.
5. Go to the destination again, this time stopping briefly at each intermediate stop.
6. Return.
7. Head toward your destination, stopping at each intermediate place. This time, however, do not travel to the destination from the second pit stop. Change direction and go to the first place that pops into your mind.
8. While in a meditative state, ask yourself why you traveled to the new destination.
9. Return to your physical body.

This exercise acquaints you with how to respond to unexpected situations, as well as offers preliminaries about how to control transitions.

TIPS FOR ENTERING DREAMING

Anything can happen once you fully enter dreaming. Here are some tips for some various situations that might arise, tips that may help you to speed up your learning.

Communication

At times you'll communicate as though you were in the physical body. Your senses will indicate a normal conversation, or indicate that you are reading a book. Most communication, however, occurs through nonverbal and nonphysical communication. Your heightened senses will help you accurately send and receive mental and emotional images. A distinct advantage of telepathy is that you may automatically translate foreign information into your native language.

You'll learn to sense the meaning of symbols. Depending on your personality, these may paint a picture, which directly indicates its meaning, or you may enjoy the intrigue of developing and refining your internal, nonverbal language.

Internal Guidance

Internal guidance is composed of the impressions, feelings, visions, and physical sensations that let you know what is going on within yourself. An upset stomach may mean you ate food that disagrees with you, or it could mean you have too much tension somewhere in your life. A recurring dream may mean you are not paying attention to, and therefore not resolving, some aspect of your life. Just like learning a foreign language, you will develop a rich, nonverbal language.

To help you to start cultivating the ability to dialogue with inner processes and maintain open channels of communication and guidance:

1. Find a place and a time where you won't be interrupted.
2. Feel for any sensations in your physical body: tingling, pain, or pressure. Place your attention in that area. Allow the sensation to expand and capture your full attention. Quietly ask the sensation what it represents, and why it is there.
3. Use as many forms of communication as possible. You might perceive images, sounds, and kinesthetic sensations in your muscles and tendons.
4. During meditation, prior to sleep or while relaxing, notice your visual imagery. What are the colors, symbols, or actual scenes? Hold within your consciousness specific questions. Anything will do. Should I change my diet? What do I need to learn most right now? Is _____ a good movie? Send the question away from you into the region of your visions, and release it. Watch what

happens. Do you see another scene? Do symbols come directly to your awareness? Do you feel differently?

5. Throughout the day, assess your feelings. While walking down a street, you may feel like heading in another direction. While driving home, you may feel like changing your career. While talking with your spouse, you may feel like going out for dinner.

6. Play with these thoughts, feelings, and images. Notice if symbols intuitively mean something to you. Further attend to them by following their lead and using them as guidance. Start with minor suggestions at first, like walking in another direction and going out to dinner on the spur of the moment. For larger, life-changing directions, investigate further. Enter a full, inner dialogue with yourself, using as many modes of perception as possible.

7. You will develop your own internal language from the symbols, sensations, and other perceptions you experience. Use, test, measure, and retest different forms of guidance. With time you will isolate those that work best for you.

8. Trust this information. You will discover that this information has your best interests at heart.

Light Beings

Many people have told me that they receive visits from entities made of light who try to assist them out of their bodies. Usually the light beings somehow grab hold of the person's nonphysical energy and attempt to pull it out of the physical body. The major difficulty here seems to be relaxing enough to allow the experience to unfold. Most of these people tell me that even though they feel no danger and sense that the light beings are benevolent, they pull back from the experience simply because it is so out of the ordinary. Frequently, the light beings try again and, with time, the people adjust and relax enough to allow them to be pulled into a DBE.

Negative Situations

Even with your protection in place, at times you may find yourself in a negative situation. Aside from feeling pulled against my will into a river during one DBE, I have not had a bad experience while completely in the dreaming body, except for the shark attacks discussed in an earlier chapter. When I recognized that they represented pent-up emotions, and occurred after I had eaten a shark dinner, they ended.

Once while *seeing* during dreaming, I had a vision of three Indians who were plotting to harm me. I felt I had three responses. One: I could react with fear, providing them energy with which to perceive me as their prey. If I reacted in that manner, they would have had a marked edge on me, as I would have placed myself in the midst of their endeavor. Two: I could have joined them, suggesting that we all band together and harm someone else. Three: The way I did react was to saunter right up to them, asking with mock curiosity, "Hey, are you guys still into this stuff?" Acknowledging their activity without supplying energy to it dissipated their energy, rendering the entire scenario harmless to me.

While some situations are not harmful by intent, the interpretation of them often produces fear and fearful reactions. For example, in the time-travel film, *The Navigator*, several men and a boy in fourteenth-century Great Britain tunnel their way into the twentieth century. As they row a boat across a channel, a submarine surfaces and they react as though it were a monster. Interpreting the vessel as a submarine was beyond their grasp.

As you travel the vastness of consciousness, at first most of it might be beyond you. Practicing nonpatterning prevents premature interpretations and allows you to gather more information, which allows you to venture further the next time out.

Protection

A frequent concern is that another entity will try to inhabit the physical body after the dreaming body leaves it, or that malevolent entities will attack the dreaming body. Perhaps the most common method of protection for both the physical and nonphysical bodies is to surround them in white light prior to entering the dreaming state. Thinking and visualizing this light as the Christ Light is not uncommon. Along with immersion in this light, many people use an affirmation such as, "I am in no danger and I will not encounter any harmful experiences," or, "I will remain protected by the Light of Christ."

I've had to use this method only two or three times in over twenty years of DBEs, and then only as a preventative measure when I became unsure of my whereabouts. I have found, however, that an excellent means of protection results from how I live my life; in other words, by how well I'm following my path with heart. The more balance there is in my daily life, the less I have to worry about harmful experiences. Developing predilections pertains specifically to this form of protection. As you find your deepest predilections, you automatically embrace more of the light within you. The more you walk in light, the less darkness you have. You're in light and so don't have to create it. At the same time, I think summoning light is simply a way to refocus intent, thereby removing awareness from the situation at hand.

Predilections also focus energy, which is a principle determinant of your experiences. If your intent is aimed at wholesome, productive DBEs, experience tends to follow that intent. This is another reason for knowing why you want DBEs. The more you refine and purposefully direct all of your energies, the more you align yourself with constructive experiences. Yet don't ignore your less desirable feelings. Refusing to acknowledge exactly how you feel—even though it may be considered by others as negative—almost always ensures that at some time you will encounter those issues during a DBE.

Shapeshifting

Often the dreaming body resembles the physical body. However, I found that if I stayed out for any length of time during any one experience or if I went out frequently, my form automatically became a sphere of energy. It is also possible to deliberately change form during a DBE. Many people find they enjoy shapeshifting into a leopard, bird, snake, or other life-form. Shapeshifting can be fun and educational.

Silver Cord

When reading or talking about DBEs, you may have run across the mention of a silver cord, a strand of light connecting the physical and nonphysical bodies. I've often heard it said that if the cord breaks, you'll die. I've also heard that if you go too far, you'll snap the cord. While I've never seen this cord, based on my travels it seems to me that it's pretty hard to snap, if it has a limit at all. Relating to it in this way places physical limitations on nonphysical experiences.

Perhaps the cord acts as a symbol representing a connection with the physical body, reassuring the person that death isn't occurring. Or perhaps there is a nonphysical umbilical cord and I just haven't mustered up enough interest to see it.

Suicide

A friend of mine captured a scorpion in a jar. He jiggled the jar simply to irritate it. To our surprise, the scorpion arched its tail and stung itself in the back. Rather than endure its torment, it killed itself.

With this in mind, I've heard a few tales of someone killing himself through a DBE. The person decides enough is enough and ends his life by not returning. But I think the people who know this method of suicide dearly love life. Every time I've heard such a story, the person in question has had his life taken away, usually through captivity. Rather than endure the torture of imprisonment, the person goes into dreaming, never to return.

Even when having no thoughts of suicide, people sometimes feel afraid of not returning from a DBE. Usually these people say that, since their daily life is a shambles, they might stay gone once they're out. Again, a good way to deal with this fear is through predilections. If you have a good life, you'll want to return. This also facilitates separation, since you can let go and go out knowing that all is well. The attitude that DBEs occur naturally during sleep also helps tone down this concern.

TIPS FOR REENTRY

Ready to return to your physical body perceptions? It's not that hard. In fact, most of the time you'll probably find yourself back before you want to return.

Returning

Basically, the return transition consists of refocusing on your physical body and getting back in touch with your physical senses. Usually just by thinking or wanting to return, you will. However, I've found the "Dorothy Technique" provides a useful model to ensure a gentle, successful return.

☀ The Dorothy Technique

1. Just as Dorothy did in the *Wizard of Oz*, click your heels together or otherwise move part of your physical body. Sometimes a person feels physically paralyzed while dreaming. If this happens, simply move part of your dreaming body and allow that movement to symbolize movement of your physical body. This focuses physical energy toward your physical body.
2. Think "There is no place like home." Think about returning. This directs mental energy toward your physical body.
3. Feel the desire to return. This focuses emotional energy toward your physical body.
4. Think and feel that you want a smooth, gentle return.

With three types of energy directed toward returning, the odds are significantly in your favor that the DBE will end. Rarely, if ever, will something block your return. If something does prevent it, use internal, nonverbal dialogue and guidance techniques to discover why. Usually you just need to stay out a little longer in order to experience something else, whereupon you return. Or you may need to explore a barrier in your life, which keeps you from growing. Whatever you experience, relax and calmly deal with the situation rather than entering fearful or anxious states.

Through experience, you'll learn how to return smoothly and easily. Sometimes a hasty return produces physical sensations of nausea, sluggishness, or light-headedness. Through thinking and feeling, tell yourself you want to return effortlessly, gently, and with all your energies balanced.

These perspectives work together to start you on your way into nonordinary realities. As with most endeavors, start with little steps. Nonattachment, reducing self-importance, and using death as an advisor, for instance, might keep you from getting angry just because the refrigerator repairman didn't show up on time. Nonattachment provides distance between the event and yourself, reducing self-reflection prevents you from taking the inconvenience too seriously, and using death as an advisor requires that you ask yourself if you really want to lose your temper and expend the energy that might instead be used for dreaming. While a display of temper might be a worthwhile form of communication in some instances, in this example it may represent a useless loss of energy, energy that could be applied somewhere else.

The basic discipline outlined in this chapter also sets the tone for the continued exploration and development of perception. Exercising perception enables the invisible to become visible. Through discipline, you not only think about but actually travel into lands beyond the ordinary. Using those journeys, you can set a true and accurate course, thereby reflecting the most meaningful aspects of yourself. On a lasting journey of continual growth, you will find that you have harnessed your energies, enabling your growth from vague and unclear perceptions of nonordinary reality to sharp and clear knowledge of specific, nonordinary abilities.

11

EXERCISING
THE DREAMING BODY

Dragon

He comes through the mist
with water dripping down.
His scaly body slops mightily on the ground.
He lifts himself into the air
and flies in the spirit sky.
He looks around the magical place.
He races birds like a thunder bolt.
He beds down in his misty cave,
and rests.

As a result of my experiences with don Juan, the Monroe Institute, talking with people who have had DBEs, perusing the Edgar Cayce psychic readings, and my own explorations, I developed a three-step process for inducing, or bringing about DBEs. This "3E" method focuses on expectation (opening perception), excitation (balancing perception), and exploration (focusing perception). Most of the exercises in this approach involve preparation. Expectation, for example, concerns opening and clearing awareness so that achieving a DBE can be considered an attainable goal. During this stage, you begin sensing the movement of energy.

Excitation involves taking raw energy and beginning to shape and balance it. Where expectation generates new awareness, excitation starts refining that energy. You begin molding your energy with the objective of harmonizing your activities in daily life with nonordinary reality goals, (in this instance with DBEs). You blend your actions with your goals, balancing mental, emotional, and physical energies, which, in turn, provide greater energy and direction for your goals.

The exercises already provided are designed to help you establish solid connections throughout your life. Meditation and following a path with heart, for instance, work together, taking your awareness further into your heart and into the center of your being. Meditation helps you discover what you want to develop in your private and professional lives, and shields strengthen your life, thereby helping you to meditate more proficiently. Finding uses for DBEs that are related to your occupation weaves your total life together, providing even more energy, balance, and direction.

The exploration stage involves simulating actual DBEs, or deliberately focusing energy toward DBEs. This chapter is designed to develop the exploration stage. As you work with various techniques to develop awareness of the dreaming body, you gradually develop the DBE intent. This intent is the focus of energy that produces a DBE. To arrive at this intent, gather the feelings associated with DBEs that you learned from simulation exercises. As these feelings coagulate and form a compact unit of energy, you may then dispense with technique as you proceed to engage a DBE itself. The DBE then becomes another technique of exercising perception, a more refined technique than those used to develop it.

You will find that the 3E method also provides an approach to increase general dreaming activity. The expectation stage now reflects your openness to enhancing a DBE. The excitation stage requires further balancing of mental, emotional, and physical energies. You begin building and harmonizing this energy as your experiences allow you to familiarize yourself with different landscapes of awareness, which then allows you to formulate how you want to use a DBE. During the exploration stage, you develop control of the DBE as you realize your goals for application, such as with a learning task. You travel to precise locations, for example, or you perceive written material (books, lyrics, business proposals) that you can put to paper after you return to your physical body.

Before presenting specific dreaming body exercises let's go over a few more issues, concerns, and considerations regarding DBEs. When you do have a DBE, knowledge of these areas will help you to have a pleasant and rewarding experience.

CONSIDERATIONS REGARDING DBES

Intent

For stable dreaming, you need a stable cohesion. For this, intent is the key. We've discussed intent earlier in this book, but there is always more to know about it. If you intend to walk down a street, for instance, you'll most likely have a stable experience of walking down a street. This is because you've learned how to handle that intent. You don't think about it, you do it. If you can handle intent a bit better, you can control your dreams. Like walking, it's a learnable skill.

As you practice these techniques, keep in mind that they are superficial. Through empowering yourself, what you're trying to achieve is the ability to transcend technique in order to arrive at the actual experience. To do this, you develop a DBE intent, a compact feeling, which acts as a vehicle or tunnel that begins or causes a DBE.

For me, a DBE intent from an approach undertaken while I'm awake feels centered inside my physical body. This energy is then projected outward. From the hypnagogic and dream approaches (provided later), the intent feels like I'm connecting with something outside of my body and I am pulled by it, or else I'm reaching out and grasping it in order to pull myself out. From one angle, the accent is on internal awareness, from another angle the accent is on external awareness.

As you align your energy through clear thinking about your goals, refining your desires and emotions about them, and behaving in ways that support realization of your goals, you consolidate energy. Shaping and then focusing this energy delivers you to the experience. The more exacting and purposeful your quest, the more power you place behind your intent. Once you consolidate your intent, you may dispense with the exercises. You now have the means to induce DBEs more rapidly.

Staying in the Physical Body

Staying centered within the physical body offers one of the most powerful exercises for DBEs. This consists of remaining relaxed and centered during the course of everyday life—not the easiest proposition. Think of how many times your attention wanders off through the course of a day. Staying in the body until you want to go out of it develops your control. Dreaming awake is dreaming while solidly in the body and in the daily world. Staying in the body at a professional level is *being*.

Furthermore, if we assume that DBEs occur naturally and regularly during sleep, then the more we act naturally the more we become aware of that which is natural to us; in this instance, the DBE. You might say the most effective technique is not a technique at all, but a true balance between oneself and the world.

Here are some specific recommendations and exercises to help you on your journey.

☀ A Gift from Vixen Tor

1. You are responsible for your life and your world. Live accordingly. (More rules and steps for this? No. You're responsible for you.)
2. Let go from time to time. Let new thoughts and sensations enter your awareness.
3. Don't judge everything all the time. Let the world breathe.
4. Respect your life, others, and the world . . . no matter what world it is.
5. Keep pushing forward on your quest, even when you don't feel

like it, and especially when things become difficult. (Laziness has many crevices.)

6. No matter how large or small your resources or your abilities, trust yourself.

7. Be present. The here and now contains the gift of your life.

☼ In The Flow

To warm up, stimulate your feelings a bit:

1. Relax.
2. Rest comfortably with your eyes closed.
3. Let your feelings flow without censorship. Entertain them without holding on to them or pushing them away. Experience any and all of them.
4. Sink deeply into yourself, into your internal world.
5. Gently push your energy out. Reach out and attend to your external world while you're resting with your eyes shut.
6. Try to combine all these steps. In other words, pay complete attention.
7. Pay attention to what is happening *now*.

With a bit of care, attention, and practice you can turn your perception of your daily world into a dream. You may also use this awareness to learn how to actually *enter* the world of ordinary nighttime dreaming; how to turn ordinary dreaming into something magical and alive. Preliminary energy-body athletic exercises follow.

DREAMING

☼ Entering Your Dreams

1. Relax.
2. Develop your purpose(s) for entering your dreams.
3. Relax some more. Build your thoughts toward dreaming from inner relaxation, not an outer hardness of "I must do this."

4. Take a nap.

5. Intent is the vehicle, movement, or tunnel that brings about conscious dreaming. To arrive at your intent gather the feelings associated with practicing with nonphysical energies (such as those given above). Aim these toward entering your dream world, and then isolate the very personal feeling that arises from this quest. This is the hook to remember your intent.

☼ Nova

1. Extend two beams of light energy outward and perpendicular to each side of your physical body: one beam out of the right side, one beam out of the left side.

2. Retract these energies to a specific location inside your chest. Your breath may help you build these energies. For example, exhale as you extend the light, inhale as you retract the light.

3. Again extend two beams of light energy from your body. This time extend one out of the top of your head and one out of the bottom of your feet.

4. Retract these energies to the same location as in step 2.

5. Form the energy within your chest into a sphere (or other form natural to yourself, such as another geometric form or that of an animal), then gently project it away from your physical body.

☼ Too Tired?

When you're too tired to do an exercise, that may be the time to push forward. But you don't have to make yourself miserable either. Try this one when you are just too tired.

1. Allow your fatigue to saturate your physical body. This facilitates relaxation and the notion that it is okay to be fatigued. (This also feeds over into actual dreaming as you learn to deal with the unexpected. Stay relaxed; it's okay.)

2. Perceive a hollow core at the center of your physical body.

3. From that core push or expand the fatigue energy outward in all directions. As you do so the core of the energy also expands.

4. Contract that energy. The core of the energy will contract as well. Again, your breath may facilitate your experience. Exhale as you expand the energy away from you; inhale as you retract the energy.

5. As you fall asleep, expand and contract your fatigue energy at your own pace. As you expand and contract the energy, know within yourself that you are doing so in order to build dreaming intent.

DREAMING AWAKE

Initially dreams occur as you place your attention on the second energy field. Dreams then shift about, scene to scene and dream to dream, because your attention is not stable. Therefore entering a dream is one skill, stabilizing it is another.

With practice, the first and second fields merge, elevating your daily life into a dream, and making your dreaming more usable and practical. You're also more in the here and now, perhaps the most practical feature of all.

☼ The Light Body

1. Perceive through imagery, thoughts, and/or feelings, light energy entering the bottom of your feet and coursing up your physical body.

2. Allow the energy to exit the top of your head.

3. Perceive it flowing, tumbling, rolling, or twirling downward, outside of your physical body, whatever method is most comfortable for you.

4. Perceive it reentering your feet and back up your body.

5. Maintain the flow.

6. Extend the light energy outward, away from you in all directions.

7. Return to full waking consciousness and remain aware of the energy flow.

8. To add versatility to this exercise, imagine that all of the tensions and toxins in your physical body are chunks of black or brown substance. As you maintain the flow of energy, visualize and feel these black chunks being removed by the flow of light, exiting the top of your head, and sailing away from you while the pure energy flows downward and reenters your feet.

☀ Connect with Your Path

While in your gazing posture, open yourself to feeling. Then reflect on the following:

1. What makes you love the world? Connect that feeling to a point six inches away from your body.
2. What makes you stronger? Connect that feeling one foot away.
3. What makes you happier? Connect that feeling two feet away.
4. Now extend yourself into your entire world, then into the entire universe. Return to your center, your place of balance within yourself. (If you can't feel it immediately, feel around for it. You know how.)

☀ Tracking Dreams

1. Relax. (Sense a pattern?)
2. Walk about slowly. Anywhere will do.
3. Take it easy. Feel the environment. Feel what's going on inside yourself. *Feel.*
4. Pay attention. (Another pattern?)
5. Feel yourself to be completely a part of your world.
6. Connect the feeling of your "external" dream to a place deep within yourself.
7. Imagine the air is full of viscous energy, awareness itself. Feel around you for peak energies, for energies that have more snap.
8. Expand your feeling so you're aware of as much as possible simultaneously.

9. Practice walking and talking while performing these exercises. Learn to feel the energy about you. Listen for it with your body. Let it speak to you, and you to it.

☀ *The Vıxen Adventure*

1. Stop telling yourself over and over and over what you think and feel the world is. In other words, don't make the world concrete, inflexible, and unyielding.
2. Allow yourself to step into new worlds.
3. Know what you want out of life so you can return to this world.
4. Is all of this difficult? Yes, it is. The remedy?
5. Put your mind to the task.

Now you will take the nonphysical energy you have been working with in previous exercises and direct it specifically toward DBEs. By applying those exercises, you have opened to and stimulated energy, and then have given it constructive direction in your life. Here, you narrow expression of that energy to a specific goal—the DBE.

Not only will these exercises help lead you to DBEs; they will better prepare you by acquainting you with sensations that occur during different phases of a DBE, such as preparation, transition, and separation. You will approach the DBE from three perspectives: while awake, during the hypnagogic state (between wakefulness and sleep), and during a dream.

EXERCISES WHILE AWAKE

Several of the following exercises are known as "Robert Monroe" techniques. He popularized them in his book *Journeys Out of the Body.*[1] I also offer a few related techniques that I discovered during my DBEs. They all provide an excellent way to perceive distinctions between physical and nonphysical energy, and between the first and second energy fields. Repeat the individual exercises often during practice sessions. And practice as often as you can. Notice as many sensations as you can.

Later you will recognize these sensations and what they represent to you personally.

☼ Model A

1. Find a comfortable place to lie on your back.
2. Inside of and down the length of your body, perceive a log of energy slowly rotating as though it were spinning along the axis of your spine. If you require assistance feeling this rolling energy, imagine a swirling hurricane symbol that television weather forecasters use. Place the eye of the hurricane in the middle of your physical body. Let the clouds extend through your skin and a few feet away from your body. Imagine the formation rotating, following the direction of the swirling clouds. Use that imagery to apply friction to the log of energy to get it rolling. The log assists in heightening your sense of nonphysical energy.
3. When you feel the log rolling, gently stop it.
4. Lift or project the log straight out of your body as though you were levitating from a lower to an upper bunk bed. Allow it to float about four to five feet above your physical body.
5. Reverse your intent and allow it to lower and return within you. This is a good time to learn how to regulate the return of your nonphysical energy body into your physical body. As you return, tell yourself you want a smooth, gentle transition where all of your energies are aligned and in harmony.
6. To add a little zest to this exercise, intend the nonphysical energy to pivot so that instead of hovering parallel to your body, it floats perpendicularly. Moving it about the room or playing in other ways exercises concentration and control.

☼ Model B

1. Repeat steps 1 through 3 in Model A.
2. Just as you levitated up, slowly sink down through your resting area, and through the floor.
3. Return your energy body to your physical body.

4. A variation of the sinking method involves partially sinking and then meeting that energy with an equal and opposite force. As you begin to sink, mentally create another force that comes from below you and send it upward toward the sinking energy. Use the upward force to exert pressure on the sinking force so that both energies rest motionless in a state of equilibrium. When the pressure in between the two forces feels even, reverse the intent of the sinking force and lift out, using the momentum of the lower, upward force to assist you.

☀ Model C

1. Repeat steps 1 through 3 in Model A.
2. This time, rather than lift up, imagine that the energy log is hinged at your ankles. Then lift out so the energy log stands straight up at a ninety-degree angle to your physical body. This is like stepping on the teeth of a rake and having the rake handle jump up at you.
3. Reverse your intent and return within your body.
4. Exit your body, again standing upright.
5. While your nonphysical body is standing up, just for the fun of it, do a back flip.

☀ Model D

1. During these exercises, you may feel vibrations. It may seem as though your entire body is shaking, while to an observer there is no movement whatsoever. Sounds may accompany these vibrations. It may even sound as though a freight train is hurling through your room, or ocean surf is crashing about you. Maintain your concentration. Learning to control these vibrations facilitates a DBE. The Chakra Tune-Up provided on page 38 is a suitable exercise to learn how to do this. The vibrations and sounds will ease and abate when you have fully entered your dreaming body.

☀ Model E

1. The last of this series of exercises involves collecting or bundling energy inside your physical body in a manner similar to the way you created the energy log. You might even think of it as stuffing a sack full of potatoes.
2. Allow this energy to exit the top of your head as though it were vapor, gas, or fog.
3. Collect or bundle it again outside of your body.
4. Travel away from your physical body.
5. Pull it back into your physical body.

DURING THE HYPNAGOGIC STATE

The borderland between wakefulness and sleep provides fertile ground to explore consciousness. Often creative insights well up from within as the solution to a problem presents itself. It also offers a natural bridge to develop nonphysical energies, since much of the attention and energy given to maintaining physical perspectives shifts to nonphysical perspectives. The hypnagogic exercises may seem more like meditation than the exercises undertaken while awake, and may be used as a general, all-purpose meditation when not focusing on DBEs. This exercise is a composite drawn from talking with people who use parts or variations of it to try to induce a DBE.

☀ Model F

1. Find a comfortable place to lie down or sit.
2. Stimulate your physical senses. Feel your chair or bed; notice the texture of your clothes. Listen to the air conditioner or heater, the traffic, the clock ticking. Smell dinner in the oven, the remnant of hair spray, and the flowers nearby. Feel comfortable in your physical body.
3. Close your eyes and gently look toward the middle of your forehead. You are now shifting from physical to nonphysical energies.
4. Relax the attention to your physical senses and pay attention

to nonphysical sensations of color, images, intuition. Mentally travel with any sounds that present themselves.

5. If pressure in your head or elsewhere in your body suggests looking in another direction, do so. Dialogue with the pressure and find out why it is there. Release the pressure and return your vision to the middle of your forehead.

6. If any image appears, stay with it through relaxed concentration. If you try too hard, the image will disappear. If you don't try hard enough, the image will vanish as well. Do not project immediately toward it. You might interfere with an actual projection or a preferred destination. Relaxed concentration is the key.

7. Look for a sequence of images where you perceive a field of color, then a static image like a photograph, and then a fluid image like a motion picture. You may not experience this progression, however. You may start off perceiving a fluid image, or not get past the field of color. The goal is to get to the fluid image so if you start there, you're that much better off. If you can only perceive color, practice longer and more often. Don't censor or edit the images. Perceive them however they appear to you.

8. You may feel pushing or pulling within your physical body as though something inside you wants to merge with the fluid image. You will probably notice that these moving images have a deeper feel to them, or are more vivid than most mental images. Now the trick is to exercise patience. Wait until you sense sufficient energy, enabling you to completely merge with the image.

9. Merging with the fluid image, so that you perceive the environment from the perspective of the image rather than from your physical body, indicates that you have made a successful transition to a DBE.

☼ Model G

1. Repeat steps 1 through 5 in Model F.
2. Rather than a sequence of colors and images, you may perceive a speck of white light or an eyeball.

3. Through relaxed concentration, allow the light or eye to enlarge.

4. You may then feel as though a force from within the light or eye is pulling you to it. Gently hold back until you feel this force becoming stronger.

5. Allow yourself to be pulled into and through them. This often produces a DBE.

☀ Model H

1. Repeat steps 1 through 5 in Model F.

2. As you focus your concentration in the region of your forehead, do not concern yourself with what you perceive.

3. Remember the feelings associated with the Light Body exercise presented earlier in this chapter (page 226).

4. Split and balance your awareness between steps 2 and 3. Maintain both the visual perceptions and the feeling.

5. As though the source of a stream of energy were within your physical body, allow this energy to flow outward and away.

☀ During Dreaming

This is an excellent exercise for stabilizing perception. It is also the most natural approach to DBEs because it works directly with dreaming. It capitalizes on the view that DBEs occur regularly during sleep, but we usually don't remember them. Rather than having to totally create a DBE, we need only remember what is happening.

1. Before sleep, command yourself through thoughts and mental imagery to find your hands during a dream. Tell yourself you want to find your hands. Imagine lifting your hands to eye level. Finding your hands is an exercise in concentration and induces lucid dreaming. If you have the alertness to find your hands during a dream, you definitely know you're dreaming. Psychotherapist Kenneth Kelzer, in his book *The Sun and the Shadow*, tells how he uses this technique to develop lucid dreaming for his spiritual growth.[2]

2. As you fall asleep, be sensitive to changing levels. You might bypass the exercise and go directly through vivid and lucid dreaming to a DBE.

3. When you find your hands, remember why you did so. As mentioned earlier, a few times, I found my hands and, since I didn't remember why I was doing this, nothing happened.

4. If you wake up, tell yourself that you will return to dreaming; better yet, feel that you will.

5. Break patterns of falling asleep. For example, if you roll over on your side, you might be sending a big message to fall asleep. Try remaining on your back until sleep comes on—which sends the message to have a DBE.

6. Stabilize the dream. Remember, the difference between a lucid dream and a DBE is that during a DBE the dream environment is stable. Scenes in a DBE don't shift unless your dreaming body moves to another location. As discussed earlier in this book, you can stabilize the dream by picking three or four objects in the dream and hold them in your awareness without them shifting or dissolving. If the objects begin to change, return your attention to your hands until you feel that the energy has stabilized or evened out. Look back at the objects. When the objects no longer shift, you have entered your dreaming body.

7. To refine your control, practice traveling to other locations. Fly around your neighborhood. Zoom off to England or Asia. Discover the magic of the moon. Allow your internal guidance to direct you.

8. To refine your control even more, learn to correspond the time of day or night where your physical body is in sync with the time zone your dreaming body is in. Locate both of these bodies in the same time zone. By this point you will know where you want to take your DBEs. This step is only an exercise for enhanced control, not something you must do to have DBEs.

CORRESPONDENCE OF TECHNIQUES

Deliberately inducing a DBE often involves four distinct stages: First, you may experience a high-energy state and possibly feel lightheaded. Second, you perceive marked distinctions between physical and non-physical energy. Third, you enter the transition where the energy intensifies and possible disorientation occurs. Fourth, you achieve a complete separation of nonphysical and physical energies. The following chart relates these stages to the three general induction approaches.

Stage	Waking	Hypnagogic	Dream
1. High-Energy	relaxation	color	recognize dreaming
2. Distinction	log roll	static images	find hands or object
3. Transition	direction out	fluid image	sense of shift
4. Separation	out	participation	stabilize environment

Blending Techniques

You may not necessarily bring about a DBE from the methods presented here. Use techniques as guidelines, not as hard and fast rules. Keep yourself open to new ways and shortcuts. If you bypass the color and static image portions of the hypnagogic technique, for example, and get right to the fluid image part, good for you. Don't hold yourself back just because you read or heard it was *supposed* to happen a certain way. Once, for example, while practicing the exercise of levitating straight up (undertaken while awake), just for fun I pivoted ninety degrees while hovering in mid-air. Suddenly, without my intending it to, the energy came back down and went inside my abdomen, where it formed into a sphere of energy and then floated out of my body.

You may also find yourself purposefully blending different techniques. For instance, the deep meditative experience of the hypnagogic exercises offers a superb situation to program yourself to find your hands during a dream, as the dream exercise suggests. As a general rule, find or create techniques that work for you. Tailor your entire life to fit you well.

Supportive Techniques

Many other exercises facilitate further development of DBEs. Use them in conjunction with general induction techniques or by themselves. The more energy you aim toward your goal, the more likelihood of success. Try these:

1. Visualize yourself from the point of view of the dreaming body.
2. Relax and cultivate feelings of flying, or floating weightless.
3. Mentally project yourself to a target destination. See if you can perceive what is going on there.
4. Feel like you're a rocket taking off or a plane flying to simulate a sense of lift-off.
5. Determine a destination, and then gather nonphysical energy within you. Permeate this energy with color, preferably orange or yellow (these colors seem to offer a better sense of the DBE, but experiment with other colors). Rather than mentally projecting to the destination, project the colored energy.
6. Allow your feelings to roam wherever they want while trying to keep them centered in your physical body. On one hand, allow the feeling of complete freedom. On the other hand, keep feeling centered within yourself. For instance, a radio antenna picks up or feels many frequencies from near and distant locations; yet the vibrations always register in the antenna.
7. When you feel sexually aroused, allow that energy to saturate your being, without acting on it. Just flow with it without surrendering to it. Not owning up to it is like refusing yourself and what goes on inside. That automatically constricts energy. It doesn't mean you have to succumb and wallow in it either. Try to let it flow into other perceptions; in doing so it will transform into another kind of energy. You may take this extra energy and apply it to almost anything, including DBEs.

EDGAR CAYCE ON ASTRAL PROJECTION

An interesting source of light for DBEs comes from the Edgar Cayce psychic readings, which are housed in the Edgar Cayce Foundation library in Virginia Beach, Virginia. As a body of knowledge, the readings provide insights on all of the processes of perception presented thus far. They contain a worldview and techniques to explore that world.

The readings also offer a good example of how philosophy and practical suggestions can aid in the development of DBEs. Although only a handful of the over 14,000 documented readings pertain to astral projection (as DBEs in the readings are catalogued), the ones that deal with astral travel point the way to an avenue that might aid the spiritual seeker in the ultimate challenge of consciousness development.

The comprehensive, nonordinary worldview in the readings offers tips as it selectively cues facets of perception outside of normal, physical senses. If we keep perception open and clear, reading or hearing about something maneuvers awareness to explore in that direction. Hence, reading about physical and astral dimensions of being, each with its own type of body, begins to align perception to distinguish between, and then experience, those dimensions.

The readings define the astral body as the form of the cosmic body when it is absent from the physical body (reading 900–348).[3] This body is something everybody has, and something everybody uses. Furthermore, as one reading states, "Each and every soul leaves the body as it rests in sleep" (853–8). Since we naturally go into dreaming during sleep, the task is to find out how to become aware of this natural shift in awareness and then harness it.

To do so, one reading mentions that astral travel ". . . should be a result and not an attempt, unless ye know for what purpose ye are using same" (853–9). That is, astral projection should come as a byproduct of spiritual development, not from the specific attempt to project—unless you are well-grounded in knowing why you want to astral travel in the first place. From experience, I think that having a constructive desire to apply what you learn during astral travel gets you off to a good start. This desire helps eliminate unwanted and sometimes totally nonsensical experiences while projecting. To develop this desire, examine your astral goals as they relate to your spiritual, mental, and material concerns (853–8). If you find your attitudes and desires about astral projection intermingled with your spiritual ideals, then you have a solid foundation.

According to Cayce, astral travel enables you to obtain direct knowledge of realities beyond physical reality. In providing information about these realities, the readings use *astral body* and *soul body* interchangeably, along with using *astral, cosmic, celestial,* and related terms synonymously (900–348). This terminology paints a portrait where the physical is but a fraction of the whole, and where the deepest soul drive is to return to the awareness of its individuality within the whole, to return to the knowledge of its oneness within all creation.

As a feature of the whole, the readings state, ". . . the body-physical has the attributes of the physical body. The body-celestial or cosmic body has those attributes of the physical with the cosmic added to same, for all hearing, seeing, understanding, becomes as one" (900–348). This overlapping unity of levels becomes very important in considering astral travel. For the Cayce readings indicate that a premier effect of astral projection is the recognition of these levels.

Moreover, as you gain experience in recognizing them, you gradually reach the core of consciousness (900–348). In other words, you have layers, or sheaths, binding your consciousness together as a unit, in much the same manner as an onion has layers. Each layer of an onion contributes to the total unity known as "onion." One way to learn of the layers that make up "you" is through astral travel.

As you gain experience in one layer, you naturally begin to experience another layer, then another layer, and so on. Each layer has its own characteristics, be they physical, emotional, or mental. By experiencing these layers, you eventually recognize your core awareness. This core awareness is a universal awareness shared by the totality of creation. Yet, even though you may rest within this core, you retain your individuality.

Developing this line of thought, the readings state that "there is the pattern in the material or physical plane of every condition as exists in the cosmic or spiritual plane . . . for all force is as one force" (5756–4). As a result, as though a part of a cosmic holograph, the physical is a replication of a cosmic order. From this comes the axiom "as above, so below," or "as it is in heaven so it is on earth."

During one reading, a person posed the question to Cayce regarding entities the person had met during an astral projection. It seemed some of the astral entities were animated, and some were like waxen images. The response indicated that those who were images were "expressions or shells or the body of an individual that has been left when its soul self has projected on, and has not yet dissolved—as it were—to the realm of that activity" (516–4). These images, you might say, were echoes of the individuals who no longer fully participated within that region. The animated people, on the other hand, were those individuals who still remained active within that sphere.

In the same reading, the person asked why his father and two brothers appeared young during his astral experience, even though when they had died, they had been older and had white hair. "They are growing, as it were," came the response, "upon the eternal plane. For, as may be experienced in every entity, a death is a rebirth. And those that are growing then appear in their growing state" (516–4).

A major theme in the Cayce readings is that as you develop spiritually, you shed the binding and restrictive forces isolating you in a three-dimensional, physical reality. Other facets of your being emerge, such as the ability to communicate with those in the spiritual planes. However, the capacity to do so rests directly with your desire to communicate (5756–4), because desire, and then that which you attune or align yourself with, generates the experiences during astral travel (5754–3).

After noting the caution regarding astral projection (knowing why you want to project), the readings contain several methods to help you develop or enhance the experience. Here are a few:

1. "First, do those things that will make thine body—as it were—whole. Projections, inflections, astral experiences, are much harder upon those who are not wholly physically fit" (516–4).

2. "Allow self to go out of the body if and when it has learned to surround self with the influence of the Christ Consciousness as to prevent the use of self's abilities by those that would hinder" (489–1).

3. "[Attune] self in mind to spirit, until there is the ability in self to see self levitated from its own body. See it pass by. See it stand aside. See it act in all of the activities" (2533–8).

4. "Do not become self-important, nor self-exalting. Be rather selfless, that there may come to all who come under the sound of thy voice, to all that come in thy presence, as they look upon thine countenance, the knowledge and feeling that, indeed this man has been in the presence of his Maker; he has seen the visions of those expanses we all seek to pull the veil aside that we may peer into the future" (294–155).

5. "And in Patience then does man become more and more aware of the continuity of life, of his soul's being a portion of the Whole" (1554–3).

6. Experiences of the astral body are governed by ". . . that upon which it has fed. That which it has builded; that which it seeks; that which the mental mind, the subconscious mind, the subliminal mind, seeks!" (5754–3). Therefore, "Keep self attuned. Keep in that way and manner as befitting that as is desired by the body, for first there is the desire—then there is the proper seeking of that desired" (599–8).

7. Study to show thyself approved unto God, a workman not ashamed of that you think, of that you do, or of your acts; keeping self unspotted from your own consciousness of your ideal; having the courage to dare to do that you know is in keeping with God's will" (853–8).

You might have notice that "attunement" is the same as "alignment," that "nor self-exalting" is akin to reducing self-reflection, and that his suggestions also speak to such things as having a path with heart; all different terms, not different content.

I find the common denominators among Monroe, Cayce, and don Juan striking, as this provides one more indication that we're dealing with universal characteristics of what it means to be having the "human" dream. Moreover, even though these suggestions came from readings pertaining specifically to astral projection, they recur throughout the entire collection of Cayce's legacy. This in itself is a strong indication of the value of astral travel. As such, astral projection can be seen as a small portion of the readings, yet supporting the readings' thrust of spiritual development.

DAILY EFFORT

Like any skill, the more you practice, the greater your chances of realizing your goal. Based on feedback from those who have used the exercises in this book, daily practice of one general exercise, in addition to one DBE exercise, produces results. In particular, people have found great value in the Chakra Tune-Up (page 38) and the Waterfall Meditation (page 144), combined with any one of the DBE exercises in this chapter.

As you develop the DBE, the initial emphasis rests on building awareness of what it entails. Later, the emphasis rests on simply allowing it to happen. By then, you'll have explored many related techniques and perspectives. And yet later, the emphasis is on developing the skill. Delving into these exercises and viewpoints expands your overall awareness, and enabling a DBE is only one dividend of investing energy in the development of perception.

By continually developing and refining your goals, connecting them and integrating them with DBEs, you'll make your entire life supportive of your goals. Separation of energy into dreaming is not a matter of having a separate life where you focus on overall life goals during the day and focus on another set of goals at night. It's a matter of having a full, well-rounded, and complete life. This promotes an allowing or accepting attitude, which keeps awareness open. The rest comes of itself, by itself, no matter what the dream!

NOTES

INTRODUCTION

1. Carlos Castaneda, *The Art of Dreaming* (New York: HarperCollins, 1993); *The Eagle's Gift* (New York: Simon & Schuster, 1981); *The Fire From Within* (New York: Simon & Schuster, 1984); *Journey to Ixtlan: The Lessons of Don Juan* (New York: Simon & Schuster, 1972); *The Power of Silence: Further Lessons of Don Juan* (New York: Simon & Schuster, 1987); *The Second Ring of Power* (New York: Simon & Schuster, 1977); *A Separate Reality: Further Conversations with Don Juan* (New York: Simon & Schuster, 1971); *Tales of Power* (New York: Simon & Schuster, 1974); and *The Teachings of don Juan: A Yaqui Way of Knowledge* (New York: Simon & Schuster, 1968).

2. Ken Eagle Feather, *Traveling with Power* (Charlottesville, Va.: Hampton Roads Publishing, 1992); *A Toltec Path* (Charlottesville, Va.: Hampton Roads Publishing, 1995); *Tracking Freedom* (Charlottesville, Va.: Hampton Roads Publishing, 1998); and *The Dream of Vixen Tor* (Charlottesville, Va.: Tracker One Studios, 2001).

CHAPTER TWO

1. I have provided physical-organ locations of the cornerstones based on the most accurate conjecture possible, conjecture being fully within the bounds of Toltec training. I triangulated don Juan's description of locations (*Tales*, 99–100) with physical anatomy as well as with other metaphysical systems. For the purposes of this book, awareness of various modes of perception is

more important than knowing their precise location. A superior doctoral research study, however, would be to map these out. In the meantime, we are left to our own devices of academic study and *seeing*.

CHAPTER THREE

1. Robert Monroe, *Journeys Out of the Body* (New York: Doubleday, 1971).
2. Francis Jeffrey and John Lilly, M.D., *John Lilly So Far . . .* (Los Angeles: Jeremy P. Tarcher, Inc., 1990), chapter 7.
3. Glen O. Gabbard and Stuart Twemlow, *With the Eyes of the Mind: An Empirical Analysis of Out-of-Body States* (New York: Praeger, 1984), 150.
4. Glen O. Gabbard and Stuart Twemlow, 8–13.

CHAPTER FOUR

1. Arnold Mindell, Ph.D., *Dreaming While Awake: Techniques for 24-Hour Lucid Dreaming* (Charlottesville, Va.: Hampton Roads Publishing, 2000), 6.
2. Raymond Moody, Jr., M.D., *Life After Life* (New York: Bantam, 1976).
3. The technology is called Hemi-Sync. Sound patterns placed in the ears via headphone or speakers facilitate balancing the left and right hemispheric activity of the brain. Through entrainment, the brain responds and then maintains an EEG pattern associated with the frequency a person is listening to.

CHAPTER FIVE

1. Taisha Abelar, *The Sorcerers' Crossing: A Woman's Journey* (New York: Viking, 1992), 232.

CHAPTER SIX

1. Shunryu Suzuki. *Zen Mind, Beginner's Mind* (New York: Weatherhill, 1970).
2. Florinda Donner, *Being-in-Dreaming: An Initiation into the Sorcerer's World* (New York: HarperCollins, 1991), 219.
3. Francesa Fremantle and Chögyam Trungpa, trans., *The Tibetan Book of the Dead* (Boston: Shambhala Publications, 1992).

4. Daniel Goleman, *Emotional Intelligence* (New York: Bantam Books, 1995), 36.

5. Ram Dass, *Be Here Now* (New York: Crown Publishers, 1971).

CHAPTER SEVEN

1. Statements attributed during conversations from 1984 through 1989 when I was a subject in The Monroe Institute's laboratory as well as being on staff at the Institute.

2. Taisha Abelar, *The Sorcerers' Crossing: A Woman's Journey* (New York: Viking, 1992), 231.

3. PSI Research, "Visualization Improves Athletic Success," *Venture Inward* 11, No. 4 July/August (1995).

4. James Gleick, *Chaos: Making a New Science* (New York: Penguin Books, 1987).

5. Julian Jaynes, *The Origin of Consciousness in the Breakdown of the Bicameral Mind* (Boston: Houghton Mifflin, 1977), 236–46.

6. William James, *The Varieties of Religious Experience* (New York: Signet Books, 1958), 292–94.

7. Mihaly Csikszentmihalyi, *Flow: The Psychology of Optimal Experience* (New York: HarperPerennial, 1990).

CHAPTER NINE

1. Shunryu Suzuki, *Zen Mind, Beginner's Mind* (New York: Weatherhill, 1970), 119.

2. Robert Monroe, *Far Journeys* (New York: Doubleday, 1985), chapter 7.

3. Dennis Tedlock and Barbara Tedlock, eds., "The Clown's Way" in *Teachings from the American Earth* (New York: Liveright, 1975).

4. Taisha Abelar, *The Sorcerers' Crossing: A Woman's Journey* (New York: Viking, 1992); Victor Sanchez, *The Toltec Path of Recapitulation: Healing Your Past to Free Your Soul* (Rochester, Vt.: Bear & Company, 2001).

5. Taisha Abelar, *The Sorcerers' Crossing: A Woman's Journey* (New York: Viking, 1992), 50–57.

6. A. M. Gray, *Warfighting: The U.S. Marine Corps Book of Strategy* (New York: Doubleday, 1989), 13.

CHAPTER TEN

1. Andrew M. Coleman, *A Dictionary of Psychology* (New York: Oxford University Press, 2001), 588.

CHAPTER ELEVEN

1. Robert Monroe, *Journeys Out of the Body* (New York: Doubleday, 1971).
2. Kenneth Kelzer, *The Sun and the Shadow* (Virginia Beach, Va.: A.R.E. Press, 1987).
3. Edgar Cayce Readings © 1971, 1993–2006 by the Edgar Cayce Foundation. Used by permission.

Bibliography

Abelar, Taisha. *The Sorcerers' Crossing: A Woman's Journey*. New York: Viking, 1992.

Castaneda, Carlos. *The Art of Dreaming*. New York: HarperCollins, 1993.

———. *The Eagle's Gift*. New York: Simon & Schuster, 1981.

———. *The Fire from Within*. New York: Simon & Schuster, 1984.

———. *Journey to Ixtlan: The Lessons of Don Juan*. New York: Simon & Schuster, 1972.

———. *The Power of Silence: Further Lessons of Don Juan*. New York: Simon & Schuster, 1987.

———. *A Separate Reality: Further Conversations with Don Juan*. New York: Simon & Schuster, 1971.

———. *The Second Ring of Power*. New York: Simon & Schuster, 1977.

———. *Tales of Power*. New York: Simon & Schuster, 1974.

———. *The Teachings of don Juan: A Yaqui Way of Knowledge*. New York: Simon & Schuster, 1968.

Coleman, Andrew M. *A Dictionary of Psychology*. Oxford: Oxford University Press, 2001.

Csikszentmihalyi, Mihaly. *Flow: The Psychology of Optimal Experience*. New York: HarperPerennial, 1990.

Dass, Ram. *Be Here Now*. New York: Crown Publishers, 1971.

Deikman, Arthur J. "Deautomatization and the Mystic Experience." In *Altered States of Consciousness*, edited by Charles T. Hart. New York: HarperCollins, 1990.

Donner, Florinda. *Being-in-Dreaming: An Initiation into the Sorcerer's World.* New York: HarperCollins, 1991.

Feather, Ken Eagle. *The Dream of Vixen Tor.* Charlottesville, Va.: Tracker One Studios (distributed by Hampton Roads Publishing), 2001.

———. *On the Toltec Path: A User's Guide to the Teachings of don Juan Matus, Carlos Castaneda, and Other Toltec Seers.* Rochester, Vt.: Bear & Co., 2006.

———. *Tracking Freedom: A Guide for Personal Evolution.* Charlottesville, Va.: Hampton Roads, 1998.

———. *Traveling with Power: The Exploration and Development of Perception.* Charlottesville, Va.: Hampton Roads, 1992.

Fremantle, Francesca, and Chögyam Trungpa, trans. *The Tibetan Book of the Dead.* Boston: Shambhala Publications, 1992.

Jeffrey, Francis, and John Lilly, M.D. *John Lilly So Far . . .* Los Angeles: Jeremy P. Tarcher, Inc., 1990.

Gabbard, Glen O., and Stuart Twemlow. *With the Eyes of the Mind: An Empirical Analysis of Out-of-Body States.* New York: Praeger, 1984.

Gleick, James. *Chaos: Making a New Science.* New York: Penguin Books, 1987.

Goleman, Daniel. *Emotional Intelligence.* New York: Bantam Books, 1995.

Gray, A. M. *Warfighting: The U.S. Marine Corps Book of Strategy.* New York: Doubleday, 1989.

James, William. *The Varieties of Religious Experience.* New York: Signet Books, 1958.

Jaynes, Julian. *The Origin of Consciousness in the Breakdown of the Bicameral Mind.* Boston: Houghton Mifflin, 1977.

Kelzer, Kenneth. *The Sun and the Shadow.* Virginia Beach, Va.: A.R.E. Press, 1987.

Mindell, Arnold, Ph.D. *Dreaming While Awake: Techniques for 24-Hour Lucid Dreaming.* Charlottesville, Va.: Hampton Roads Publishing, 2000.

Moody, Raymond, Jr., M.D. *Life After Life.* New York: Bantam, 1976.

Monroe, Robert. *Journeys Out of the Body.* New York: Doubleday, 1971.

———. *Far Journeys.* New York: Doubleday, 1985.

Sanchez, Victor. *The Toltec Path of Recapitulation: Healing Your Past to Free Your Soul.* Rochester, Vt.: Inner Traditions/Bear & Co., 2001.

Seuss, Dr. *Oh, the Places You'll Go!* New York: Random House, 1990.

Suzuki, Shunryu. *Zen Mind, Beginner's Mind.* New York: Weatherhill, 1970.

Tedlock, Dennis, and Barbara Tedlock, eds. "The Clown's Way" in *Teachings from the American Earth.* New York: Liveright, 1975.

Index

About the Author and the Poet

Ken Eagle Feather is the author of *On the Toltec Path*, which explores the teachings of Toltec seer don Juan Matus as presented by anthropologist Carlos Castaneda. His other books include *Traveling with Power*, *Tracking Freedom*, and *The Dream of Vixen Tor*.

Concurrent with his apprenticeship to don Juan, Ken obtained degrees in education and mass communications. He later served on staff of the Association for Research and Enlightenment, which is part of the Edgar Cayce legacy, and the Monroe Institute, founded by Robert Monroe, a pioneer in using sound technology to facilitate the exploration of consciousness. A former vice president of sales and marketing for a publishing company, he is currently communications director for a medical science research organization. He lives in Richmond, Virginia.

Harriet Coleman penned the poems in this book while dreaming awake, and did so at the age of twelve. Now in college, she is exploring creativity through Irish dancing, photography, and contemporary art. She lives in Andover, England.

BOOKS OF RELATED INTEREST

On the Toltec Path
A Practical Guide to the Teachings of don Juan Matus,
Carlos Castaneda, and Other Toltec Seers
by Ken Eagle Feather

Don Juan and the Power of Medicine Dreaming
A Nagual Woman's Journey of Healing
by Merilyn Tunneshende

Twilight Language of the Nagual
The Spiritual Power of Shamanic Dreaming
by Merilyn Tunneshende

Don Juan and the Art of Sexual Energy
The Rainbow Serpent of the Toltecs
by Merilyn Tunneshende

Dreamways of the Iroquois
Honoring the Secret Wishes of the Soul
by Robert Moss

The Dreamer's Book of the Dead
A Soul Traveler's Guide to Death, Dying, and the Other Side
by Robert Moss

The Teachings of Don Carlos
Practical Applications of the Works of Carlos Castaneda
by Victor Sanchez

The World Dream Book
Use the Wisdom of World Cultures to Uncover Your Dream Power
by Sarvananda Bluestone, Ph.D.

Inner Traditions • Bear & Company
P.O. Box 388
Rochester, VT 05767
1-800-246-8648
www.InnerTraditions.com

Or contact your local bookseller